ENERGY HEALING

for Trauma, Stress & Chronic Illness

About the Author

Cyndi Dale (Minneapolis, MN) is an internationally renowned author, speaker, healer, and business consultant. She is president of Life Systems Services, through which she has conducted over 65,000 client sessions and presented training classes throughout Europe, Asia, and the Americas. Cyndi is the author of twenty-five-plus books, including *Llewellyn's Little Book of Chakras*, *The Spiritual Power of Empathy*, and *Awaken Clairvoyant Energy*.

ENERGY HEALING

for Trauma, Stress & Chronic Illness

Uncover & Transform
the Subtle Energies That Are
Causing Your Greatest Hardships

CYNDI
DALE

Llewellyn Publications
WOODBURY, MINNESOTA

FIRST EDITION
First Printing, 2020

Book design by Rebecca Zins
Cover design by Kevin R. Brown
Figurative illustrations by Mary Ann Zapalac

Llewellyn is a registered trademark of Llewellyn Worldwide Ltd.

Library of Congress Cataloging-In-Publication Data
Names: Dale, Cyndi, author.
Title: Energy healing for trauma, stress & chronic illness : uncover &
    transform the subtle energies that are causing your greatest hardships /
    Cyndi Dale.
Description: First edition. | Woodbury, Minnesota : Llewellyn Publications,
    2020. | Includes bibliographical references and index. | Summary: "Cyndi
    presents the physical and subtle energy origin and potential remedies
    for diseases and chronic illnesses such as autoimmune disease, mental
    health, mast cell issues, epigenetics, psychoneuroimmunology,
    transgenerational inheritance, effects of stress, trauma, EMFs and the
    concern of 5G, and more"—Provided by publisher.
Identifiers: LCCN 2020017395 (print) | LCCN 2020017396 (ebook) | ISBN
    9780738761046 (paperback) | ISBN 9780738761084 (ebook)
Subjects: LCSH: Energy medicine. | Healing.
Classification: LCC RZ421 .D34 2020 (print) | LCC RZ421 (ebook) | DDC
    615.8/528—dc23
LC record available at https://lccn.loc.gov/2020017395
LC ebook record available at https://lccn.loc.gov/2020017396

Llewellyn Worldwide Ltd. does not participate in, endorse, or have any authority or responsibility concerning private business transactions between our authors and the public.

All mail addressed to the author is forwarded but the publisher cannot, unless specifically instructed by the author, give out an address or phone number.

Any internet references contained in this work are current at publication time, but the publisher cannot guarantee that a specific location will continue to be maintained. Please refer to the publisher's website for links to authors' websites and other sources.

Llewellyn Publications
A Division of Llewellyn Worldwide Ltd.
2143 Wooddale Drive
Woodbury MN 55125-2989

www.llewellyn.com
Printed in the United States of America

CONTENTS

Part 1
Physical and Subtle
*The Energies of Trauma, Stress,
and Chronic Illness*

Part 2
Breaking Free
*Techniques for Recovering
and Healing the Self*

CONTENTS

SUBTLE ENERGY HEALING TECHNIQUES

ILLUSTRATIONS

Disclaimer

The information in this book is not intended to be used to diagnose or treat a medical, emotional, or behavioral condition for you or another person. To address social, emotional, mental, medical, behavioral, or therapeutic issues, please consult a licensed professional such as a therapist, psychiatrist, or physician.

The author and publisher are not responsible for any conditions that require a licensed professional, and we encourage you to consult a professional if you have any questions about the use or efficacy of the techniques or insights in this book. References in this book are given for informational purposes alone and do not constitute an endorsement.

All case studies and descriptions of persons have been changed or altered so as to be unrecognizable. Any likeness to actual persons, living or dead, is strictly coincidental.

INTRODUCTION

*Acts must be carried through to their
completion. Whatever their point of
departure, the end will be beautiful.*

—Jean Genet, *The Thief's Journal*
(tr. Bernard Frechtman)

I've been a professional intuitive and energy healer for more than thirty years. Most of the 65,000 people I've engaged with in that time have been dealing with the effects of unhealed trauma.

That's a big statement, I know. But that's how prevalent unhealed trauma is.

Moreover, most of my clients with unhealed trauma are also struggling with chronic illness and other chronic life challenges such as relationship, financial, or self-esteem problems. To me, an energy healer, this overlap is no coincidence. Time after time, person after person, I've been able to trace a clear, if complex, connection between chronic challenges and unhealed trauma. It doesn't surprise me at all when I read that 6 in 10 adults in the United States have a chronic disease, and 4 in 10 of those adults have more than one.[1]

When people with chronic illnesses and challenges come to me, they usually tell me similar stories. They've addressed their problems in a wide variety of ways, including various branches of allopathic medicine, psychotherapy, and complementary and alternative medicine practices, and maybe they've experienced a certain degree of healing or relief, but something is still missing. They may not know what it is, but *something* is keeping them from feeling the way they want to feel—the way they know, deep in their hearts, they *could*

---

1 Centers for Disease Control and Prevention, "Chronic Diseases in America."

1

feel—whether that's happy or comfortable, safe or loved, whole or free. Something is keeping them from healing to their optimal potential.

The piece they're missing is *energy*—or, more specifically, subtle energy. In our work together, I introduce them to the unseen but very powerful energies that govern everything in our world, including us. Together, we look at the various parts of their subtle anatomy, including the invisible centers, fields, and pathways within and around our physical body, and how these parts have been or are being affected by subtle energies. I show them how, very often, the unaddressed energetic damage from traumatic stressors and our subtle anatomy's response to them eventually manifests in the physical body as chronic illnesses, which include autoimmune disorders. It can manifest on the physical level as other chronic challenges, too, such as addictions, learning disabilities, behavioral concerns, or recurring psychological, emotional, or relationship patterns that don't seem to shift no matter how they're addressed.

Together, my clients and I uncover the subtle energies of trauma, the energies involved in the stress response the trauma has triggered, and the energies underpinning their chronic illnesses and challenges. Then we work with their subtle anatomy and other, more helpful energies to move them toward the healing they seek.

I've watched as a young mother with lupus gradually became healthier, finally able to hold her toddler son without wincing. I've seen an agoraphobic grandfather track his fear of the world back to an early childhood event and, for the first time in twenty years, grab his cane and start walking to the store. I've been honored to support military veterans experiencing the long-term effects of witnessing the events of war, individuals with addictions and allergies, codependents stuck in bad relationships, and people with nearly every other type of concern.

With this book, it is my honor to share with you the same concepts and techniques I've shared with them so that you can experience the same help and healing.

Your Guide to Addressing the Energies of Challenge

In chapters 1 and 2, you'll learn more about the nature of energy, including how it operates, and the two different kinds of energy: physical and subtle. The end of chapter 1 presents a special explanation: a case study of how you might approach SARS-CoV-2, the virus that caused a world pandemic through the disease of COVID-19, starting in 2019/20. Then, in the rest of part 1, I'll describe in detail how specific forms of subtle energy, called *forces,* impact us first during a crisis and can then cause ongoing challenges if their effects are left unaddressed.

Chapter 1: how trauma begets challenges. Trauma leads to chronic challenges, and energy is the core reason. In this chapter you'll become acquainted with this book's fundamental concepts. The first of a multi-chapter guide lists various types of trauma and challenges the book can help you address.

Chapter 2: all the energetics you must understand. In this chapter you'll learn more about energy, including energetic signatures, forces, and our energetic/subtle anatomy.

Chapter 3: your physical anatomy under stress. This chapter explores all things physical in relation to the energetics of trauma and chronic illness. Basically, I'll present an up-to-date biology lesson about trauma and trauma-related stress, including a reference guide listing how the body's various systems react to the stress of trauma.

Chapter 4: your subtle anatomy under stress. Here I'll show how your subtle self, consisting of organs, channels, and fields, reacts to—and can be damaged by—the energies of trauma and subsequent trauma-related stress. This chapter also covers several subtle energy (or spiritual) factors that can contribute to the effects of trauma and our chronic challenges.

Chapter 5: how the physical and subtle interact in response to trauma. When we're under siege by disrupting energies, both our physical and subtle anatomies respond immediately and over time—sometimes even over multiple lifetimes. Case studies will reveal why the energies of trauma stick around so long and are often complex. The trauma and challenges guide from chapter 1 will be expanded on here, giving you insights on specific concerns.

Chapter 6: the roles of grieving and codependency in healing. We need to grieve life's traumas. If we don't, not only do we become stuck in a shock response, but we can also develop codependent attitudes, behaviors, and relationships. This chapter will explore both grieving and codependency and the energetic bridge between them. The third section of the trauma and challenges guide will address how grieving and codependency affect specific trauma and chronic challenges.

The effects of trauma, trauma-related stress, and chronic challenges can be complex, and part 1 contains a lot of in-depth information. To help you sort out how the details apply to you, I've included personal assessment tools at the end of chapters 2–6. The insights you glean from these assessments will prepare you for part 2, where you'll find a wealth of healing techniques that apply the concepts from the previous chapters.

Chapter 7: foundational techniques for healing trauma and challenges at the subtle energy level. Ready to fill up your subtle energy toolkit? In this chapter you'll learn my top ten subtle energy techniques for transforming trauma and subsequent challenges. If you're acquainted with some of my other twenty-five-plus energy medicine books, you'll recognize a few of these processes; however, they have been customized for the purposes of this book.

Chapter 8: a subtle energy approach to healing trauma. Building on techniques from the last chapter, you'll also acquire new ones in order to become freed from traumatizing experiences.

Chapter 9: addressing the subtle energies behind chronic illnesses. The deep inner healing wisdom and processes offered in this chapter will help you alleviate chronic illnesses, including autoimmune disorders. Subtle vehicles for addressing chronic illness are primarily covered here; physical assists are covered in the next chapter. A special guide at the end of the chapter lists subtle energy insights for a variety of specific chronic illnesses.

Chapter 10: additional techniques to support your healing. Subtle healing processes are greatly enhanced when supported by real-life changes. This chapter will address challenges related to issues like addictions and allergies, using both subtle energy and physical antidotes.

Appendix: a four-phased technique for energetically healing SARS-CoV-2/COVID-19. This staged healing will enable you to clean up the viral attachments, clear the pathways of involved forces, disempower any present or potential viruses, and enable protective energetic boundaries.

Before you embark on your own healing adventure, let me share a few additional insights that I've gleaned from my years of working with clients.

First, the healing you'll be doing will be deep, and deep healing frequently takes time. Your chronic illnesses and challenges didn't develop overnight, and they usually don't disappear overnight either. While I have seen people experience sudden and dramatic improvements as they work with subtle energy, other changes happen gradually. Sometimes you make what you regard as a great leap forward, and then nothing seems to happen for a time. Please trust that however your healing unfolds, it will do so on exactly the schedule that is ideal for you.

Second, subtle energy healing is a piece usually missing from our overall healing efforts. It is not a replacement for other pieces, such as allopathic care or other forms of complementary care. The effects of trauma and our responses to it are multifaceted, and your approach to healing needs to be multifaceted too. Sometimes subtle energy healing can help conventional treatments work more effectively; sometimes conventional treatments are needed to set the stage for successful subtle energy work. Don't deny yourself the benefits of medicine or medical advice or the support of well-trained therapists or practitioners. If you do, you're just leaving out other important pieces of your healing.

Finally, know that you're not alone. As I shared at the beginning of this introduction, trauma and its effects are so prevalent that they're almost a universal experience. But as the many people I have worked with will tell you, it's also something that you can address and heal—and by doing so, you're contributing to a greater healing. In our chaotic world, darkness can so easily seem to eclipse the light. For this reason, every single soul on this planet is called to shine right now. By healing your deep-seated challenges, you'll emerge as the burnished ember of goodness that you are, ready to contribute your unique light to the world.

You've had the strength to live with your trauma and the challenges that evolved from it. Now it's time to gain the power you need to free yourself from them. Because you're reading this book, I believe that you're ready, I believe in your ability to heal, and I believe in you.

Part 1

Physical and Subtle

The Energies of Trauma, Stress & Chronic Illness

You want to make significant strides in your health and wellness, and you deserve to. It's far easier to recover from your life challenges if you understand what created them.

The storyline of hardship isn't as straightforward as basic biological or therapeutic approaches assert. We are made of energy, physical and subtle. That means the stuck spots in our life are anchored by both types of energy. In fact, I like to tell clients that they are composed of light, sound, soul, and clay (or earthly elements). All of these components vibrate at both substantial and insubstantial levels.

Part 1 provides you with in-depth explanations of your *complete* human self, which is concrete, immaterial, and everything in between. As we progress through the first six chapters of this book, prepare for the final landing place: the grieving heart. Above all, healing involves honoring our feelings. At one level they can act like adhesives, binding our traumas, stress, and chronic illnesses, but they also help set us free.

Along the way, personal assessment questionnaires will guide you to look at your own challenges through the lens of each chapter's information. You'll be ready to put all this information to good use in part 2.

CHAPTER 1

All Challenges Are Energy Challenges

*Healing is a matter of time, but it is
sometimes also a matter of opportunity.*
—Hippocrates (tr. W. H. S. Jones)

Maureen was a sixty-year-old high school teacher suffering with constant fatigue, aches and pains, arrhythmia (an erratic heartbeat), lung infections, depression, anxiety, and uncontrollable moods. By the time she came to me, she'd already been to dozens of medical doctors. Their diagnoses included an autoimmune disorder, hormonal imbalances, and idiopathic pain, which basically means "pain we don't know the cause of." Her holistic practitioners had suggested she had Lyme disease, leaky gut syndrome, past-life challenges, mold infections, and more. The treatments she'd tried included a mild form of chemotherapy, cognitive therapy, vitamin supplements, and hypnosis.

I could tell that lying deep inside Maureen were problematic energies that had never been addressed and cleared; in fact, there was an aspect of Maureen's self that was locked away, trapped in these energies, unable to become free and healthy. It wasn't hard to identify the events that put these energies in place: over a few months in her childhood, Maureen had undergone one catastrophe after another. A tornado had wiped out her family's farm. Soon after, her father had died from a heart attack. Her mother then developed a serious mold infection in her lungs and began losing control of her emotions, often yelling at the kids.

Maureen was still experiencing the suffering she'd been through during that horrific period of her childhood because the energies associated with those events were still present and active not just in her physical body, but also in her energy anatomy.

What do I mean by "energies"? In this chapter I'll provide you a simple snapshot of energy and trauma to prep you for the detailed information in the rest of this book.

Why All Challenges Are Energy Based

Energy is information that moves, and it comprises absolutely everything, including both the tangible and intangible aspects of ourselves. Energy underlies every life disrupter and resulting hardship—physical, psychological, and spiritual. It also underlies every good thing in life and the resulting joy and peace—physical, psychological, and spiritual. This means that powerful changes can occur if we work on an energetic level to fix them.

To understand how, you first need to know that there are two types of energy: physical and subtle. Most healing processes, such as the use of prescription medicine, specific diets, physical therapies, simple cognitive processes, and even the old adage "Time heals all wounds" are based on physical energy. The physical universe certainly counts when we're working toward alleviating our adversities. In fact, there are biological reasons why our body requires (but also resists) healing, and there are physical energy modalities that support healing. The key to freedom, however, often lies in the other energetic domain—that of subtle energy.

Subtle energies—also called psychic, intuitive, and quantum energies—are inseparable from the material self. They aren't just some mystical phenomena that float around haphazardly. They actually underpin and organize physical reality, including your physical body. I propose that very specific subtle energies are the main causes of chronic illness and other intractable challenges.

During a crisis, we're hit with a type of subtle energy called forces. Any of the six vital forces—environmental, missing, modern, physical, psychological, and spiritual—can create problems during the crisis itself, but it's the stress response set off by the forces that can eventually lead to chronic illness and other lingering hardships. As we continue to be afflicted by the original forces, those forces trigger mechanisms within us that surround the wounded self (the aspect of our psyche most afflicted by the traumatic event) in a bubble of shock. Unless this wounded self is freed from the shock bubble, it will continue to suffer in darkness, triggering new energetic responses that cause even more damage.

What makes forces destructive or harmful is not the energies themselves but whether or not they're compatible with our original energetic signature. This is our master energetic code, the culmination of everything unique about our body, mind, and soul. This signature determines what external energies will nourish us or harm us, whether they enter during life events, through food or other physical substances, or as subtle feelings and thoughts. Whether we're facing a one-time crisis or an ongoing challenge, we'll be able to respond to the energies that match our original energetic signature, and we'll react negatively to those that don't.

I define trauma as the damage caused by the initial disruptive, incompatible force, which is delivered from outside of ourselves. Because trauma is inflicted outside to inside, it must be healed the same way. We require help from another person, living being, or even a spiritual guide or the Spirit. In part 2 I'll give you a plethora of techniques that will enable you to energetically heal trauma in this way, from the outside to the inside.

Beyond that initial trauma there is the damage caused by secondary energies or secondary forces. These secondary energies or forces are created from within, during our system's physical and energetic response to the initial trauma. If they aren't addressed, they remain stuck in our body and our energy systems, continuing to cause more harm—harm that, over time, most often manifests as chronic illness or other ongoing challenges. Because these secondary energies are self-generated and harm us from the inside, they must also be energetically healed from the inside. I'll provide you with insights and techniques that will allow you to accomplish this deep inner metamorphosis.

When I looked at Maureen's conditions from an energetic point of view, I could see that her physical and subtle energy anatomies had been compromised and traumatized by forces that greatly mismatched her original energetic signature. Because no one had been available to help her grieve and recover from the traumatic childhood events, the aspects of her that had been traumatized and encased within a shock bubble had never been freed. Meanwhile, the original force and its energetic effects had been absorbed into both her body and energy systems, where they lingered, morphed, and began damaging her physical and subtle anatomies from the inside, eventually triggering a chronic illness. She needed help to heal both outside to inside and inside to inside.

In chapter 2 we'll delve more deeply into our physical and subtle energy anatomies, our original energetic signatures, and the forces and their energetic effects. You'll learn what helped Maureen as well. But first I want to illuminate how important this brave new approach to trauma is by discussing a crisis that has impacted the entire world: the SARS-CoV-2 pandemic. In the next section, I will show you how to look at the virus from an energetic point of view, and then I will provide a fourfold technique in the appendix to actually work with issues related to this virus.

Energetics and SARS-CoV-2

In 2019 a new plague, caused by a virus, began to spread across the globe. It was officially named SARS-CoV-2. In its wake was a disease called COVID-19. SARS-CoV-2 is one of many types of coronaviruses, which have been around for centuries. They typically affect birds and mammals and are named for the crown- or corona-like spikes on their surfaces.

SARS stands for "severe acute respiratory syndrome" and CoV means "coronavirus." A "2" was added to the label to distinguish this SARS virus from the first that caused an outbreak in 2002 (SARS-CoV). The actual disease caused by SARS-CoV-2 is labeled COVID-19 as an acronym for coronavirus disease 2019. Said again, SARS-CoV-2 is the virus that causes the disease named COVID-19.

At every level, SARS-CoV-2 is the source of significant trauma. It can and does kill, regardless of race, age, or gender, but is most serious to the elderly and people with compromised immune systems. Transferred airborne, it lives for various ranges of time on surfaces, but it doesn't just stay in place. It spreads—fast. And it doesn't read the stop signs we use to separate one country or street from another. This virus has no bounds.

Equally tricky is the fact that not everyone with the disease knows they have it. Often it causes few to no symptoms. This means that the infected can distribute the virus without their knowledge. Microbes like SARS-CoV-2 can turn any of us into an agent of death.

People most seriously impacted become very sick. The most common signs are fever, tiredness, and a dry cough. The disease can also result in aches and pains, congestion, sore throat, diarrhea, and a loss of taste. The most serious turn is signaled by difficulty breathing, and then a patient is near the end.

I'm sure you'll have noticed that so far, I've mainly been talking about a few of the physical facets of the disease. Why? After all, aren't we going to learn an energetic approach to healing in this book? We are energetic beings, but that means we are physical as well as subtle. The physical counts. As the pandemic taught us, physical isn't enough. We must also arrive at healing assessments and antidotes by peering beneath the physical surface of a challenge to consider all other factors.

And there are a lot of angles through which to view SARS-CoV-2. We know it causes stress. Just the thought of living on the same planet as this virus creates anxiety and worry. As I'll point out over and over, stress can all too easily lead to trauma—even more so when the enemy is invisible.

We are dealing with a virus that is distributed environmentally and endangers our lives, even while it potentially threatens our ability to make a living, create intimacy, and feel safe in the world. Grief lies in its wake, either because of a loss of innocence, our own health, or loved ones' lives. The psychological toll is great, but so is the spiritual. The spread of this disease, the fact that it is a pandemic—that there is nowhere to hide—calls for us to examine (or reexamine) our basic nature. Is there a God in charge of all of this? If so, will prayer save us? What might be the deeper meaning we can assign to this disease, if there is one? Are we being called to save the planet or just ourselves and our loved ones? Can we trust our own spiritual guidance or are humans supposed to be eliminated from the planet with one giant swipe of a disinfecting wipe?

As I outline all the ways we will eventually examine the issues involved in healing this particular virus, you'll come to better understand why this book offers such a powerful and unique set of ideas. What energetic concepts are involved?

Physical Analysis of SARS-CoV-2

We must approach healing from this virus through an understanding of its structure and function. We begin with what scientists know about viruses in the general sense.

Like all viruses, SARS-CoV-2 isn't considered alive. Rather, viruses dwell in a sort of vague in-between state: not alive, not dead. They exist only to invade and multiply, and that's what they do.

Very small organisms, viruses are only 15 to 300 nanometers in diameter. They can live in heat and cold and contain DNA or RNA that serves as their means of multiplying. RNA-encoded viruses are especially dangerous to living beings as they mutate more easily than do DNA viruses. As we might expect with that lead-in, the SARS-CoV-2 virus has a single strand of RNA in its center, which is surrounded by fat and glycoproteins. The latter look like spikes. It is through these spikes that the virus can bind to an enzyme on certain bodily cells, especially those in the respiratory tract, though it also impacts the gastrointestinal system and endothelial cells, among other physical structures.

Basically, these spikes pierce a body's healthy cell and the RNA enters and takes over that cell. It actually uses the host's ribosomes, which are protein factories within the human cell, to replicate. While operating, its only way of communicating is through electrostatic interactions, but once it is inside of a bodily cell, it disguises itself. SARS-CoV-2's hidden nature makes it hard for the immune system to detect it, which leaves it able to systematically destroy healthy tissue.

Why am I telling you so much about the physical mechanics of SARS-CoV-2? As you'll learn in the appendix, the physical structure of the virus is the basis for one phase of our healing work. In short, we never ignore the concrete.

There are other physical factors involved in situations like the spread of SARS-CoV-2 that go far beyond those typically addressed in the medical system. For instance, we'll look at the role of your epigenome, a chemical soup that holds ancestral memories. It seems that these chemicals—and your ancestors—can determine what diseases you might catch or not. But you'll also want to examine the health of any or all of your organ systems, from the neurological to the digestive.

Subtle Energetic Analysis of SARS-CoV-2

In this book you'll be mainly taught how to scrutinize and address a trauma-causing situation through the lens of subtle energy. You'll discover that this can be a complex process. For instance, we'll look at issues like these:

Primary Forces and a Shock Bubble. There are many forces potentially causing you harm in relation to SARS-CoV-2. The virus always operates through a natural environmental force. As you'll learn, this force can deliver the virus straight into your body, infecting you, but it can also bring in negative subtle energies that can cause anything from increased reactivity to the delivery of others' anxiety. This force can even bring in the idea of the virus or cause you to take on a loved one's symptoms as a way to help them out.

It is also possible that this virus was doctored through bioengineering. If so, we're also working with a human-made environmental force. Even if that theory doesn't make sense to you, the virus mutates easily within humans. Any secondary or tertiary versions of the virus could be considered part of a human-made environmental force.

At one level, SARS-CoV-2 can also cause damage through the delivery of a physical force. To illustrate, it can be caught through touch, which is a physical force. Not only can you catch the virus through that physical force, but negative subtle energies can enter that create additional harm. What if the person who last touched that surface was angry or sad?

Now their feelings get stuck into you, lowering your immune system and creating more depression or anxiety.

Whether or not your interaction with the virus involves more than the natural environmental transfer, secondary forces can create complications for healing. We can pick up on others' anxiety and thus become injured by an emotional force. We might become connected to dark entities that propel us into fright, and thus we're bonded to this virus through a spiritual force. We might become scared because of the news media, and thus be afflicted with a modern, or digital, force. In the end, we might find some part of ourselves hovering as a wounded self within a shock bubble. Toward that end, to really deal with and recover from the virus, we must uncover this self, invite grieving, and provide protection.

Energetics of a Virus. As you'll discover, every type of microbe fulfills a particular energetic task. Viruses are unique in that they are attached to some external form of energy. You'll learn more about the possible sources of attachment throughout this book and in the appendix. Suffice it to say that from an energetic point of view, it is necessary to release these attachments in order to disempower the virus.

Our Original Energetic Signature. One of the most imperative concepts to grasp is of having an original energetic signature. This is your central governing code. We want our physical and subtle energies to match rather than conflict with this key code. How might this idea apply to the existence of, and fall-out from, the pandemic? Consider the fact that there are many physical factors that determine who might be most affected by the virus or not. As said, these include age- and health-related functions. Smokers will most likely become sicker than non-smokers, and so on. What if one of the issues is our original energetic signature? If our signature is less viable and blurrier, if there are "gaps" or lots of spaces between our signature and our organic functions, we might be more vulnerable to the virus. Hence the importance of re-establishing the original code through energetic exercises.

Coinfections and Their Energetics. Many of my fellow healers, especially those who specialize in frequencies, believe that SARS-CoV-2 opens the door to coinfections. Coinfections are caused by microbes that run at a similar frequency to the SARS virus. Basically, SARS-CoV-2 opens the door, and other critters follow. While I don't list these possible coinfections, you'll learn about the meanings of the different microbes and be provided a way to help energetically eliminate them via your exercises.

Energetic Protection. We scrub our hands with warm water and soap to wash off the virus. We are told to wear masks and gloves to decrease contact and therefore the likelihood of contracting the disease. I believe it's just as important to establish the subtle energy boundaries needed to deflect or transform the virus.

Additional Energetic Factors. In approaching the virus and our relationship to it, there are any other number of energetic factors we might take into account. Are we energetically weakened by a viral connection to an energetic field called a miasm? A miasm is a familial structure of programs. Maybe we're vulnerable because of a dark entity or force or an ethnic programming. Maybe certain chakras of ours are weak; these are the subtle energy organs that will become the focus of our analyses and also healing processes. Perhaps we have too-fluid auric fields, extensions of the chakras that "decide" what will impact us or not. There are all sorts of ways to examine a situation like a pandemic, and if we love ourselves, we'll learn the basics.

As you become acquainted with the concepts covered in this chapter, and specifically in my discussion of SARS-CoV-2, remember that examining for energetics can complicate the situation but also provide you far more tools to use when seeking health and healing. After all, all challenges are energetic challenges. What energetic issues are involved in a situation will decide what steps you will take toward recovery.

Now let's dig deeper—and meet up with Maureen again.

Trauma and Challenges Guide, Part 1
Common Types and Sources

As noted earlier, I define trauma as the cause of a challenge, including the challenge of chronic illness. Any type of trauma can produce physical and subtle challenges; listed here are some of the most common. Many of the items on this list can be both an initial trauma and a subsequent challenge triggered by the stress response to trauma.

Environmental Trauma

Environmental, natural

- *natural disasters*
- *cosmic flares*
- *climactic changes*

Environmental, human caused

- *pollution (airborne toxicity)*
- *geo-pollution*
- *sound toxicity*
- *electromagnetic toxicity*

Physical Trauma

Injuries

- *accidental*
- *deliberate*

Physical abuse and violence

Sexual abuse and violence

Pain, primary or secondary (primary pain is usually the result of a physical force, and secondary pain involves the aftermath of this challenge, including follow-on injuries such as those incurred post-surgically or as emotional fallout)

Microbial infections

Genetic

Epigenetic (a chemical soup of microbes and ancestral memories that surround the coding genes)

Diseases

Psychological Trauma

Emotional abuse

Verbal abuse

Psychological abuse (includes emotional but is broader)

Moral trauma (such as being forced to act against your value system)

Digital abuse
- *bullying*
- *dating manipulation*
- *fast news cycles*
- *hyperavailability*

Learning issues
- *attention-deficit/hyperactivity disorder (ADHD)*
- *autism spectrum*
- *somatic (body) sensitivities*
- *dyslexia and similar challenges*

Psychological illnesses and conditions
- *depression (including different types, such as clinical, situational, and postpartum)*

- *anxiety*
- *post-traumatic stress disorder (PTSD)*
- *codependency (four types, including energetic codependency)*
- *additional mental illnesses, including borderline bipolar disorder, schizophrenia, and more*

Addictions and allergies

- *substance*
- *behavioral*
- *food (and other nourishment issues in particular)*

Aging

Financial problems

Relationship problems

Spiritual and psychic problems (including soul wounds, attachments, entity attacks, absorption of others' energies, hyperpsychism, and more)

Complications of grieving

Again, many of the items on this list can be both an initial trauma and a subsequent challenge, depending on the person and circumstances. For example, experiencing a learning issue can be a traumatizing long-term event for one person, while another person might develop learning issues as the result of a different trauma, such as losing a parent in early childhood and not receiving emotional support while grieving the loss. For the first person, the learning issue is a causal trauma; for the second person, the learning issue is a challenge that develops because of a trauma. So part of the healing process is determining which hardships are foundational traumas and which are challenges growing out of them.

Left unaddressed, the energies of both trauma and our system's response to it can cause or contribute to chronic illnesses. The lines between first-level traumas, second-level stress responses, and subsequent long-term disturbances blur when we're dealing with many psychological, learning, addiction, and allergy-related problems. We'll at least briefly address these concerns within this book. Know that each type of challenge can affect us both physically and energetically.

Synopsis

All challenges are, at their core, energetic challenges. Trauma is a significant life disruption that affects us not only physically, but also energetically. The force, or energy of the trauma, harms us when it doesn't harmonize with our original energetic signature, or our innate characteristic energy. Forces trigger a physical and energetic stress response; these energies and the secondary energies that are part of that stress response are the sources of our chronic challenges. These chronic challenges can include not only chronic physical illnesses, but also chronic psychological and interpersonal issues.

Now let's dig more deeply into the dynamics of energy to understand how and why, even though it's often invisible, its impact on us is so powerful.

CHAPTER 2

The Energies Underneath Our Challenges: Understanding Forces, Signatures, Our Energy Anatomies, and the Energetics of Trauma

There is a tendency at every important but difficult crossroad to pretend it's not really there.
—Bill McKibben, *The End of Nature*

In the previous chapter, I gave you an overview of how incompatible energy not only harms us during a traumatic event, but also keeps adversely affecting us over time if we don't address it. Now we're going to unpack some of the key concepts I introduced, including our subtle energy anatomy (and how it relates to our physical anatomy), our original energetic signature, forces and how they operate, and how our physical and energetic responses to trauma can lay the foundation for chronic illnesses, including autoimmune disorders. Armed with this knowledge, you'll be ready to understand how to heal from the effects of trauma and subsequent challenges, just like my client Maureen did.

To get started, it will help you to know a little bit more about energy itself.

Energy = Information + Vibration

As noted in chapter 1, energy has two components: information and movement. The information is the programming that tells something what to be. For instance, the information within your morning java tells your coffee to be coffee. If you alter that information, that coffee might change—maybe it goes from dark roast to light roast; perhaps it becomes a cup of tea.

The energy of everything in this universe also vibrates or moves. Even something as hardcore as a solid object is actually vibration, or waves of frequency. The two types of vibration are light and sound. These core units of energy are differentiated by the rates of their vibrations. We know what color something is by its vibration; we can tell the difference between a dog's bark and a cat's meow in the same way.

What happens if you adjust an object's vibration? It changes. Vibrationally, we modify reality all the time. Cold frequencies, which are low and slow, will turn water into ice. Be careful when thawing those cubes out, though. Hot frequencies are fast and quick. Make that water too hot, and you'll vaporize the cubes—and still be thirsty, having skipped the liquid stage altogether.

The twofold nature of energy—information and vibration—explains how a stressor can impact you not just physically, but also energetically. Imagine that a dog bites you, leaving puncture wounds. Not only have the dog's teeth broken your skin, but the dog's act, whether it was aggressive or defensive in nature, also inserts disruptive energetic data into your skin. That data interrupts the skin's vibration, causing a separation and an inability for the two edges to easily rejoin.

Two Types of Energy: Physical and Subtle

Governed by the laws of classical science, physical energies are measurable and respond to concrete actions. Subtle energy, on the other hand, can't always be measured and operates according to different rules, or the lack of them. There are many other names for subtle energy, such as *psychic, spiritual,* and *mystical.* I like the word *subtle* because it best describes the nature of these slippery, sly, and stupendous energies, which are explained by quantum science.

Quanta are the smallest units of reality. There are various types of quanta, including quarks, tachyons, and gluons. The truth is, we don't really know how many types of quanta exist because of the unique ways they operate. For instance, in the quantum world, an object doesn't exist unless it's observed. If two particles meet, they forever remain entangled, or interconnected. They will continue to affect each other, even when thousands of miles apart.

Quantum science offers the key to understanding reality. Classical science can't explain how everything works, although it does describe how the basic observable forces function, such as the weak nuclear force, the strong nuclear force, electromagnetic activity, and gravity. But classical science can't account for phenomena like the mystical transference of thoughts and feelings, miracle healing, mind-body interactions, clairvoyant insights, spiritual connectivity, and the blessings of creativity. The answers to these mysteries lie in the existence of subtle energy and the behaviors associated with it.[2]

Quantum laws actually underlie classical science's rules of energy's behavior. Quanta aren't concrete unless voted into reality consciously, and neither is the material world. Everything around you? Most of it is empty space; the objects in it are determined by the appearance and disappearance of quanta, or subtle energies, which are made of infinitesimally small, vibrating strings of energy. As Albert Einstein once said, matter is simply slowed-down energy waves that vibrate at different frequencies, all occupying mainly empty space.[3]

What all of this means is that a crisis like a dog bite isn't merely a physical event. If that dog was angry, hurt, or sad, those emotions, which are composed of subtle energy, can lodge in the wound. If the dog carries leftover memories from a prior abusive owner, those subtle energies can land in the punctures along with physical bacteria from the dog's mouth. And if you have a negative history with dogs, the energies of your own associations with them can stir up and potentially make it near impossible to heal from a simple bite—that is, unless you deal with the subtle energies involved with the dog bite. Remember, not every event will impact you negatively. This book is about helping you to identify and counter the energies that have proved to be harmful or hurtful to you.

How do you go about dealing with such events? First, you have to know that you're working within two different and intertwined energetic anatomies.

The Physical and Subtle Anatomies: Interdependent Structures

If you were to ask an anatomy professor where your liver is, they'd point to a specific spot on the right side of your upper abdomen. But ask a Chinese medical practitioner and they'd point to many different places in your body. That's because in traditional Chinese medicine, as in other Asian and indigenous healing modalities, the liver organ is merely the visible component of a much vaster, albeit invisible, structure.

---

2   Tiller, "What Are Subtle Energies?" 293–304.
3   Ferguson, *A Real-Life Christian Spiritual Journey*, 240.

Most of us have been educated about our physical anatomy, at least to some degree. Its components can be grouped into three major categories: organs, channels, and electromagnetic fields. The organs include the liver, heart, and spleen. The channels include the lymph and cardiovascular vessels. Every part of your body, including the tiniest atoms in your cells, generates electricity, which in turn creates fields made of electricity, magnetism, or electromagnetism. Most of these fields add up to a collection of electromagnetic fields (EMFs), or fields of light, that is the self. So, in a way, you're a giant light bulb.[4]

As well, all the fields in your body vibrate. Because everything that vibrates produces sonic waves, you're also an enormous sound generator. The resulting light and sound fields exchange energies within different parts of the body and between the body and the external world.[5] In fact, they can take in energy that is good for you—and energy that is *not* good for you.

Less well known is our body's subtle anatomy. It's formed from the same three constituents as the physical—organs, channels, and fields—but the components are more interactive and powerful.

The most influential subtle organs are the chakras, or energy centers. Every chakra regulates and impacts a region of the physical body and its related functions. It also regulates a set of psychological and spiritual tasks. When they're humming along, chakras convert physical energies into subtle energies and vice versa. This means that chakras register what happens to you not just physically and materially, but also emotionally, mentally, verbally, and spiritually. They also serve as mini brains for your body, deciding how you'll respond to stimuli.

Figure 1 shows you the twelve-chakra system I use, outlining its basic components. There are seven chakras located within the body proper and five located outside of the body. Most Western systems focus on only the seven chakras located in the body, but I believe it's vital to recognize that the self isn't a closed system. Because we are made of subtle energy, our "bodies" expand beyond their physical boundaries—even into other dimensions. Chakras basically run everything about you, so understanding them is essential to understanding our expansive nature and our energetic challenges.

---

4   Fraser, "How the Human Body Creates Electromagnetic Fields."
5   Smith, *Our Inner Ocean*, 295.

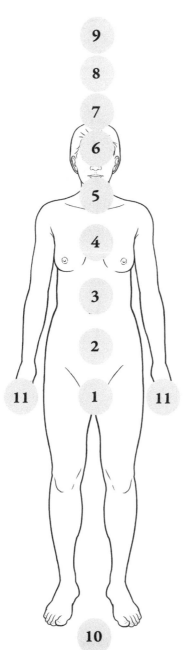

CHAKRA	GENERAL MAIN FUNCTIONS
FIRST	survival and physicality
SECOND	creativity and emotionality
THIRD	structure and mentality
FOURTH	healing and relationships
FIFTH	communication
SIXTH	strategy and vision
SEVENTH	spirituality and purpose
EIGHTH	mysticism
NINTH	harmony
TENTH	nature and ancestry
ELEVENTH	commanding of forces
TWELFTH	unique to each person

Figure 1: The Twelve-Chakra System. *The twelve-chakra system features seven in-body chakras and five out-of-body chakras. The twelfth chakra (not pictured) is an energetic field surrounding the body.*

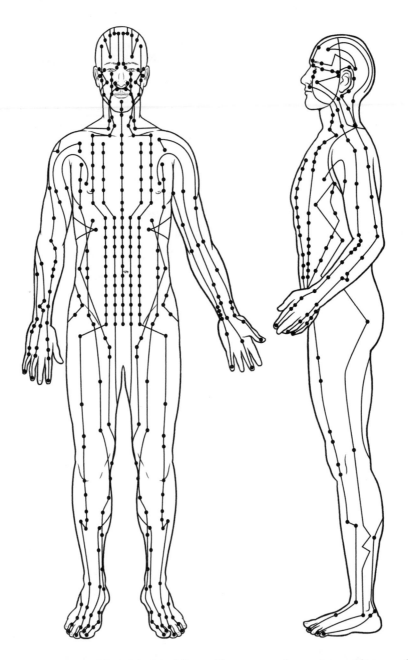

Figure 2: The Main Meridians. *There are twelve main meridians and two additional ones, the Conception Vessel and the Governor's Vessel, that are considered equally important. The Conception Vessel is shown on this illustration; the Governor's Vessel also flows down the central axis of the body but on the back side. Meridians run through the connective tissue and transport the subtle energy of chi throughout the system.*

Like the physical body, the subtle anatomy also contains channels. There are two primary subtle conduits you need to know to understand energetic challenges. One is the meridians, which distribute a subtle energy called chi throughout the body. Mainly occupying the connective tissue, meridians are riverways of light and sound that nourish the muscles and fascia while interacting with the circulatory system. They convey not only subtle energies but certain physical substances as well, and they are electrical in nature. The main meridians are shown in figure 2.

The other vital subtle channels are the nadis. There are thousands of nadis in the body. On a physical level, they primarily serve (or function as) the nervous system. The central nadi, called the sushumna, equates with the spine; the ida, which emanates from the left side of the first chakra, relates to the parasympathetic or relaxing nervous system; and the pingala, which originates from the right side of the first chakra, operates the sympathetic or reactive nervous system. The nadis are portrayed in figure 3.

As you can see, these subtle channels are both physically and subtly operational; they echo two of the body's physical systems, and they receive and distribute subtle energies, serving as feeder systems for the in-body chakras. When these channels are congested or malfunctioning, you can suffer nearly any type of issue, from physical to mystical. I will share more details about both the meridians and the nadis, including their main functions, in chapter 4.

Finally, there are the subtle fields. For this book, we'll focus on one specific set of subtle fields. Your overall *auric field* consists of twelve individual subtle or auric fields, each generated by one of your twelve chakras and layered on top of each other, like gradations of a parfait. Every auric field is an extension and expression of its chakra kin. Whatever happens to an auric field is transferred into a chakra and vice versa. While chakras regulate the you *inside* of you, their corollary fields govern the you *outside* of you.

Every chakra and its fellow auric field operates on a specific set of frequencies. As you can see in figure 4, each field is a different color, but it is the same color as its partnered chakra. Each chakra and field can also be represented as a unique sound range.

Together, the chakras and their corresponding auric fields work like conjoined communication devices. An external auric field absorbs energies matching its frequency and transfers that data to a chakra. In turn, a chakra discusses this information with the physical organs associated with it, also sending the information upward through the spine to the brain, which deciphers the messaging.

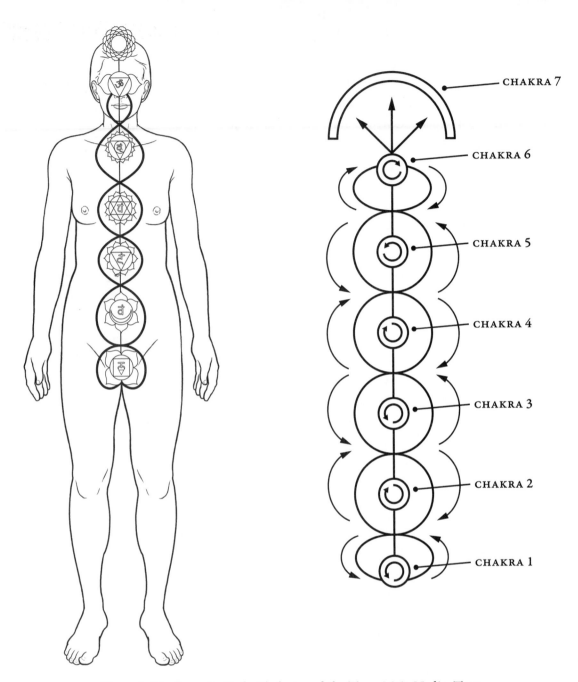

Figure 3: The Seven In-Body Chakras and the Three Main Nadis. *There are thousands of nadis, subtle energy channels associated with the nervous system. The three main nadis are shown here. The sushumna, the major nadi, runs within the spine. The ida is generated from the left side of the first chakra, and the pingala from the right. One of the reasons that the chakras spin is because of the crisscrossing energies of the ida and pingala.*

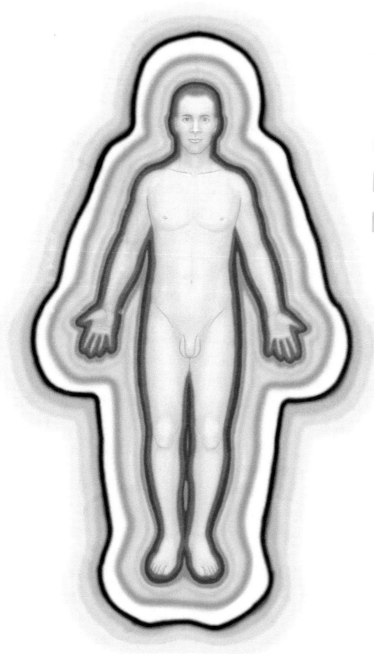

AURIC FIELD	COLOR
FIRST	red
TENTH	brown
SECOND	orange
THIRD	yellow
FOURTH	green
FIFTH	blue
SIXTH	violet
SEVENTH	white
EIGHTH	black
NINTH	gold
ELEVENTH	pink
TWELFTH	translucent

Figure 4: The Twelve Auric Fields. *In the twelve-chakra system, there are twelve auric fields. Each field is the same color as—and communicates with— its associated chakra. The first chakra's auric field begins closest to the body.*

Every field and corresponding chakra also emanates energy into the world. The decisions about what energies to bring in and keep out are complicated, but they are basically established by past life, childhood, and cultural programming, as well as your original energetic signature.

The auric fields outside of the physical body can absorb energies that don't touch your skin. They can also attune to another's thoughts, feelings, or even the memories of that person's previous experiences. They can even absorb the subtle effects of a physical blow to a person standing near you or the subtle effects of children bursting into giggles. In general, the energy of whatever happens around or to you can make its way to the auric field that matches the frequency of that event, and, depending on the programming of that field, bring those energies straight into its related chakra, as well as your body. Those incoming energies then spread through not only your subtle anatomy channels, but also the channels of the physical body.

Besides your auric fields, gazillions of other fields are part of your subtle anatomy. As explained earlier, every cellular pulse of electricity produces physically measurable fields; well, it also produces subtle fields. The quanta associated with this activity are far-flung, appearing in dimensions beyond the third and even linking with quanta in other time periods, such as the long-ago past, alternative presents, and possible futures. In fact, I believe they can connect with aspects of your soul from past lives, alternative lives, and future lives—ideas I'll discuss in chapter 3.

You Are an Original Energetic Signature

How does your system, a medley of your physical and subtle selves, decipher what energies (physical or subtle) to react to? How does it decide if these incoming energies will create healthy or unhealthy responses? The gauge that makes these determinations is your *original energetic signature.*

This signature is the sum total of the frequencies needed to unify your body, mind, soul, and spirit. It defines what frequencies you need to assimilate in order to fulfill your spirit's purpose and express yourself lovingly. It will decide which foods, liquids, colors, sounds, climactic conditions, and even thoughts and feelings will support you and which will be harmful. Hence, there are two main types of frequencies we interact with: constructive and destructive.[6] Your original energetic signature decides which is which.

---

6   Crosbie and Crosbie, "The Role of Quantum Physics."

On Soul and Spirit

Your mind, body, soul, and spirit are all different aspects of your total self. I define your soul as the aspect of you that moves across time and lifetimes, gathering experiences. As you'll read in chapter 4, I believe that the soul can be supportive or unintentionally destructive in terms of your well-being and how you address the energies of challenge.

Your spirit differs from your soul. It is your spiritual essence, the aspect of you knowingly connected to what I call the Spirit. (You may call it by whatever name you use—God, the Divine, the Universe, Allah, the Goddess, your Higher Power, the All, or something else.) Your spirit gives you the most vital and accurate information about which energies are helpful and supportive for you and which are not. It embodies your original energetic signature. You'll learn more about your spirit, as well as the role it can play in the healing of challenges, as this book goes on.

The idea of having (or being) a unique energetic signature isn't only a metaphysical concept; it is also a scientifically valid truth. For instance, every human heart exhibits an exclusive biometric so individualized that wearable technology devices are now employing a person's heartbeat as their password.[7] Research is also revealing that an individual's brain expresses innate properties and specialized ways of signaling.[8] Even our voices are distinct—various factors including vocal chord, lung, and nose functions and frequencies blend together to assure originality.[9]

Our original energetic signature is programmed into our bodies during conception. And then life happens. Right from the get-go, we interact with both physical and subtle energies that aren't constructive for us. Much of the time, we adapt. We absorb and process beneficial energies and neutralize debilitating energies. But if the absorbed energies are extremely detrimental or we are chronically exposed to incompatible energies, the following can occur:

We can't personalize our decisions. When we can't relate to our original energetic signature, we can't figure out what is good for us. We flail about, unable to select anything from healthy foods to uplifting relationship partners.

---

7 Yury, "Your Heartbeat May Soon Be Your Only Password."
8 Makin, "New Evidence Points to Personal Brain Signatures."
9 Wonderopolis, "Why Does Everyone Have a Unique Voice?"

We accept others' projections. If we're unable to relate to our inner code, we might too frequently accede to others' opinions. For instance, if we don't know what type of profession to enter, we might just join the family business—and be unhappy.

We project onto others. Somewhere inside of us, we know our true selves and what we genuinely need. If we can't own this data, we project it upon others. For instance, a parent might try to make their child become the doctor they always wanted to be themselves.

We own—and react to—energies that are not our own. As the gap increases between our original energetic signature's requirements and what we're exposed to, we more frequently absorb energies that are destructive and harmful to us. After all, there are empty holes to fill!

We react negatively to positive energies. The more hidden our original energetic signature and its signals are to us, the more apt we are to substitute other energies for our true desires. For instance, if we require love and we've never received it, through lack of recognition we might reject authentic love and keep choosing poor stand-ins.

How do we recognize our original energetic signature? Most of us have experienced flashes of our original energetic signature in childhood, at least. Those flashes of inspiration that were purely "us." Think of the times when you felt flow within yourself. The times when you knew instinctively what you liked and what you didn't, when you needed sleep and took a nap without apology, when you needed sustenance and knew exactly what food would satisfy you most, or when you chose what you wore and played with based solely on what felt best to you. The times when you felt a kind of internal, resonant harmony that felt both grounded and light. Not surprisingly, on account of the many experiences we've had, we often feel distant from our original energetic signatures, this sense of inner knowing. Technique 12, "Rediscovering Your Original Self and Signature," will show you how to strengthen your connection with your spirit, the part of you that holds your original energetic signature.

Because you're unique, an event that injures you might not hurt someone else and vice versa. For example, one of the great sociological puzzles is why one sibling is resilient in the wake of childhood abuse and another suffers major life issues. There are many reasons, including the fact that one child might be treated differently than another, but the core explanation lies in the realm of original energetic signatures.

Imagine that one child's original energetic signature is that of a warrior. He is bold, brave, and courageous. His brother's original energetic signature, on the other hand, is that of a peacemaker, calm and emotionally sensitive. In the face of severely verbally and physically abusive parents, the warrior brother could theoretically emerge from childhood as competent and forthright. The peacemaker brother, on the other hand, could enter adulthood mentally ill because the environment failed to promote his innate aptitudes. Then again, the warrior brother could develop an overly aggressive or abrasive personality in the wake of the abuse he suffered, and the peacemaker could develop a heightened sense of empathy and justice as a result of the same experience. It all depends on how each brother's original energetic signature resonates with and is able to process the unique energies of the original abuse and the secondary energies that developed afterward.

Forces Everywhere

Most traumas are caused by forces that don't suit our original energetic signature. This same principle applies to all living organisms, including animals and plants.

So what's a force? From a classic science point of view, it's a push or pull on an object. When a force interacts with an object, that object will be altered in some way. For instance, if the breeze gusts while you're taking a walk, your hat might fly off. The wind is the force, and the object is the hat.

Forces also form when two or more objects interact. Return to your walk. This time, the wind breaks off a tree branch, which in turn knocks off your hat. The first force (the wind) established a dynamic that caused two objects (the branch and your hat) to collide and create another force.

A force isn't actually a property of an object. It is energetically independent. Just as the wind can pick up and carry fallen leaves, a force can pick up and carry additional subtle energies or charges. Picture a force as a moving energy field or a wave that can carry discrete or small units of energy within it—in other words, charged subtle energies. When a force is "forced" on someone or formed during an exchange, these subtle energies can be transferred into anyone (or anything) around. The subtle energies that cause the most harm are those that are the most mismatched with an original energetic signature; the same can also be said of the physical energies related to the force.

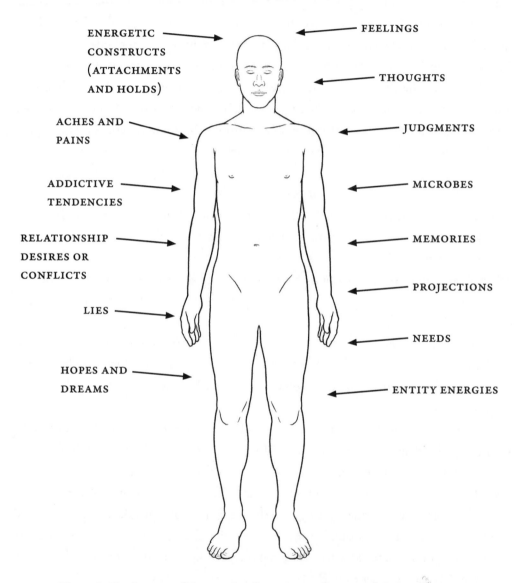

ENERGETIC CONSTRUCTS (ATTACHMENTS AND HOLDS)

FEELINGS

THOUGHTS

ACHES AND PAINS

JUDGMENTS

ADDICTIVE TENDENCIES

MICROBES

RELATIONSHIP DESIRES OR CONFLICTS

MEMORIES

PROJECTIONS

LIES

NEEDS

HOPES AND DREAMS

ENTITY ENERGIES

Figure 5: The Impact of Forces. *Any force can carry extra subtle energies into a person's system. Both the forces and subtle energies can create challenges if they don't match a person's original energetic signature. This illustration shows a few of the differing types of subtle energies that can cause or contribute to challenges.*

Back to your walk. This time, pretend that the wind had picked up measurable (physical) radioactive energies from a far-off nuclear disaster before it reached you. For sure, those radioactive energies will cause serious damage. Now imagine that the wind had wrapped itself around a seriously raging alcoholic before reaching you; it picked up the man's anger and attitudes, maybe even a few of the reasons he drinks. His emotions and attitudes are examples of the small units of energy or charges that an environmental force (or any type of force) can carry with it. The gale of the wind—the potency of a force—can deliver these subtle charges directly into your auric fields. These energies might bounce right off and you'd walk on, unconcerned, or they might be particularly damaging to you. The latter might happen if you don't relate well to anger or if frequencies in your original energetic signature were sublimated because your father was an alcoholic. The rest of the day, you might feel frustrated, maybe even drunk, without knowing why.

Forces don't always cause a negative outcome. As mentioned, you might not react to a particular force, and you might not react to the subtle charges it carries, whereas someone else might react to both. Forces can also carry positive energies, such as joy, love, hope, and goodness. Even then, however, the "positive" energies that are good for one person might not be good for another. For example, someone who exudes high, vibrant energy may impact your system with a feeling of overwhelm or imbalance. And, as pointed out earlier, you might start responding negatively to the exact energy needed to sustain your original energetic signature.

Figure 5 shows how forces impact you.

Types of Forces

There are six major types of forces relevant to trauma. Each one can affect us physically and carry subtle charges that can create a negative impact, depending on how they interact with our original energetic signature.

Environmental forces can be delivered through events such as climactic changes, weather disruptions, and pollution. Physical energies connected with these forces can be so strong that they can dismember a house or dam. Subtle charges riding on these forces can include the victims' horror, animals' fears, poverty worries, and even the subtle energies of the microbes that grow in the wake of these disasters (an issue I'll address in chapter 4).

Physical forces involve some type of physical interaction—the kind that occurs in car accidents, bodily abuse, falls, or even witnessing one person physically harming another.

Besides the follow-on bodily or material damage, physical forces can carry the subtle charges of anything from dark memories to dysfunctional beliefs.

Psychological forces break into three types: emotional, mental, and verbal. Feelings can be transported through someone's words but also through the intuitive airwaves, as can mental ideas, like criticism and cruelty. Verbal forces, or messages shared audibly, are frequent vehicles for dispersing both audible information and subtle feelings and thoughts. For example, you've likely experienced a conversation in which someone sounds happy to see you, but deep inside, you sense that they are actually unhappy about running into you. Our subtle self is often more aware of energies than is our everyday self.

Spiritual forces encompass a plethora of invisible sources of energy that can wield disruptive influences. This list includes ghosts, deceased ancestors, and the negative energies programmed into a house or object. (We'll discuss these matters in chapter 4.)

Modern forces include the energies continually emanating from power lines, cell phones, the internet, television, and the like. This category also encompasses the content of digital media, which is physical if we're looking at a horrifying website, but also perceptible intuitively. For instance, we might sense the violent energy of the pornographic material another person has just perused or pick up on the negativity of a news report that hasn't yet been broadcast.

Missing forces constitute those forces we should have received in our lifetime but didn't. For instance, all infants are innately programed to assume unconditional love. If we didn't receive it, we'll have an empty space that we might try to fill later with other means. In chapter 5 I'll show you how missing forces are the source of many types of allergies, addictions, and other chronic challenges and illnesses.

The Energetics of Trauma and Chronic Illnesses

From an energetic point of view, life's most disruptive, harmful energies cause two main hardships: trauma and chronic illnesses, including autoimmune disorders.

Typically, trauma is considered to be an infliction that causes an overwhelming amount of stress. The more intense its impact, the greater the chance we'll continue to suffer from its influences—at least, until we're able to integrate the physical, psychological, or spiritual outcomes of the event. For the purposes of this book, I offer a broader understanding of trauma: it is the detrimental outcome of a force wielding damage to the inside of us from the outside. Again, we'll be most adversely affected by the incoming forces, both physical and subtle, that don't match our original energetic signature.

Complicating the matter is the fact that an incoming force often leaves any or all of the following in its wake:

An entrance wound: where the force enters our physical and/or subtle anatomies.

An exit wound: where the force exits our physical and/or subtle anatomies, if it does.

A pathway: the path of the force as it moves through our anatomies.

Stuck points: Sometimes a force doesn't exit but gets stuck. That blockage must therefore be cleared and replaced with positive energy.

Missing energies: These forces ought to carry loving energies but don't. Bringing in the needed energies is key to healing many traumatic and chronic illnesses.

If a force's wounds and pathway are actually physical, such as when a bullet enters the physical body, physical actions are needed for healing. We need to treat the initial wound site(s) and any other parts of the body affected by the impact of the force. And we probably need to provide medicine to support the body's healing response and prevent secondary problems from developing. The subtle energy effects of the force's impact should be dealt with in much the same way: we need to address the entrance and exit wounds. The pathway must be cleansed, filled, or refilled, and perhaps reconstructed. Missing energies must be provided.

When the impact of a trauma goes unhealed, any secondary subtle charges the force was carrying can attract additional similar traumas, triggering a trauma cycle. For instance, if a young girl is sexually abused in childhood, she has a greater chance of being sexually abused as an adult.[10] This statement isn't only based on social science research; the subtle injuries caused by the abuse, as well as the subtle charges launched into her subtle anatomy by the perpetrator (remember the raging alcoholic?), will cause her energetic fields to attract the same types of traumatizing energies from outside of herself and fail to protect her from them.

---

10   Ogloff et al., "Child Sexual Abuse and Subsequent Offending and Victimization"; Crime Victims Center, Inc., "Statistics—Child Sexual Abuse," and Office of National Statistics, "People Who Were Abused As Children Are More Likely To Be Abused As an Adult."

And there's yet another factor that makes healing trauma even more complex: both the physical and subtle anatomies react automatically to encapsulate the injured part of the psyche in a shock bubble. Until liberated and lovingly supported, this stuck part of the self remains trapped in the bubble, where it continues to re-experience the original trauma. It remains locked away, endlessly stuck inside the energy of the trauma, while the rest of the self continues on. Eventually, the self in the bubble might not even want to be found. Who wants to be hurt again? If this wounded self remains entrenched too long, the physical and subtle anatomies will eventually develop a set of secondary forces. These self-created injurious internal secondary forces are what underlie chronic illnesses, including autoimmune disorders.

Modern society has seen an incredible rise in chronic illnesses and a corresponding inability of the medical community to respond. I believe this is because modern treatments miss the fact that the physical body isn't actually trying to harm itself. Rather, it's often seeking to destroy or rid itself of the disruptive, harmful subtle charges that entered during a trauma or that developed as a result of the body's response to trauma. These subtle charges and secondary forces register in the body biochemically but are more like ghosts than solid entities. The physical body can't actually clear them, but it tries to anyway. In the case of autoimmune disorders, when striking at the vaporous subtle charges and secondary forces, the immune cells only hit healthy cells. (According to Western medical science, an autoimmune disorder is a disease in which the body's immune system attacks its healthy cells.) In the case of cancer, the immune cells are hoodwinked by the secondary charges into thinking there's nothing there. With allergies, the secondary charges trick your immune system into believing that a beneficial or benign substance is actually a threat or "the enemy." This is why I believe that chronic illnesses, including the eighty-plus known autoimmune disorders, are more of a subtle rather than a physical issue.

What can we do about either trauma or chronic illnesses?

In a nutshell, we must heal trauma the same way it impacted the system: from outside to inside. Thus, trauma relief requires the assistance of another person, helper, or even a spiritual guide or the Spirit. We must also assist the wounded self that remains trapped within its shock bubble, applying qualities such as compassion and forgiveness to help this wounded inner self grieve and emerge. Chronic illnesses, at least the subtle components of them, require an inside-to-inside fix. We must also treat the secondary effects of unhealed trauma, including ongoing self-injurious processes.

Returning to Maureen

Remember Maureen, the sixty-year-old high school teacher whom you met in chapter 1? It took about a year, but eventually Maureen's conditions—the fatigue, aches and pains, arrhythmia, lung infections, depression, anxiety, and swinging moods—cleared. Our treatment plan was complicated. It started with me acknowledging her major childhood traumas and figuring out what energies were linked to each.

The first layer of healing focused on clearing the forces and subtle charges from the tornado that destroyed her family's farm. This environmental force had sent part of young Maureen's self into a shock bubble; it also filled her body and subtle anatomy with the subtle charges of terror and horror that had emanated from her family and community. These charges had remained locked into the tenth chakra and filled her tenth auric field with the same agonizing emotions. Using love and the types of subtle energy techniques I'll share in later chapters, we helped release her wounded self and the interfering subtle charges.

We did much the same inside of her fourth chakra, located in the heart area. Here she had taken in subtle charges generated from her father's heart attack. None of us can heal energies that aren't our own. We worked with this issue spiritually, inviting her father's soul into our session. Maureen communed with him and was able to gently return the energies of his emotional challenges to him.

Maureen, an energetic sponge, had also absorbed energies associated with her mother's mold infection. (In chapter 4 you'll learn how microbes impact us both physically and subtly.) As she processed the subtle energies held within her own mold infection, her lungs began to heal. She had also transferred her mother's moods into herself in order to protect her younger brothers and sisters; these, too, we needed to lovingly release.

Finally, we discovered a cord of subtle energy in her first chakra. This cord was attached to her still-living mother. Through these types of energetic constructs, we exchange energy with another person or being. Maureen's extreme fatigue was due to the fact she was giving her life energy to her mother and taking on her mother's issues in their stead. Children often unconsciously "agree" to these types of connections in order to support those they love. After we dealt with this cord, Maureen's energy immediately bounced back to normal. You'll learn about cords and similar energetic constructs in chapter 4, and in chapters 9 and 10 you'll learn how heal them.

To support our sessions, Maureen altered her diet, mainly by abstaining from inflammatory foods. (You'll learn more about these foods in chapter 10.) She also undertook body work, focusing on emotional grieving and eye movement desensitization and reprocessing

(EMDR) therapy. EMDR is extraordinarily beneficial, as it transforms the challenging energies locked into physical cells and the infra-low brain waves; we'll discuss these layers of trauma in chapter 3 and infra-low brain waves in chapter 7.

Maureen never would have wanted to relive her traumas. But in the end, she decided that she could leave her past behind, as well as the feelings of shame and terror that so often accompany trauma. Instead, she would embrace the wisdom of her healing process and mentor her students; she worked in an inner-city school district, and she knew firsthand that they were already experiencing more than their share of life's challenges.

Maureen's story is only one of many you'll read about in this book. In the next few chapters, you'll meet other people whose stories will demonstrate the energies of challenge. There is a story for everyone and everything. Fortunately, we are more than our stories.

Personal Assessment: *Your Current Life Challenge*

This short questionnaire will help you reflect on the cause or causes of a current life challenge. You'll need writing instruments, paper, and about twenty minutes of uninterrupted time.

1. Take a few deep breaths and focus on a present-day challenge. Now respond to these statements:

    ▸ *I would describe the challenge in the following way:*

    ▸ *I would rank the negative influences of this challenge in the following ways, using the number 1 for the most severe effects and the number 4 to describe the least influential:*

    > physical _____
    >
    > emotional _____
    >
    > mental _____
    >
    > spiritual _____

    ▸ *This challenge adversely affects _____ percent of my everyday life.*

    ▸ *This challenge impacts _____ percent of my life every month.*

    ▸ *My life would improve by _____ percent if this challenge were to resolve or transform.*

2. I believe that the following types of forces might be underlying this particular challenge: (you can write down more than one)

    ▸ *environmental*

    ▸ *physical*

    ▸ *psychological*

    > emotional (feelings-based forces)
    >
    > mental (thought-based forces)
    >
    > verbal (forces you've heard either audibly or psychically)

    ▸ *spiritual*

    ▸ *modern*

    ▸ *missing*

3. Look at the forces you wrote down in question 2. Next to those selected, indicate if you are experiencing the wounding in the following ways:

   ► *As trauma-induced stress:*
   ► *As a chronic illness or other chronic challenge, such as learning difficulties or a pattern of financial struggle:*
   ► *As both trauma-induced stress and chronic illness/challenge:*

4. Have you experienced any silver linings because of the dark cloud of this challenge? Reflect upon any wisdom gathered, then write down your perceptions.

5. Are you willing to go through any grieving necessary to move through this challenge? If not, what would you need to allow yourself to grieve what has occurred or is occurring?

Hold on to these results; you'll add to them in the next chapters. The personal assessments at the end of the part 1 chapters will help you see how the symptoms of your chronic illness or challenge are connected on both the physical and subtle energetic levels. That information will then help you as you dive into the healing techniques in part 2.

Synopsis

This chapter examined the energetics of a challenge. In it, you learned that energy is information that moves and that there are two main types, subtle and physical. Our system includes a subtle anatomy and a physical anatomy to manage each type of energy as we interact with it. These anatomies are interdependent, although the subtle anatomy is more thorough in its functions.

Both anatomies will operate optimally if they can take in and process energies matching your original energetic signature, the personal spectrum of frequencies that define your true self. Energies that nourish and sustain this original energetic signature create well-being, and energies that don't cause disruption and challenges.

The ultimate challenges are delivered via forces, invisible waves of energy that can cause physical effects and can also carry extra subtle charges. Forces and subtle charges that don't match our original energetic signature will cause the most harm.

There are six major types of forces: environmental, physical, psychological, spiritual, modern, and missing. Impacting us during a traumatizing event, all of these forces create pathways of injury that must be found, cleansed, and healed. The most challenging of events will send the wounded self into a shock bubble, where it remains trapped. We can't fully recover from or transform through the results of such a force until we release the wounded self from the shock bubble and enable grieving, and until we clear out the intrusive subtle charges that came with the force.

There are two main conditions that result from these traumatizing forces, and they must be dealt with in different ways. Traumatic injuries must be healed outside to inside, which is how they were caused. Chronic illnesses, including autoimmune conditions, which involve a self-injurious process, must be shifted inside to inside.

Now turn the page to chapter 3 and learn more about how the physical anatomy responds to life's harmful disrupters.

CHAPTER 3

The Physical Anatomy: What Happens When We're Hurting

That was a long time ago, but it's wrong what they say about the past, I've learned, about how you can bury it. Because the past claws its way out.
—Khaled Hosseini, *The Kite Runner*

The body is so wonderful. It holds our soul, illuminates our spirit, and reflects life's vicissitudes. Our body's strengths are matched by its fragility, making life poetic but also scary. And because the body remembers everything, we can't hide from anything—a fact that both serves us and challenges us.

Stress is the basis of trauma and chronic illness. So in order to truly undo the harm inflicted by trauma and challenges, it's vital to understand the complex cascade of chemical and neurological activities that the body goes through when stressed. Ultimately, if our life feels too challenging, it's because our body hasn't finished dealing with a stressor. The major stressors might lie in the past or exist in the present, but no matter what, they are the root of our problems.

This chapter is an in-depth biology lesson and crash course in how the various bodily systems respond to stress. At the end I've provided a special guide that serves as a reference for this and later chapters. I encourage you to refer back to this guide when assessing stress and trauma and seeking recovery, as it contains data more in-depth than I cover in the main flow of the book. I have found that healing often requires "feeding our brain," or understanding the nuts and bolts behind a challenge or disease process. The greater our understanding of the biologics of an issue, the lower the fear we feel when approaching our recuperation—and the more apt we are at a successful recovery.

For instance, if you're struggling with a chronic illness and are aware of the microbe involved, you can reference that microbe in the guide and better comprehend how it operates in your body. You can then construct a clear plan for dealing with it.

In the next two chapters, you'll learn more about the subtle energetics of these matters, such as microbes. You can combine the physical and subtle perspectives to build an even more on-point healing approach.

The Cycle of Stress

Any of the forces described in chapter 2 can be a stressor to our body. Those stressors that most seriously affect us create what I picture as a loop of interlacing physical, physiological, and spiritual reactions. As you can see in figure 6, no matter what stressor begins the stress cycle, it also can potentially harm you in the other two ways.

For instance, I worked with a woman named Hannah who was an office manager and the mother of three children. Through these roles, she received up to 1,500 emails a day. She was completely overwhelmed, mainly because she believed she should be able to keep up with the incoming missives. What began as a psychological misunderstanding rooted in her belief that she had to be picture-perfect resulted in insomnia, fatigue, headaches, nightmares, and eventually a near physical and nervous breakdown (physical effects). It also birthed a bigger question about her ultimate life purpose (spiritual effects).

Over time, I helped Hannah with every level of her challenge. She altered her belief and began accepting her human limitations. She set limits on her email interactions, even with her boss. She dealt with her deep-seated perfectionist issues, coming to peace with this need for limits. Finally, she addressed the spiritual aspect of the matter by asking herself what she really wanted to do with her life. Eventually, she changed careers, focusing on one that didn't require the same level of online activity and that gave her a sense of satisfaction. None of these outcomes would have been possible, however, if she hadn't paid attention to her body's reactions to both short- and long-term stress.

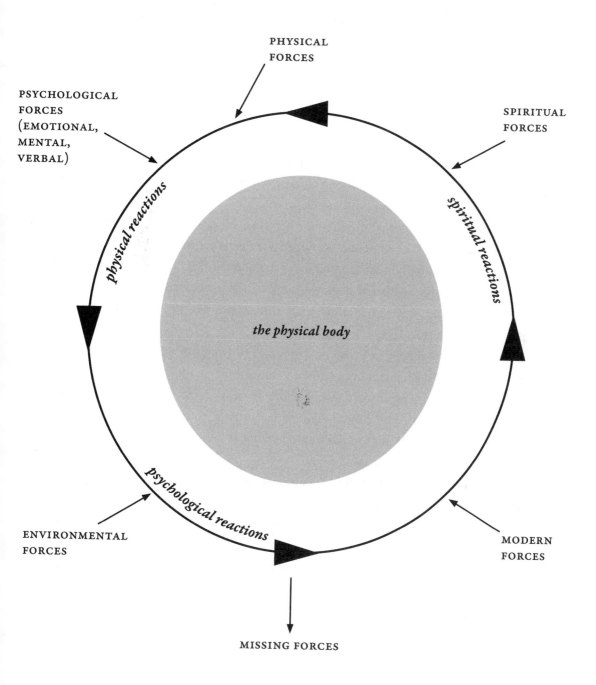

Figure 6: The Cycle of Stress. *The cycle of stress is such that no matter which of the six forces—environmental, physical, psychological, modern, spiritual, and missing—cause a stressor, the body's responses can lead to physical, psychological, or spiritual challenges.*

In general, if we fully deal with a stressor in a relatively short amount of time, the body can return to normal. If we can't—if the stressor is too acute, it becomes chronic, or we get stuck in our reactions to it—the cost can be phenomenal. We'll become fatigued, irritable, and suffer mood swings. We might become hyperaroused, experiencing nighttime insomnia and daytime exhaustion. Our concentration, learning, and memory retrieval can be impaired, and if we have a learning issue, the symptoms can worsen. We can also develop any other number of challenges, including chronic illnesses, mental disorders, food issues, addictions, relationship hardships, and more.

It's important to point out that stress is quite personal. What will stress you out might be different than what will stress someone else out. Never shame yourself for not being "strong enough" to deal with something. Stressors can be great or small. They might even be positive or negative. I once worked with a woman who got the hiccups every time something happy happened. Her mother used to yell at her when things went her way, and so, for her, joy became a negative stressor.

The truth is that anything that makes us respond to an event can count as a stressor. For example, I once worked with a middle-aged man named Marcos. He felt guilty about every penny he spent. The more expensive a purchase, the stronger his reaction. When he bought a much-needed family van, he was up all night with a horrible stomachache and a migraine. He'd experienced these types of physical symptoms when spending money since he'd started a lawn-mowing business as a teenager.

What did Marcos's serious physical and emotional symptoms stem from? His parents had run a restaurant and laundered money for their relatives through it. Consequently, every time they spent money on him, he felt filthy. His childhood experience made him think that all monies spent by him were "bad monies." Once Marcos understood the power of this deeply held perception, he began to see money as a neutral life tool. The physical symptoms he experienced when spending money disappeared. He found it fascinating the way his body had become so stressed in response to such a simple action as spending money, but that's exactly the nature of the body's stress response.

How Stress Affects Our Body's Systems

Under stress, the body reacts in fairly predictable ways. It has to; it is hardwired to respond to change in order to handle a crisis. Every bodily system reacts to a stressor. The nervous system is our first responder, but its actions are swiftly followed by immediate and interactive responses within the respiratory, cardiovascular, musculoskeletal, endocrine, digestive, and immune systems. Even our cellular and genetic makeup get involved, as do various processes involving sound and light frequencies. This chain of internal events leaves us more alert and able to focus when going through a predicament. We only get into trouble if we can't return to baseline.

The Nervous System Under Stress

Under pressure, our nervous system is the first of many bodily systems to kick in. After all, its job is to calculate and respond to risk. Key is our central nervous system (CNS), composed of the brain and the spinal cord, but it's our autonomic nervous system (ANS) that gets things going.

The ANS is exactly what it sounds like: a non-conscious and autonomic processor of data. Standard science tells us that the most essential stress responses involve two ANS subcomponents: the sympathetic nervous system (SNS), which is the excitatory and activating part of the ANS, and the parasympathetic nervous system (PNS), the calming and de-escalating aspect of the ANS. Recently, science has spotted a third actor on the stage: the vagus nerve, the longest nerve in the body.

When prompted, the SNS immediately triggers the production of excitatory hormones, chiefly adrenaline, noradrenaline, and cortisol. This initial hormonal blast-off is called the *stress response* and triggers the flight, freeze, fight, and fawn reactions regulated by the mammalian/limbic brain system (see guide 2 at the end of this chapter for more on this part of the brain). Depending on the circumstances, we'll take flight, or try to escape the situation; freeze, or duck and cover; fight, or attack an element of the situation; or fawn, which involves trying to please others involved in the situation.[11]

Once the crisis is over, the body returns—or is supposed to return—to the pre-emergency, relaxed state via marching orders from the parasympathetic nervous system. However, long-term and intermittent stress or really acute problems stop the PNS from kicking in. In addition, overactivity in the PNS can stimulate a new set of problems, such as asthma, dilation of the blood vessels, and more.[12]

The nervous system's stress response can be triggered from an external event, but it can also arise because of internal circumstances, such as an upset stomach or nagging thought. Basically, if there is a problem, the nervous system will find it, as it constantly scans to assess situations as safe, dangerous, or life threatening. The vagus nerve is actually the "intelligence" behind the operation, however, making the snap decisions.

---

11   Walker, "Codependency, Trauma and the Fawn Response."
12   American Psychological Association (APA), "Stress Effects on the Body."

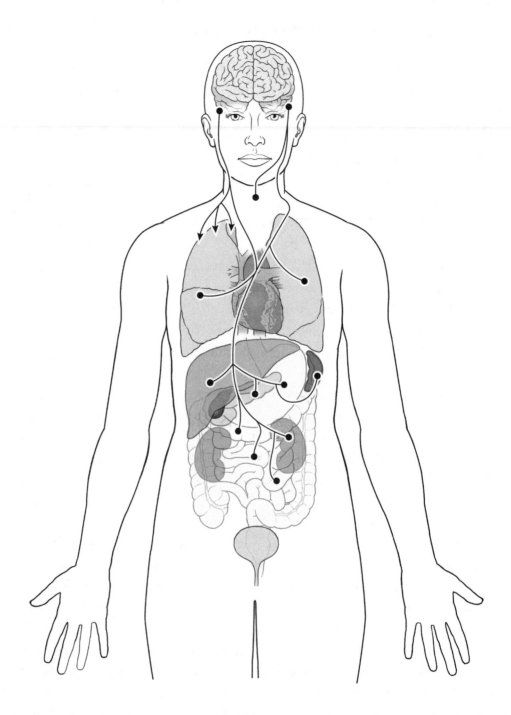

Figure 7: The Vagus Nerve in the Body. *The vagus nerve runs along a gut-heart-brain axis (also called the gut-brain axis) and plays a primary role in determining our physical stress reactions. As you can see, it interfaces with all of our organ systems.*

The vagus nerve is the tenth pair of twelve cranial nerves descending from the brain, specifically from the brain stem; the brain stem is part of our reptilian brain, which is rigidly dedicated to safety. The vagus nerve actually splits into two parts at the neck. Called the left and right vagus, these nerves then branch throughout much of the torso.

The vagus nerve is the longest pair of cranial nerves and is made of motor and sensory fibers. Its travels interconnect the brain with the heart, lungs, gut, liver, spleen, gallbladder, ureter, female fertility organs, neck, ears, tongue, and kidneys. Essentially, it uses the neurotransmitter acetylcholine to cause muscle contractions in the PNS, which in turn controls our automatic bodily functions. Figure 7 shows you the pathway of the vagus nerve. (In chapter 4 you'll see how this nerve relates to the chakras.)

I cannot emphasize enough the importance of this nerve. The vagus nerve keeps our heart rate constant; regulates our breathing, sweating, blood pressure, and blood glucose balance; and assists with digesting our food. It also helps create and regulate our emotions.[13]

How does this single nerve accomplish this latter task? The most vital bond formed by the vagus nerve is between the heart, brain, and gut. Each of these is considered an emotional center, though they operate differently. The heart, for instance, is a port of entry for the psychophysiological experience of feelings. Basically, positive emotions cause a balanced heart-rhythm pattern and better health throughout the body. Negative emotions trigger the opposite, creating disabling heart-rhythms and bodily conditions.[14]

There are many brain areas that serve as emotional processing centers. These include the amygdala, involved in our primal emotions; the hippocampus, which holds the memories that cause emotional reactions; and several cognitive brain centers that regulate our belief systems.[15] But it's our gut that plays the biggest role in our feelings, as well as in many disease processes.

When I say "gut," I mean the enteric nervous system, also called the "gut brain" or the "second brain." This is our digestive system's processing center. Containing more neurons than the spinal cord, it is composed of two networks of neurons that are embedded in the walls of the digestive tract and run from the anus to the esophagus. This system controls our physical digestion, but its operations are so critical to our stress response that it is often

---

13 Ropp, "12 Ways to Unlock the Powers of the Vagus Nerve."
14 HeartMath Institute, "The Making of Emotions."
15 Tarasuik et al., "Understanding the Neurobiology of Emotional Intelligence," 307–320.

considered a third part of the ANS. Not only that, it also secretes neurotransmitters that link it to the CNS and establish protocols for our emotional responses to events.[16]

Of particular importance is the gut-brain axis formed by the vagus nerve. The interplay between the vagus nerve, the gut, and the ANS means that emotions can trigger a stress reaction and vice versa. In that at least 90 percent of the signals passing along the vagus nerve run from the enteric nervous system to the brain, the lead determiner of our well-being is actually our gut, not our brain. Those butterflies in your stomach? That's your gut determining that you're emotionally stressed about giving a speech. As such, the vagus nerve informs your brain, and you get wheezy and scared. But the physical conditions in the gut are equally vital to causing emotions.

At least 100 million bacteria dwell in our gastrointestinal tract, along with fungi, parasites, and viruses. We usually live symbiotically with these microbes, which form a microbiome in our enteric nervous system. In fact, these microbes are quite helpful, aiding in our metabolic functions, fat distribution, immunity, and even in keeping us from getting sick. The vagus nerve conveys to the brain what's happening physically in the gut, and when something is off in this secondary brain, it stimulates reactions in the head brain.[17] You're taking antibiotics? The resulting upset in the gut's microbiome can influence the brain and make you more aggressive.

Any number of conditions can damage the vagus nerve—including diabetes, poor food choices, an influx of toxins, alcoholism, infections, and any sort of stressor—thereby creating uncontrollable challenges.[18] In fact, so influential is the vagus nerve and its effects that a brand-new theory about its importance has emerged. Called the polyvagal theory, we owe much of our knowledge about this nerve to Stephen W. Porges, a psychiatrist and research scientist.[19]

The polyvagal theory explains that the vagus nerve programs our reactions to stress based on our social interactions and relationships. The theory is more particular than most about highlighting the specific physical structures that coordinate our stress reactions. These players are the dorsal branch of the vagal nerve, a part of the PNS that causes us to freeze when we're scared; the entirety of the SNS, which adds the fight-or-flight elements; and

---

16   Bowen, "The Enteric Nervous System."

17   Zhu et al., "Microbiota-Gut-Brain Axis and the Central Nervous System."

18   Ropp, "12 Ways to Unlock the Powers of the Vagus Nerve."

19   Porges, The Polyvagal Theory.

the ventral branch of the vagus nerve, a mammalian parasympathetic communication and social interactive system. This particular part of the vagus nerve, called the "smart vagus," assesses social behaviors.

Says Porges, if a situation seems safe, we engage with the ventral vagus. We'll be relaxed and share freely. If we're not feeling secure, the SNS will take over. If the SNS can't alleviate our fear, the dorsal PNS will shut us down. The perceptions that lead to recognizing these three steps are called neuroperceptions.[20]

The Respiratory System Under Stress

Under stress, the SNS hormones send our respiratory system into overdrive. We breathe harder and more quickly in order to let the blood distribute more oxygen to the body. If we get too wired, however, we'll breathe too fast and can hyperventilate, which can cause a panic attack or anxiety. Heavy emotional stress, such as the death of a loved one, can actually cause an asthma attack. Lacking relief from the stress response, we may incur respiratory damage and oxygenation issues.

The Cardiovascular System Under Stress

Just like that, stress hormones increase our heart rate and blood pressure, which return to normal if the stress passes. In the meantime, the blood vessels that direct blood to our large muscles and the heart dilate so we can physically respond to the stressor. Repetitive or chronic stress, however, damages the blood vessels, leading to hypertension, heart attack, and stroke, as well as inflammation in the circulatory system.

The Musculoskeletal System Under Stress

Our muscles tense when we're under stress in order to guard against injury and pain. If these muscles don't release when an event has passed, we'll remain in a state of guardedness, which can trigger problems, including headaches, migraines, and back pain.[21]

Connective tissue is part of the musculoskeletal system. We know that mechanical or physical stress can create tissue damage in connective tissues as well as muscles. Research in animals also reveals that animals under emotional stress are predisposed to connective tissue damage, with an increased potential for tissue hemorrhages, edema, and mast cell

---

20   Friedland-Kays and Dana, "Being Polyvagal."
21   American Psychological Association (APA), "Stress Effects on the Body."

proliferation. Mast cells are immune cells produced in the bone marrow; when overpopulating the body, they cause inflammation.[22]

The Endocrine System Under Stress

Our endocrine (hormone) system, which regulates mood, growth, development, tissue functions, reproductive system functions, metabolism, digestion, and more, is a vital part of our stress response.

The part of the brain known as the hypothalamus is the link between the nervous system and the endocrine system. The hypothalamus is actually part of a greater bodily system called the hypothalamic-pituitary-adrenal (HPA) axis, a three-way driver of the endocrine system's stress response. It causes an increase in steroid hormones called glucocorticoids, which include cortisol, one of the three main stress hormones that the SNS causes the body to produce.

Under stress, the hypothalamus asks the pituitary gland, located in the brain, to produce a hormone that tells the adrenal glands, atop the kidneys, to increase the manufacturing of cortisol. Cortisol is like jet fuel. It gives us immediate energy by mobilizing the glucose and fatty acids in the liver. (We need the energy from that extra glucose, or sugar, but if the liver keeps making it, we'll have a higher chance of developing type 2 diabetes.) Cortisol also helps regulate the immune system and reduces inflammation, thus compensating for the inflammation incurred during stressful situations.

Chronic exposure to the hormones fabricated by the members of this axis, however, can cause psychological, immune, and metabolic disorders and conditions such as depression, chronic fatigue, obesity, and chronic illnesses, including autoimmune disorders such as the many types of diabetes. It can also affect the reproductive system, which can lead to negative changes in a woman's menstrual cycle and impotence in men. It can even speed up our biological aging. Basically, chronic stress impairs the communication between the immune system and the HPA axis.[23]

---

22 Sukakov, "Connective Tissue Under Emotional Stress."

23 American Psychological Association (APA), "Stress Effects on the Body," and Aguilera, "HPA Axis Responsiveness to Stress."

The Digestive and Immune Systems Under Stress

The digestive system reacts immediately under stress. In fact, changes in the digestive system are so intertwined with responses from the immune system because of the gut-brain connection that I have to discuss both systems together.

On a simplistic level, after the SNS stimulates the stress hormones, the response from the CNS can cause the esophagus to spasm; these spasms increase the acid in the stomach, causing indigestion, nausea, heartburn, and acid reflux, which can result in constipation and diarrhea. If the balance in our nervous and digestive systems isn't restored, we'll absorb fewer nutrients through the small intestine.

After digesting the food passed from the stomach, the small intestine passes micronutrients into the bloodstream. Fewer nutrients entering the bloodstream mean an increased chance of malnutrition. This intestinal permeability, caused or made worse by stressors like poor diet, infections, emotional upheaval, and toxins, breaks apart the junctures of the intestinal wall. Now bigger particles, such as toxins, microbes, and undigested food, can get through the small intestine's wall. The liver, which cleans the blood, struggles to filter these substances out of the bloodstream and becomes overworked; in turn, the kidneys, which also filter waste and extra fluid from the body, become tired. Then your entire body lags, becoming fatigued and inflamed. This multi-organ breakdown is called leaky gut syndrome.

With a lowered intestinal barrier, harmful gut bacteria can also enter the bloodstream, causing additional inflammation and infection. Your immune system marks these properties as invaders and attacks them, inviting food allergies, brain fog, fatigue, skin problems, mood challenges, hormonal imbalances, asthma, seasonal allergies, chronic fatigue syndrome, and fibromyalgia. Additional challenges can include irritable bowel syndrome (IBS), diverticulitis, Crohn's disease, and other chronic illnesses, many of which qualify as autoimmune disorders.

How can simple stress cause such maladies? Nearly 80 percent of your immune system lives in your gut, as does 95 percent of the serotonin responsible for your mood.[24] Those one to two pounds constituting your gut's microbiome regulate anxiety, depression, and your emotional behavior, and they also protect you from respiratory and other infections.

---

24   Myers, "9 Signs You Have Leaky Gut," and Iliades, "How Stress Affects Digestion."

Certain of these intestine's microbes also produce vast amounts of antibodies, which can attack incoming pathogens. If this process is disrupted, so is your health.[25]

Did you know that these gut microbes can also trigger diseases in your brain? Yup. The vagus nerve monitors the health of the gut and communicates that information with the CNS. If the vagus nerve is stressed (due to inflammation caused by an infection, for example), its ability to function properly is compromised, which can cause erroneous messages to be sent to the immune system via the CNS. There is increasing evidence that the abnormal shaping and clumping of alpha-synuclein, a protein that helps in the chemical exchange between nerve cells in the brain, found in Parkinson's patients is due to a disturbance in the gut's microbiome. Other intestinal microorganisms can damage the vagus nerve and convey chemical marching orders that can lead to neuropsychiatric and metabolic disorders, such as schizophrenia, autism, anxiety, obesity, diabetes, depression, multiple sclerosis, and more.[26]

There is such an obvious relationship between the gut, immune system, and neurological system that science has recently invented new terms to convey it. These terms include *psychoneuroimmunology*, which is the study of the connections between the brain, immune system, illness, stress, and mood, and *neuroimmunology*, which is the study of the connections between the nervous, immune, and endocrine system.

I'll give you yet another example of how important it is to track the connections between systems. Let's say you're depressed or anxious and decide to see a neuroimmunologist. Their first step would probably be figuring out your levels of the neurotransmitter serotonin, an important mood stabilizer made in both the brain and the gut. In both areas it is the same molecule, but it's produced by different types of cells, about 95 percent of which are in the gut.

Low serotonin in the brain can lead to anxiety and depression, conditions that especially occur in reaction to stress. Selective serotonin reuptake inhibitors (SSRIs), the most common treatment for anxiety and depression, put more serotonin not only into the brain, but the gut too. Too much serotonin in the gut causes "mental illness" in our second brain, such as feelings of anxiety, autism symptoms, and even illnesses like irritable bowel syndrome. In other words, when you're depressed in the brain, you can become anxious in your gut. But even if there is enough or too much serotonin in the brain, you can potentially have too

---

25   Krans, "6 Surprising Facts About the Microbes Living in Your Gut."
26   Kwon, "Does Parkinson's Begin in the Gut?" and Bonaz et al., "The Vagus Nerve at the Interface of the Microbiota-Gut-Brain Axis."

little in the gut, which can cause conditions like osteoporosis, a bone disease, as well as other problems.[27]

The neuroimmunologist might also decide that to treat your depression and anxiety they need to test your body for inflammation and get to the underlying cause. According to the World Health Organization, depression is the leading cause of disability worldwide.[28] However, up to 70 percent of all patients aren't helped by available treatments, including antidepressants.[29]

Maybe that's because bodily inflammation worsens and can sometimes even cause depression. When the immune system attacks pathogens—or even our own healthy cells, in the case of an autoimmune disorder—the entire system enflames, releasing cytokines (proteins that regulate the immune system) and other substances, causing sleepiness, fatigue, cognitive struggles, and lack of appetite—in other words, depression symptoms. In fact, markers of inflammation are higher in depressed people than non-depressed ones.[30]

What else might a psychoneuroimmunologist or neuroimmunologist notice in your combined digestive-immune system? Well, stress—even emotional stress—will decrease the body's lymphocytes, the white blood cells that fight infection, putting you at increased risk for various diseases and even cancer. The resulting suppressed immune system will also put more pressure on other systems. For instance, the circulatory system has to work harder, which can lead to coronary heart disease.

One very challenging result of stress, especially acute or long-term stress, is the overproduction of mast cells (immune cells) by the bone marrow. As I've already mentioned, too many mast cells lead to inflammation and chronic illnesses, but this process also stirs the overproduction of cytokines. Cytokines are formed from proteins that enable cross-cellular communication. Created in the right amount, they regulate our immune responses to challenges. When overproduced, which happens when we're under too much stress, they cause inflammation and corresponding diseases such as rheumatoid arthritis.[31] (Both cytokines and mast cells are discussed further in guide 2 at the end of this chapter, as well as other parts of this chapter and the book.)

---

27 Hadhazy, "Think Twice: How the Gut's 'Second Brain' Influences Mood and Well-Being."
28 World Health Organization, "Depression."
29 Oaklander, "New Hope for Depression."
30 Azab, "The Brain on Fire: Depression and Inflammation."
31 Eustice, "Cytokines and How They Work."

Our contemporary researchers will also point out that psychological well-being influences the immune system. For instance, research on a group of students under great pressure showed that their immune systems were dampened during that time. The loneliest students were found to have the weakest immune systems.[32] This is yet another example of how each aspect of the self influences all other aspects of the self.

Seven Essential Nutrients

The nutrients we receive from food are vital to dealing with and recovering from all challenges. Like the body, they have both physical and subtle aspects. Here are the ways seven important nutrients contribute to our physical health; chapter 4 will discuss the subtle aspects of these nutrients.

Carbohydrates: Sugars for energy.

Fats: Calorie-rich acids that store energy, provide insulation, protect our organs, and help proteins do their job.

Proteins: Grow and repair muscles and other tissues.

Fiber: Indigestible part of the diet. Important because it serves as a vehicle for taking out waste through the large intestine.

Minerals: Inorganic but necessary elements.

Vitamins: Water and fat-soluble nutrients necessary for all bodily functions.

Water: Carries nutrients, clears wastes and toxins, and composes 70 percent of the body's material.

The Cellular and Genetic Systems Under Stress

Under stress, all of our cells, including the cells that carry or affect our genes, take a beating. (See the cellular and genetic systems section of guide 2, which defines all of the terms included here.) The DNA in your genes, the sequence of which carries the qualities of your ancestors, can become injured, and the results can include cancer, infection, and disease. As well, environmental challenges, whether they occur inside or outside of the body, can cause epigenetic alterations, or alternations to material in genes that are responsible for all the other functions of the gene not related to DNA. Stressors that impact the epigenetic material include unhealthy foods, air, and the lack of basic needs; alterations in family structures

---

32   McLeod, "Stress, Illness and the Immune System."

or the environment such as famines, hurricanes, radiation, and more; exposure to severe socioeconomic alterations; biochemical stress; and more.

Not only might you be affected by epigenetic alterations, but you can experience problems handed down to you from at least fourteen generations in your past.[33] This process is called transgenerational inheritance, and it affects you more than you realize. Imagine that, as a member of the "clean plate club," you constantly gulp your food. That tendency, which causes you to be overweight, might be a result of your life experiences; then again, it might be something you inherited from your grandparents, who nearly starved to death during the Great Depression in America. You might be acting out their behaviors, which were born out of food scarcity.

Another interesting cellular stressor exists because of the presence of microchimeric cells. These cells are remnants of other people, and they can exist within a body for decades, either supporting the body's immune system or establishing the conditions for problems, including cancer, diabetes, heart conditions, and more. There are many sources of these microchimeric cells. The most common ones are those that we inherit from our mother; as well, cells from our bodies can remain within our mother's body after we are born. Likewise, cells from our older siblings can be absorbed into our bodies while we are in utero. Microchimeric cells can migrate to nearly any organ or place in the body and multiply there. Sometimes they travel to an injury site, reproduce, and help repair the wound.[34] But other times they stir up the immune system, which attacks them, causing chronic illnesses, including autoimmune disorders. I've actually worked with a client who had a tumor in her uterus. The doctors couldn't figure out if it was cancerous or not. Using my intuition, I perceived it to contain a part of a "disappeared twin"—part of the body of a twin that was absorbed in utero. Indeed, when surgeons removed the tumor, they discovered teeth and hair in it. The microchimeric cells had begun to grow and had solidified into a tumor.

I've found that the influence of these cells isn't well known within the medical community, but it ought to be. For instance, microchimerism is more common in patients with multiple sclerosis than in their healthy siblings, suggesting it plays a role in this disease process.[35]

---

33   Hurley, "Grandma's Experiences Leave a Mark on Your Genes," and Weinhold, "Epigenetics: The Science of Change."

34   Shute, "Beyond Birth."

35   Matone, "Scientists Discover Children's Cells Living in Mothers' Brains."

We don't yet fully understand the subtle energy connections between the physical and subtle anatomies and microchimeric cells or the factors that cause these cells to become supportive or destructive. In my work, however, I've come to believe that the connections and effects are multilevel.

For one, I believe microchimeric cells that match our original energetic signature will be more beneficial than those that don't. Equally important is the nature of the relationship between the people whose cells we carry—or the people who carry our cells—and ourselves. The more loving the relationship, the more supportive the microchimeric cells will likely be. The more problematic the relationship, the greater the chance the microchimeric cells will cause negative side effects.

One exception to this last statement involves trauma. I've worked with clients who were exceptionally close to a relative with whom they exchanged microchimeric cells, such as twins or biological parents and children. Time after time, I noticed that my clients would suffer symptoms or stressors similar to those their loved ones experienced. For instance, if a beloved daughter experienced panic attacks, her mother might start to have them too. I believe the microchimeric cells act like a carrier device, bringing the subtle energies from one person to their loving relative, who absorbs the energies unconsciously. When you consider that subtle energy can pass from auric field to auric field, it can certainly pass from a mother to the maternal cells within her child or from a twin to their sibling. Not all transferred energies will have a negative effect. If a son gets a pay raise, his mother might too!

Under stress, another interesting phenomenon occurs in the cellular membranes of bodily cells, which contain integral membrane proteins, special proteins that respond to energetic signals from the environment. When these cells receive healthy energies from outside of themselves, such as when we direct or allow into the body positive intentions, thoughts, prayers, and the like, certain physical patterns form in specific parts of the body, such as in the DNA in our mitochondria and within certain capillaries. Basically, Mobius loops form. A Mobius strip or loop looks like a twisted figure eight formed from a material with only one side and one boundary (see figure 8).

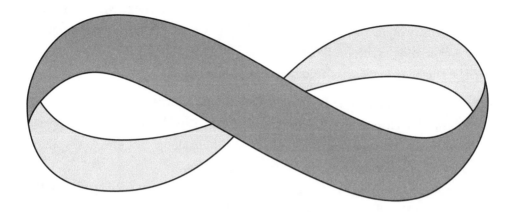

Figure 8: The Mobius Loop. *A Mobius loop or strip has only a one-sided surface, which remains in one piece when split down the middle. The flow of bodily fluids or the flow of subtle energy in many areas of the body create this shape when healthy, supporting good health and optimum functioning.*

As explained by Stephen Linsteadt—founder of the Scalar Heart Connection, a process for connecting with the heart's innate knowledge—when we're healthy, the DNA in our mitochondria, the organelles in the cells that make energy, assume the shape of a Mobius loop. The flow of blood through our arteries and veins also creates the shape of a Mobius loop within our body. The blood flows one way through the arteries and the opposite way through the veins; thus, our blood flow creates subsets of figure eights in our capillary networks, especially near the endocrine glands (the sites of the chakras). What shape appears where the venous blood intersects with the right atrium, crossing over the arterial flow of blood in the process? A figure eight. As well, there is a Mobius shape in front of the lungs that serves as a battery storage for scalar waves, a very special and powerful energy.

Scalar waves are electromagnetic frequencies that form vectors and keep our body healthy, and they are produced by Mobius loops. When we're stressed—if we are defensive or scared, for instance—our cells stop responding to growth signals and close down. Significant growth signals can be produced internally and externally, and they can include our own and others' positive thoughts and feelings, as well as positive environmental occurrences. When cells are in need of repair, such as when we're in stress mode or we are feeling pessimistic or hurt, the cells retract to conserve energy, thus decreasing the formation or intensity of the scalar wave–producing Mobius loops. Therefore, negativity limits the creation and intensity of our body's internal sources of power. For instance, our immune cells stop growing, leading to chronic illnesses.[36]

You'll be taught an exercise to "recoil" your system in chapter 9.

Subcomponents of Biology: Light and Sound Under Stress

As established in chapter 2, we are composed of sound and light. When we're operating at our original energetic signature, we'll "glow" and "hum along" just fine. Stress alters the light and sound sub-aspects of our signatures in many ways.

One of the harshest results of negative experiences is subsequent negative self-talk. Equally brutal are the effects of others' critical words and actions. One of the most important effects occurs through a particular quantum energy called the phonon.

Phonons are tiny quantum energies that arise from atoms oscillating in a crystal. They can actually slide through certain types of solids, delivering the messages they carry when doing so.

In the body, phonons are created when pressure waves, or sound waves, are produced because of motion within the crystalline tissues of the body. These types of tissues include the blood and connective tissue, both players in your immune system. In fact, when your heart beats, the resulting phonons imprint on the lipids, or fats, in your blood and are carried through the body. They also stream through the blood plasma to carry data from the CNS to the hemoglobin, which brings oxygen throughout the body.[37] If you are focusing on positive thoughts and feelings or listening to supportive messages or music, the resulting phonons will support health throughout the body. If you're focusing on the opposite, your organs and overall health will suffer.[38] As well, if the people around you are mean, judgmental, or rude, the phonons inside of your body can reflect this negativity, causing serious disruption in your nervous system and also harmful immune responses.

Another "tiny energy" impacting your health—and your DNA—are photons. Photons are units of light. Your body actually emanates photons that are 1,000 times less intense than what your eyes can see. This light fluctuates according to the time of day and your metabo-

---

36   Linsteadt, excerpts from *The Heart of Health.*
37   Fraser and Massey, *Decoding the Human Body-Field*, 206–214.
38   Kshatri, "Sound Healing: More Than Just a Good Vibration."

lism.[39] You also produce visible light from your heart, but this light is reduced when you're under stress.[40] Overall, the more supportive a situation, the healthier our photon flow and emission; the more stressful, the greater the chance that our photon flow will be disrupted.

Imagine that you're having coffee with friends, and they are supportive and sweet. The photonic flow within your body will be smooth and strong, as will the light emanating from your heart field. You'll be able to receive their love and also send them love. Now pretend you are sitting in a meeting at work, offering an unpopular opinion. Guess what happens to your photonic flow? That's right—it's inhibited, setting off a stress response in your nervous system.

Stress also impacts a mini version of the photon called the biophoton. Biophotons are quantum-size photons that transmit information patterns of a particular DNA sequence to another, a process explained in a new science called wave genetics. Russian researchers, in particular, have been studying the activities of the body's biophotons. The most amazing results have demonstrated that universal messages or knowledge can actually pass into the DNA via wormholes related to the biophotons given off by our DNA, thereby providing us with telepathic downloads. Stress distorts this process and cancels out the intuitive leaps that our DNA biophotons can enable us to make. When our DNA biophotons are active, we can pick up information from the universe and also groups of people. Imagine what comes in—and collapses our DNA functions—when we're exposed to group violence and cruelty. Imagine what comes in when we encounter the opposite.[41]

Biophotons have become the focus of even more emerging research, as they've been shown to span several ranges of frequencies, including the infrared, visible, and ultraviolet ranges of the electromagnetic spectrum. One particular study in this body of research (which is, interestingly, about a body of light) is investigating if we can detect disease by observing biophotons. For example, when cells were collected in a culture dish, the study found that the cancer cells emitted more biophotons than the normal cells.[42]

Biophoton emissions are also involved in a variety of biological functions, including the regulation of certain neurotransmitters, respiratory activity in white blood cells, seed

---

39   Mercola, "Your Body Literally Glows with Light."
40   Bair, "Visible Light Radiated from the Heart with Heart Rhythm Mediation."
41   Baerbel, "Russian DNA Discoveries."
42   Muehsam, "The Energy That Heals Part II: Biophoton Emissions and the Body of Light."

germination, and more. Studies also show that biophotons allow our cells to communicate with each other, even when they aren't next to each other.[43]

My interest in biophotons is strong because they are the anatomical equivalent of one of the things I see in my own work. I work with the concept at least a few times a week. I frequently track the flow of biophotons in someone's physical and subtle bodies in order to figure out what might be happening physically or psychologically. I intuitively see the biophotons as tiny bubbles of energy that move between the physical and subtle anatomies. These effervescent balls vary in color, sound, and flow, and based on those three factors, I can often detect problems.

For instance, I've found that cancer cells emanate biophotons, but the shape of those bubbles is distorted and often appear murky brown-green. As well, their flow is frantic and frenzied, unlike the slow, oscillating flow of biophotons that come off healthy cells. If a client shares that they have a genetic disorder, I often detect distorted biophoton bubbles lurking around the cells affected by the challenge. Besides appearing warped, these biophotons often look brownish, brackish, or murky. Moreover, I included the Russian study about biophotons cited above because I've witnessed the phenomenon of the DNA's biophotons creating a wormhole that allowed transformative healing.

I once worked with a client who had barely survived a major heart attack and was taking four or five medications as a result. He knew he needed the medications, but he wanted to decrease the dosage levels because of the side effects. Intuitively I saw warped biophotons clustered around a representative gene in his heart, so I knew we were dealing with some sort of genetic predisposition to heart issues. My client confirmed this. I could also track those warped bubbles to the epigenetic material.

Psychically, the chemical soup of epigenetic material looks like a sort of alphabet soup to me. When I tapped into my client's ancestral issues, I sensed that one of the core issues related to the family heart disease was an entrenched belief in being unlovable. I saw an intuitive image of a little boy being put into an orphanage. My client confirmed that his great-grandfather had been put in an orphanage at age four and left there by his parents, who didn't have the money to raise him. The little boy had, understandably, felt completely abandoned and unlovable. My client confirmed how that ancestor had died from heart disease.

---

43   Ibid.

As my client and I worked with the issue, which included the sending of healing to all his ancestors' souls imprinted with that painful belief, I watched the photons emanating from the epigenetic material begin to swirl and turn white. Then a bright vortex opened up around the epigenetic material. I saw a flash of white pass into the epigenes and, from there, into the genes. By this time the biophotons were all evenly shaped and distributed. And guess what? My client actually experienced a sudden flash of feeling lovable.

Soon after our session, he called me and said that he'd been able to greatly reduce the dosage of his heart medications.

The Next Level of Stress: Trauma

Stress always leaves a short-term imprint. Sometimes stressors remain longer, in which case they turn into full stress traumas. In other words, traumatic stress is stress that remains. Because of its influence, clearing it requires outside-to-inside assistance, as the stressor is delivered from outside of ourselves and involves the capturing, or dissociation, of the self in shock.

Most experts recognize that traumatic or severe stress can be caused by many experiences. You can be personally involved in an event but also wounded if you witness something negative. Adverse affects can occur after you learn about an event harming another or continually hear about hardships, as you might if you were volunteering for a first-responder organization, for example. As we learned earlier in this chapter, you can also inherit traumas—through transgenerational epigenetics, for example.

Most experts also insist that it takes an intense or severe event to qualify a stressor as a trauma. I disagree. A hurricane might cause long-term psychological distress in one person but not in another. The perceptions that vote yay or nay on trauma are programmed into us right from the get-go—yes, in the womb. In fact, while in utero, our body begins building the neural networks that make sense of our experiences, encoding every biological system with the perceptions that will make us feel excited or limited about possibilities.

For example, if we receive love and nurturing when young, we'll expect goodness from the world around us. Our perceptions will be more or less limited to positivity. We'll be able to take in nourishment from a variety of sources. Our available epigenetic stream will trigger happy events and choose "healthy" DNA responses.

Conversely, if we're met with anger or contempt, we'll experience fear, anxiety, or guilt in relation to our needs. These interchanges are tucked within the limbic circuits running our nervous systems, mainly regulated by the vagus nerve. We'll believe the subjective truth that life is dangerous and become tense in reactions to life events that might not actually be frightening.[44] Basically, negative experiences remain encoded in our nervous system unless we can unlock them. Fortunately, this phenomenon of neuroplasticity is beginning to be recognized and addressed by the medical community, and it's led to the development of treatments such as the Dynamic Neural Retraining System (DNRS), a drug-free process for retraining the limbic system, and Neurosculpting, a meditation process designed to repattern the neural pathways of the brain to decrease the stress responses.

It's often far easier to relate to our challenges if we can point to a physical cause, such as a traumatic brain injury received in a football game. Even the resulting stress cycle—the replaying of emotions and physical symptoms felt during and after we incur an injury—seems explainable. But as explained in the last chapter, there are a lot of forces that bring about trauma. One of the keys is that a full-on traumatic stress response involves the imprisoning of the traumatized self.

As explained by Bessel van der Kolk, a leading trauma expert, dissociation is the essential core of trauma. An overwhelming experience, along with all the feelings, senses, images, and physical sensations associated with it, causes fragmentation, or a separation of the wounded self from the remainder of the psyche. If lacking reparation, that injured self will continue to trigger the initial stress response. In other words, that injured self becomes trapped in a chemical cycle of stress and can cause the same to the remainder of the body, as the stress hormones related to the event continue circulating ad nauseam.

One key player is the thalamus, the brain's gatekeeper, which tells us what to focus on or not. When we perceive that a stress is over, the thalamus shuts the floodgates and we can move on. When the stress continues looping, the floodgates remain open and we'll keep re-experiencing all of the sensations related to the original trauma. We'll also be hyper-alert to everyday events. In order to shut down what we feel, we'll often adopt negative strategies, such as using drugs and alcohol. When these addictive behaviors don't work or stop working, the stress pops up again.[45]

---

44 Badenoch, *The Heart of Trauma*, 21–22.
45 van der Kolk, *The Body Keeps the Score*, 66–71.

The energies related to the injured self become trapped even on the cellular level. When we're going through stress, two amino acids attempt to create balance. These are glutamate, which surges when we are vigilant and challenged, and gamma-aminobutyric acid (GABA), which calms us down. Glutamate also helps us store memories so we can retrieve them.

Normally, GABA doesn't interfere with memory storage or retrieval. However, there are two types of GABA receptors on our cells. One set works with the glutamate. The other, which is considered a sort of free agent, encodes scary memories, making them unavailable to our consciousness. Many of our challenges are the result of these subconsciously stored memories. Because the memories are locked away, we often don't recall what caused our traumatic experience.[46]

Yet another set of concerns arises when trauma caused by occurrences outside of ourselves gets turned inward. These are chronic illnesses, including autoimmune disorders.

Chronic Illnesses and Challenges: Trauma Turned Inside-Out

As I've explained, the trapped, wounded self calls for attention and help, and it usually marks where your subtle anatomy was initially injured by the energetic forces of trauma. The body senses and continuously attempts to heal that still-unrepaired injury, as well as rid itself of the secondary charges that came in on the wave of the initial force. But the body can't register energetic invaders the same way as it can physical invaders. Its attempts to heal itself can therefore become self-injurious, eventually leading to full-blown chronic illnesses, including autoimmune disorders.

Chronic illnesses such as fibromyalgia, chronic fatigue syndrome, cancer, asthma, allergies, and Lyme disease occur when the incompatible energies essentially fool the immune system into thinking there's either nothing there or that a beneficial or benign substance is a threat. In both cases, the incompatible energy is free to exist within our bodies.

Autoimmune disorders specifically occur when the body's immune system attacks healthy cells. This happens when there is a low or overly high activity of the immune system, decreasing the body's chance of fighting invaders. Autoimmune disorders show up when the body's antibodies go awry. Instead of confronting antigens, they attack good cells or

---

46   Paul, "How Traumatic Memories Hide in the Brain, and How to Retrieve Them."

bodily systems. There are over eighty known autoimmune disorders,[47] including rheumatoid arthritis, lupus, type 1 diabetes, celiac disease, multiple sclerosis, psoriasis, thyroid diseases, and myasthenia gravis. Research scientists are now finding evidence that some diseases, such as Parkinson's and testicular cancer, may also be partly autoimmune in nature.[48]

How do you know if you have an autoimmune disorder? You'll often experience fatigue, joint pain and swelling, digestive issues, swollen glands, skin problems, and overall stiffness. Then again, you can feel just about any sign of stress, including multiple illnesses and disease. But I believe that the root cause, which sometimes baffles doctors, is trauma. In one study done in Stockholm, Sweden, at least one-third of participants with autoimmune disorders also suffered from a stress-related disorder resulting from trauma such as physical, sexual, or domestic abuse; war experiences; assault; major accidents; and family history of anxiety and depression.[49] An even more well-known study conducted between 1995 and 1997 in San Diego, California, revealed that of the 15,357 adults affected by autoimmune disorders to the point of requiring hospitalization, 64 percent had experienced at least one adverse childhood experience, such as household substance abuse, mental illness, or a parent in jail.[50] Many other studies show similar results.

My own research and experience with clients strongly indicate that autoimmune dysfunctions are an extension of traumatic stress. In a nutshell, the trapped or dissociated self continues stirring the cascade of stress responses in the body along with the all-too-frequent post-traumatic stress reactions. The body becomes so overcome with mast cells, as well as cytokines, that the immune system finds itself searching for predators.

In the meantime, our ancestral issues trigger and stir epigenetic reactions, making it seem like ancestors with similar traumas are alive within us. In fact, we probably will start mirroring their experiences, behaviorally and physiologically. Physically, epigenetic memories can actually create a hyper-reactivity in the particles leaking through the gut into the blood, leading to food and environmental allergies and sensitivities. The immune cells might even

---

47   National Institute of Environmental Health Sciences, "Autoimmune Diseases."

48   Columbia University Medical Center, "Parkinson's Is Partly an Autoimmune Disease, Study Finds," and Kurtzman, "Scientists Discover Autoimmune Disease Associated with Testicular Cancer."

49   Levine, "Stress-Related Disorders Linked to Autoimmune Diseases, Study Finds," and Song et al., "Association of Stress-Related Disorders with Subsequent Autoimmune Disease."

50   Merrick et al., "Prevalence of Adverse Childhood Experiences from the 2011–2014 Behavioral Risk Factor Surveillance System in 23 States."

react to any microchimeric cells that mimic our ancestral energies. Thus can ghosts assert their authority over us.

How can we convince the body that all is safe when it doesn't feel safe? The answer lies in examining what occurs in the subtle anatomy under stress. We will explore that topic in chapter 5.

Your Body and Its Systems
A Compact Reference Guide

Following are the various parts of the physical anatomy affected by short- and long-term stress reactions. Organized by the major systems in the body, it describes the basics of each bodily area and salient facts about trauma and chronic illnesses, including autoimmune disorders. This guide contains extra details so that you can better understand what is happening in your own body under stress. This information will fill in the blanks in your brain and, in doing so, help you begin to create a recovery plan. While you're reading, it's important to remember that your body is amazing in its intelligence and in its ability to respond to healing. Having an open curiosity about and understanding of your anatomy can help you befriend your own body.

Many of the bodily systems are grouped together based on commonalities and close relationship in response to stress: respiratory system with circulatory, excretory with digestive, reproductive with endocrine, and cellular with genetic. Connective tissue is partnered with the muscular system, and bone marrow is described under the immune system, as are the major microbes.

Nervous System

There are four key components to the nervous system, as well as several other important features that are important to understand to fully appreciate the body's response to stress.

1: Central Nervous System (CNS)

The CNS is composed of nerve tissues that control the body. There are two main subdivisions: the brain and the spinal cord.

▶ **Brain:** The most complex organ in the body, the brain consists of about 100 billion neurons. It manages our thoughts, memories, movements, emotions, and automatic functions like breathing, heart rate, body temperature, and more.

The "triune brain" model describes three basic sections of the brain.[51] Although neuroscientific research has held a more sophisticated understanding of both animal brains and the human brain since the inception of the triune brain model decades ago, I'm including it in this guide because it is simple to understand. In addition to describing these three brain sections, I've included details about the thalamus because that organ plays a significant role in our stress response.

These four major parts hold our brain's functional capacities:

Reptilian brain: Oldest brain structure. Includes the brain stem and cerebellum. Rigid, instinctive, and compulsive.

Mammalian/limbic brain: Emerged in the first mammals. Stores memories and manages behaviors that produce pleasant and painful reactions. Very reactive, producing fight, flight, fear, or fawn responses. Includes the amygdala, which runs the body's alarm system; the hippocampus, which runs memory and spatial activity; and the hypothalamus, which stimulates hormone production in the pituitary when we're under stress. Helps establish heart rate, blood pressure, appetite, digestive hormones, and more.

Higher/neocortex: Responsible for language, abstract thought, and consciousness. Allows sorting, thinking, and learning.

Thalamus: Plays a role in states of sleep, wakefulness, and consciousness, as well as regulation of stress, moods, and negative emotions. Influential in creating a shock state after trauma.

▶ **Spinal cord:** Runs almost the full length of our back and carries information between the brain and the rest of the body.

---

51 The triune brain model/theory was created by neuroscientist Paul D. MacLean in the 1960s. He described it in his book *The Triune Brain in Evolution* (New York: Springer, 1990).

2: Peripheral Nervous System (PNS)

The part of our nervous system that runs through the skin, muscles, and joints. Made of sensory neurons that cluster in groups called ganglia, it consists of two major subdivisions: the automatic nervous system and the somatic nervous system.

▶ *Autonomic nervous system (ANS):* Regulates the involuntary functions of the body. Traditionally considered to include two major parts, although the vagus nerve and enteric nervous systems, described under "neurons," are also part of it.

Parasympathetic nervous system (PNS): The relaxing side of the ANS helps us rest and digest. Hormones associated with it include acetylcholine, prolactin, oxytocin, and vasopressin. When we're under severe stress or afflicted with life's challenges, this system becomes seriously depleted, leading to serious illnesses.

Sympathetic nervous system (SNS): The excitatory part of the ANS, mobilizing our fight, flight, fear, or fawn responses. Makes us contract and close up before putting us in hyperarousal, or the acute stress response. Associated hormones include adrenaline and catecholamines (such as norepinephrine and epinephrine). Also affected by hormones including estrogen, testosterone, and cortisol (see "endocrine/reproductive systems" in this guide). Trauma triggers the SNS, which then directs the body to make cortisol, adrenaline, and noradrenaline.

▶ *Somatic nervous system (SNS):* Associated with the control of voluntary body movements made by the skeletal muscles. Consists of afferent (sensory) nerves, which relay sensations from the body to the CNS, and efferent (motor) nerves, which send commands from the CNS to the body.

3: Neurons

Also called nerve cells, neurons process and transmit information through electrical and chemical signals via synapses. They connect to each other to form networks in a way that makes them look like branches on a tree. Two important nerves or nerve-like structures implicated in stress and trauma are the vagus nerve and glial cells.

▶ *Vagus nerve:* The longest and most complex of the twelve nerves that emanate from the brain. It carries information from the brain to the body and vice versa, interconnecting the brain with the tissues and organs throughout the body, including the ANS, heart, lungs, abdomen, and neck. It is a modulator in the gut-brain axis (see "enteric nervous system" below); plays a role in changes in moods, immune responses, digestion, and heart rate; and frequently influences psychiatric and neurodegenerative diseases.[52] It is an essential player in causing or furthering chronic stress and chronic illnesses. As you'll see in chapters 4 and 5, it interacts with the subtle anatomy.

▶ *Glial cells:* Non-neuronal cells that are technically part of the neurological system. They maintain fluid balance, form myelin or protective sheaths for nerve cells in the brain, and destroy brain pathogens, while also removing dead nerve cells.

4: Enteric Nervous System

The enteric nervous system is the part of the PNS that links to the brain via the vagus nerve to form a "gut-brain axis" or connection. Often called the "second brain," it is located in the abdominal area and organizes 100 million neurons, often called neurotransmitters, which enable us to feel the inner world of our gut and its contents while processing emotions. It also gestates millions of different microbes that form the body's microbiome. These microbes aid in everything from digestion to mood regulation. This gut brain also influences our weight, mood, and long-term health and is sometimes considered a third part of the ANS.

Circulatory/Respiratory System

The transport system of the body, the combined circulation and respiratory system have several key components.

Blood

The fluid that delivers oxygen and nutrients to all parts of the body and carries away wastes, transports hormones that regulate our moods and health, and conveys white blood cells vital to resisting or eliminating infections. When stressed, we breathe faster to deliver oxygen-rich blood to the body, although the stress hormones in the blood cause our blood pressure to rise.

---

52 Breit et al, "Vagus Nerve as Modulator of the Brain-Cut Axis in Psychiatric and Inflammatory Disorders."

Blood Vessels

Tubule structures that transport blood through the tissues and organs. There are three types: arteries, veins, and capillaries. Under stress, our blood pressure rises because the vessels narrow.

Heart

The organ that pumps blood through our circulatory system. The heart is significant not only because of its circulatory power, but also for the following reasons:

GUIDE 2

- The heart's electrical field is 60 times greater in amplitude than the electrical field generated by the brain.
- The heart's magnetic field is 100 times greater than the field emanating from the brain and can be detected up to three feet away.
- The heart secretes a number of hormones and forms hormonal and neural pulse patterns as well as heart rhythms. The resulting oscillations carry emotions and perceptions into the rest of the body.
- The heart's hormonal and neural pulses also share emotional and intuitive information through the electromagnetic fields (EMFs) outside of the body.
- The magnetics generated by the heart "tell" people (or animals) whether we are angry or appreciative.[53]
- The stronger the positive emotion in the heart, such as love or appreciation, the more cohesive the body's organs, bettering our health.
- The more negative emotions we experience, the more likely a disease process will occur, including neurodegenerative diseases, hypertension, heart problems, diabetes, sleep disorders, metabolic syndrome, and more.[54]

Lungs

Lungs are made of elastic sacs that enable breathing and branching airwaves that process oxygen and carbon dioxide. Psychological factors such as stress, sadness, and anger cause wear and tear on the lungs.[55]

---

53   McCraty, "Energetic Communication," chapter 6 in *Science of the Heart*.
54   McCraty, "Resilience, Stress and Emotions," chapter 2 in *Science of the Heart*.
55   Lehrer, "Anger, Stress, Dysregulation Produces Wear and Tear on the Lung."

Immune System

The body's immune system is quite complicated. It affects—and is affected by—factors including diet, exercise, air quality, emotions, belief systems, genetics, and more. In order to understand new and lingering challenges, it's important to be acquainted with the main immune players. Most of the hormones and immune cells listed interact with other bodily systems. An additional section will acquaint you with the major microbes, which play a vital role in our immune system functioning.

Lymphatic System

This is a network of lymphatic vessels that carry lymph, a special fluid, toward the heart. The lymph transports fatty acids and fats from the digestive system, removes extra fluid from the tissues, and transports white blood cells to and from the lymph nodes into the bones. The lymph nodes are small structures that produce and store cells that fight infection. Technically, the spleen is considered part of the lymph system; it controls the amount of blood in the body, contains white blood cells, and gets rid of old or injured blood cells.

Thymus

This small organ in the upper chest is involved in fighting infection. It is where T lymphocytes (T cells) are made and mature. (T cells are described later in this section.) The thymus is often considered to be a gland and part of the endocrine system because it contains glandular tissue and produces hormones.

Bone Marrow

This yellow, spongy tissue inside the large bones makes new blood cells. The following blood cells are especially important to know about:

- ▶ *Red blood cells:* Are filled with a protein called hemoglobin. Oxygen and carbon dioxide attach to the iron in the hemoglobin. (Oxygen enriches, and carbon dioxide is a waste product.)

- ▶ *Platelets:* Help the blood clot at injury sites.

- ▶ *White blood cells:* Sometimes called leukocytes, these fight bacteria, viruses, and other germs. Most circulate in the bloodstream, but some exist in the lymph fluid. They attack invaders or dangerous cells, which are called antigens.

Technically, antigens are molecules that induce an immune reaction, causing the body to produce antibodies, which are proteins that recognize and bind to antigens to stop their pathological process. Each antigen has its own distinct surface that triggers specific reactions.

Usually antigens are foreign, but they can also be created within the body. External invaders include bacteria, viruses, fungi, chemicals, pollens, or toxins. An example of an internal danger is cancer cells. In the case of autoimmune disorders, the immune system will attack healthy cells.

The main white blood cells are:

Neutrophils: First responders that tell other white blood cells to attend to the problematic area.

Eosinophils: Fight off bacteria and parasites. When overproduced, they cause allergic reactions.

Monocytes: Clean up dead cells.

Basophils: Create nonspecific immune responses to pathogens, producing histamine while they work, which in turn causes reactions such as asthma and allergy symptoms. A very important type of basophil are the mast cells, which are described separately in this section.

Lymphocytes: Flow through the lymph vessels to support the immune system. Here are the main types:

- **B lymphocytes (B cells):** Make antibodies.
- **T lymphocytes (T cells):** Destroy infectious and cancerous cells by engulfing them after attaching to the antigens. They mature in the thymus. Subcategories include killer T cells, which fight viruses and other pathogens, and helper T cells, which decide how a body will respond to different pathogens.
- **Natural killer cells (NK):** Directly attack cells infected by a virus.

In addition to blood cells, bone marrow also makes the following types of cells:

▸ *Stem cells:* Undifferentiated cells from which blood cells and other cells are made. Hemopoietic stem cells produce blood cells, and stromal cells create fat, cartilage, and bone cells.

▸ *Mast cells:* These immune cells are considered master cells. They can be found almost everywhere in the body, especially the connective tissue, small intestine, and areas invaded by a pathogen. They are influenced by the tissues they gravitate toward. Inside the mast cells are chemicals such as histamine, a compound that causes allergy symptoms, and heparin, which stops blood coagulation.

In general, mast cells are dispersed or activated because of infection but can also be triggered during an onslaught of stressors, physical and psychological. An overproduction of mast cells is a major issue in chronic illnesses, causing mastocytosis and mast cell activation syndrome (MCAS). When these conditions occur, the mast cells end up attacking the body's own cells and causing aches, pain, fatigue, allergies, asthma, and other chronic symptoms.

▸ *Cytokines:* A loose category of cells formed from proteins that help other cells communicate. There are five types, including interferon and interleukin. Cytokines direct immune cells to areas of infection. They are set loose in cascades, often by cells such as macrophages (specialized cells that destroy microbes), mast cells, and helper T cells. Cytokines often stimulate the production of more cytokines, some of which are anti-inflammatory, some of which are pro-inflammatory. Too many pro-inflammatory cytokines will cause chronic pain conditions.

Interstitium

This is the fluid-filled space in the connective tissue underneath the skin. It also lines the digestive tract, urinary organs and vessels, and many other organs, providing a collagen barrier that keeps the fluid and solid exchanges healthy within the tissues. Some researchers have suggested that all of the interstitium in the body, taken collectively, could be considered a single organ.

Major Microbes

There are five basic classifications of microbes. Microbes aren't all bad; a few of the microbes listed below are essential to our health.

▸ *Viruses:* Typically consist of a nucleic acid molecule in a protein coat. Able to multiply only within a host.

- ▸ **Bacteria:** Single-cell microorganisms without internal cellular organelles or a distinct nucleus. Many of the million living in the gut are necessary for maintaining good health.

- ▸ **Fungi:** Organisms with nuclei that usually create a spreading network and secrete enzymes at their tips. They can cause poisoning and allergies and lead to parasitic infections. The latter grouping includes fungi that cause issues like candidiasis, ringworm, and athlete's foot.

- ▸ **Protozoa:** Single-cell organisms that have organelles and nuclei. They are parasitic; in other words, they need an external source of energy to survive. Examples include malaria and giardia.

- ▸ **Worms:** Also called parasitic worms, types include tapeworms, flatworms, and flukes, which can live in the body. Because they breed, they steal an organism's nutrients and can cause blockages.

Digestive/Excretory System

Your digestive system allows your body to take energy from food and liquids, while the excretory system rids your body of toxins and waste. These systems are critical to dealing with and recovering from stressors, and they play vital roles in immunity. The most important parts to know about are as follows:

- ▸ **Esophagus:** Moves food from the mouth to the stomach.

- ▸ **Stomach:** Breaks down food, kills microbes, and passes its products into the small intestine.

- ▸ **Small intestine:** Further breaks down the stomach's products so the body can absorb the nutrients it needs. It needs help from the pancreas, liver, and gallbladder to do its job. Here many nutrients are passed into the bloodstream to be delivered throughout the body.

- ▸ **Large intestine:** Receives liquid waste from the small intestine, absorbs the extra water from it, and then passes the remaining solid waste out of the body through the rectum and anus.

- ▸ *Liver:* Filters harmful substances out of the blood. It also stores healthy nutrients for later use.

- ▸ *Pancreas:* Secretes enzymes into the small intestine and makes insulin to regulate the body's sugars.

- ▸ *Gallbladder:* Stores bile, which breaks down fats in the small intestine.

- ▸ *Kidneys:* Process blood to take out waste and unneeded water. Urine consists of these waste products and extra water that the kidneys have cleared from the bloodstream.

- ▸ *Bladder:* Stores urine and controls urination.

Endocrine/Reproductive Systems

The endocrine system is a collection of glands that select and remove material from the blood, process these materials, and secrete chemicals to be used elsewhere. These chemicals are usually called hormones.

The endocrine system affects almost every part of the body. It also links with the reproductive system, which is why I've outlined both the endocrine glands and the major reproductive organs (the gonads), along with their related hormones. This list isn't all-inclusive; for instance, the kidney, liver, and heart also produce hormones.

Stress on these systems is a significant cause of disease processes. Stressors, infection, and change alter the hormone levels, which can set up problems like type 2 diabetes, thyroid disorders, kidney stones, cancers, low blood sugar, infertility, inflammation, and lack of energy.[56] This is why it's vital to have an understanding of these systems.

Major Endocrine System Glands and Hormones

The nonsexual endocrine glands, present in men and women, are as follows.

- ▸ *Adrenals:* Located at the top of each kidney, these small but all-important glands make hormones that give us energy. Receiving marching orders from several other glands, such as the pituitary, they produce adrenaline, which stimulates action, and steroids, including aldosterone, which assists the kidneys and affects the heart and blood vessels. They also make cortisol, which controls blood-sugar

---

56   Zimmermann, "Endocrine System: Facts, Functions, and Diseases."

79

levels, regulates metabolism, decreases inflammation, and aids in memory. There are many diseases associated with the adrenal glands, which usually produce lack of energy, exhaustion, and many chronic conditions and illnesses.

▶ *Pancreas:* This organ, also part of the digestive system, makes insulin, the hormone that regulates the body's blood-sugar level. (See "digestive/excretory system.")

▶ *Parathyroids:* These four tiny glands in the neck control the body's calcium levels.

▶ *Pituitary:* This small gland, located in the brain, runs many of the body's vital functions and interacts with other hormone glands to help run other bodily functions. It receives thyrotrophin releasing hormone (TRH) from the hypothalamus (a part of the brain, described under "nervous system") to produce thyroid stimulating hormone (TSH) to run the thyroid. It also makes prolactin to induce breast milk production; hormones that act on the adrenal glands (adrenocorticotropis hormones), ovaries, and testes; and growth hormones.

▶ *Thyroid:* Considered the master metabolic control center, the thyroid secretes hormones that affect heart rate, skin maintenance, temperature, nervous system activation, fertility, brain function, digestion, and growth. It works with the pituitary, which provides instructions for making more or less of these hormones. The two major thyroid hormones, triiodothyronine (T3) and thyroxine (T4), perform the work. T3 is present in the bloodstream as "free T3" but also binds as a protein in the body. Medical doctors don't always measure both; often someone can have thyroid-related symptoms and be unable to get an accurate diagnosis. Problems are usually labeled hyperthyroidism, which is an overactive thyroid that produces too much thyroid hormone, or hypothyroidism, which is an underactive thyroid producing too little thyroid hormone.

Reproductive System Glands and Hormones

The male and female reproductive systems, including their major organs and hormones, are described next.

- *Female Reproductive System:* This system enables procreation and the production of necessary female hormones. The major internal organs are the ovaries, which are hormone glands that make ova (eggs); the uterus, which is connected to each ovary via the ovarian ligaments and the fallopian tubes, holds the fertilized eggs and matures in utero children; the cervix, which serves as the doorway between the vagina and the uterus; and the vagina, which is the means by which the penis enters and connects with the female body.

- *Male Reproductive System:* The most vital task of the male system is to produce and maintain sperm. The major organs are the penis, which is used in sexual intercourse; the testicles, which are hormone glands that make testosterone and sperm; and the scrotum, which is a loose sac that contains the testicles. The prostate is another key player; it provides fluid for ejaculation.

- *Major Sexual Hormones:* There are three main sexual hormones:

  Testosterone: An androgen hormone produced in men and women. In men it regulates sex drive, fat distribution, muscle mass, and the production of red blood cells and sperm. One type of it is converted into a form of estrogen. In women testosterone is made in the ovaries, adrenals, and peripheral tissues and assists with sex drive, muscle mass, and energy.

  Estrogen: In women estrogen promotes women's sexual characteristics, such as the menstrual cycle. In males it matures the sperm and supports the libido. It is mainly made in the ovaries in women and the adrenals in men.

  Progesterone: A calming female hormone, it regulates the uterus lining and is made in the ovaries, placenta, and adrenals. In men it is made in the testicles and adrenals and helps regulate the balance of estrogen and testosterone.

Muscular System and Connective Tissue

The muscular system is an organ system that permits movement of the body, aids in digestion, maintains posture, and circulates blood and other fluid. It is made of cardiac, skeletal, and cardiac muscles.

While muscles work together, each is also an independent organ constructed of muscle tissue, blood vessels, tendons, and nerves.

The connective tissue is composed of loose connective tissue, fat tissue, blood and blood-forming tissues, dense connective tissues, cartilage, and bones. All connective tissues support and bond other tissues together, supporting the body's organs and other structures. Connective tissue is made of cells such as fibroblasts, a connective substance, and macrophages (mobile white blood cells), as well as protein fibers made of collagen that are embedded in carbohydrate-rich matter. Collagen is a protein that provides structure and strength.

Of critical importance to stress and trauma is the part of the connective tissue known as the fascia. Fascia, which some consider to be more of a liquid-crystalline matrix, lies just beneath the skin and surrounds all deeper structures, essentially providing shape to the body. Physical and emotional trauma, as well as inflammation and scarring, tighten the fascia (rather like when a spider's web is stretched out of shape when a bug has been captured within it), producing pain, lack of flexibility, headaches, and the slowing of lymph fluid, among other problems.[57] When you have a lot of mast cells in the body, which are produced by immune responses, the resulting histamine can inflame the connective tissue.

Cellular and Genetic Systems

There are all sorts of powerful activities conducted by your cells and genes. This section summarizes the basics.

Cells are the fundamental working units of the body. They contain the chemical deoxyribonucleic acid (DNA). Your DNA is made of about three billion nucleotide bases. The sequences of these bases (adenine, cytosine, guanine, and thymine) determine life instructions. On these bases are about 20,000 genes, specific sequences of bases that tell your cells how to make the important proteins that carry out life functions.

Your Coding Genetics

A gene is a sequence of DNA that determines your bodily expressions, such as blood type, disease tendencies, and eye color. The genes in which the DNA is turned on "code" for certain proteins, which in turn determine whether certain events activate in your cells or body.

You receive a set of genes from each parent. These are carried on chromosomes, which are organized as threadlike structures made of DNA that are coiled around histones, a special

---

57   Barnes, "What Is Fascia?"

type of protein, within the nucleus of a cell. Because of their appearance, these strands are called a "double helix," which is shown in figure 9. They are located in the cellular nucleus. You have two threads of DNA that replicate and are supposed to be duplicated. Challenges of any variety can cause injury to the chromosomes and alter or mutate your genes, leading to disease, infection, cancer, and other issues.

Figure 9: The DNA Double Helix. *Our DNA is carried on two chromosomes, which intertwine as a double helix.*

Epigenetics is the study of the factors that turn the DNA in genes on and off (turning them into either coding genes or noncoding genes) but don't alter the DNA sequence. This is called a change in phenotype without a change in genotype.

The noncoding genes, called the epigenome, are actually made from a complex chemical soup. These chemical compounds can attach to the genes and regulate their activity. These modifications remain attached as the genes divide, causing changes for up to fourteen generations and potentially leading to problems. A sampling of such problems includes degenerative conditions, behavioral abnormalities, and metabolic disorders, as well as cancer, learning issues, autoimmune disorders, cardiovascular dysfunctions, respiratory diseases, and psychological issues such as anxiety, depression, and even schizophrenia.[58]

---

58   Hurley, "Grandma's Experiences Leave a Mark on Your Genes," and Weinhold, "Epigenetics."

The epigenome factors alter the DNA sequence through a process called methylation, which involves the attachment of small methyl molecules to particular genes. Methyl molecules have one carbon and three hydrogen atoms. When these molecules get linked to a gene, they cause it to tighten around the histone. When that happens, the gene can't produce the protein it needs to, which causes problems such as those just described.

Most relevant to our discussion of stress, trauma, and chronic illnesses, including autoimmune disorders, are the three main types of stressors that lead the epigenetic material to alter in the DNA:

Internal environment stressors: Involves changes to the body inside of itself, such as modifications to hormones, oxidation, inflammation, fat processing, gut microbiota, aging, and biochemical stress. We control a lot of these factors through our lifestyle.

External environment stressors: Exposure to pathogens, radiation, dangerous chemicals, and pollutants; results of medical intervention; and dietary, lifestyle, and occupational factors.

Generational external environment stressors: This very important category includes factors passed down through generations. It can include psychological, financial, and other socioeconomic stressors; geopolitical effects; educational attainment; climatic conditions; and even differences in reactions to living in a city or the country. All of these stressors affect not only the original victim of trauma, but also their descendants.

For instance, one study showed that overfed male mouse pups developed a metabolic syndrome, which included insulin resistance, obesity, and glucose intolerance. These traits were then passed down to offspring that did not overeat. Fortunately, actions conducted by the successive generation, such as through a change in diet or other behaviors, reversed the problem. The vital role played by the environment, however, is critical, accounting for almost 85 percent of chronic issues.[59]

It's also important to know that events aren't king. Perceptions co-reign. As shown by Dr. Bruce Lipton, our perceptions of the environment affect us as much our experiences. This means that family dynamics, belief systems, peer ideas, and more alter our epigenetic material and, therefore, our genetics, leading to positive or negative effects.[60]

---

59   GreenMedInfo Research Group, "Epigenetic Memories Are Passed Down 14 Successive Generations."
60   Fortson, "Bruce Lipton, PhD—Epigenetics," in *Embrace, Release, Heal.*

Microchimerism: The Effects of Others' Cells

This body of study is revealing that the cause or precursor to many diseases is the presence of another's physical cells in our own body. There are many ways we become infused with others' cells, including:

Fetal cells: Cells of a mother that remain in the body of her progeny.

Children cells: Cells from an in utero child that remain within the mother after the child is born.

Older sibling cells: Cells remaining in the placenta from older siblings and are then transferred into younger children.

Twin cells: Cells (or even bodily parts) of "disappearing twins," those that don't survive in utero.

Transfusion cells: Cells from blood or other fluids given through transfusion.

Organ cells: Cells from transplanted organs.

Sexual cells: Cells remaining from sexual experiences, such as those that enter the body through the semen or from contact with a woman's vagina.

The presence of any of these cells either helps or harms the recipient. These microchimeric cells can multiply and then migrate to injury sites and repair damage, but they can also cause chronic illnesses like cancer and rheumatoid arthritis.[61]

Sound and Light Systems

There are very small units of sound and light that respond to stress and, conversely, keep us healthy if they are nourished:

Phonons: Subatomic units of sound that carry positive or negative energies throughout the body along pressure waves.

Photons: Wave particles that are the basis of light. The information in—and vibration of—our photons can impact everything from our DNA to our EMFs.

---

61   Shute, "Beyond Birth."

Personal Assessment: *Physical Symptoms Created by Your Trauma*

With this assessment, you'll create a chart listing your challenge's physical symptoms. This chart will be a concise way to see all of the physical components of your challenge and how they affect you. You'll need writing instruments, paper, and about thirty minutes of uninterrupted time.

1. On a new sheet of paper, create a six-column chart like the sample chart shown opposite. Title this chart "physical symptoms."

2. In the first column, "symptom," list your physical symptom(s). Write in one symptom per row. Feel free to list all your symptoms or start with the ones that are at the top of your mind.

   ▶ *Consider the following when you're making your list:*
     Which physical symptoms occur regularly for you, even daily?
     Which physical symptoms are low-grade but also chronic?

3. In the next column, note which body systems and organs are involved in each symptom.

   ▶ *If your challenge is a complex one, there might be a few body systems involved.*

4. In the third column, give each symptom a ranking based on how much it affects your life. Put the number 1 next to those symptoms that impact you the most every day or have impacted you the most over time. Use the numbers 2–5 for those that have correspondingly less impact.

5. In the fourth column, note which symptoms become more severe when you experience stress. Which symptoms flare or intensify under stress? Do different stressors cause different symptoms to flare? If so, which body systems are those symptoms connected to?

6. In the fifth column, write down any other notes you think are relevant to the symptom.

   ▶ *For example, you might note the specific stressors that make a physical symptom worse. Or you might write down things you've tried to lessen the impact of a symptom and which have worked (or not).*

You'll return to this chart in chapter 4 to fill in the sixth column. This chart will also be used in the personal assessments at the end of chapters 5 and 6.

Sample Physical Symptoms Chart

SYMPTOM	BODY SYSTEM	SEVERITY OR IMPACT ON DAILY LIVING (SCALE: 1 TO 5)	HOW MUCH THE SYMPTOM IS AFFECTED BY STRESS (SCALE: 1 TO 5)	OTHER NOTES	CHAKRA(S)

Synopsis

Stress reactions in the body, while caused by personally sensitive events, set off a predictable cascade of reactions, which is called the stress response. Every bodily system is affected, although the nervous system initiates the activity. Severe stress is characterized as trauma because it also involves the trapping of the wounded self within a chemical response. The resulting damage can eventually cause the immune system to malfunction, resulting in chronic illnesses, including autoimmune disorders.

Before you can consider yourself fully educated about the stress response, you must learn how the subtle system responds to life's demands. This is the subject of the next chapter.

CHAPTER 4

Subtle Stressors:
The Invisible Influences Behind Challenges
and How They Energetically Affect Us

It is only with the heart that we can see rightly;
what is essential is invisible to the eye.
—Antoine de Saint-Exupery, *The Little Prince*

The effects of stressors, especially traumatic stressors, on the subtle anatomy are as dramatic as they are upon the physical—maybe even more so. After all, the invisible self often determines the health of the visible self.

In this chapter I'll briefly reintroduce the three main structures of the subtle anatomy, which were presented in chapter 2, in order to explore the impact of stress on them. I'll then explain the true purpose of the subtle anatomy, which is to integrate our four essential selves. As I describe these four selves, I'll illustrate both how they might react to and create stress. For instance, you'll learn that the soul can carry trauma from a prior life into a new life.

Finally, I'll outline the myriad of subtle energy constructs underlying many hardships, including the exchange of external energies; attachments; microbial, nutritional, and hormonal programs; and microchimerism concepts. I'll provide lots of examples along the way.

What to Know About Your Subtle Anatomy

As explained in chapter 2, there are three basic units to your subtle anatomy: organs, channels, and fields. Respectively, our main concerns are the chakras, the nadis and meridians, and the auric fields.

The Three Faces of Your Chakras: Physical, Psychological, and Spiritual

Chakras are an integral part of your nervous system function and therefore of your stress response and trauma recovery as well. Each chakra links into the physical body through a specific neural center (nerve plexus), as well as through a specific hormone-producing gland/organ or other body part. Each is also considered to be located in a general region of the body and to regulate specific physical parts or functions in that region. At the same time, each chakra manages a set of psychological (mental and emotional) concerns and promotes a unique aspect of spiritual development, along with managing a specific intuitive function.

The spiritual function of the chakras is extremely important; in fact, most esoterics believe that the highest chakric job is to stair-step us toward enlightenment. For instance, once we've mastered the physical and psychological well-being of our first chakra, which regulates our hips and security issues, we begin trusting our own essential identity. In turn, we can then perform physical empathy in a loving way. Before this first chakra shift, however, our physical empathy gift might have caused us to absorb others' physical aches, pains, and even microbial infections, perhaps out of a desire to "help" them. Once we've faced all first chakra issues, including any misapplication of our intuitive efforts, we climb into the second chakra, where we embrace our emotions and work toward the related spiritual activity of attaining emotional well-being.

The following chart will give you a working understanding of your chakras' different aspects. This information will be used throughout the rest of this book to help you pinpoint which chakra is most strongly reacting to—or causing—a stressor. With this knowledge, you can interact with that particular chakra to ease the related challenge. This chart also includes each chakra's associated color and Western-assigned tone, both of which signify its main frequencies. (I'll cover the Hindu *bijas*, or mantra sounds, for each chakra in chapter 8.)

Chakra Summary Chart

CHAKRA	BODY REGION IT GOVERNS	IN-BODY LINKS	PHYSICAL ASPECTS IT GOVERNS	PSYCHOLOGICAL PROCESSES IT GOVERNS	MAIN SPIRITUAL ATTRIBUTES & INTUITIVE FUNCTIONS	COLOR	TONE
First	Hips	Coccygeal plexus/ adrenals	Hips, genitals, anus, rectum, large intestine, adrenals, skin, parts of kidneys, part of enteric nervous system	Safety and security; primal emotions	Identity as a spiritual being; physical empathy	Red	C
Second	Abdomen	Sacral plexus/ ovaries or testes	Sexual organs, abdomen, small intestine, parts of the kidneys and enteric nervous system	Emotions and creativity; all major feelings	Emotional well-being; emotional empathy	Orange	D
Third	Solar Plexus	Solar plexus/ pancreas	Most digestive organs, including parts of the kidneys and enteric nervous system	Power issues, structure, self-esteem, feelings related to empowerment	Higher beliefs; mental empathy	Yellow	E
Fourth	Heart	Cardiac and pulmonary plexi/heart	Cardiovascular and respiratory systems and parts	Love, relationships, and healing; feelings about relationships	Love; empathic healing	Green	F
Fifth	Throat	Cervical plexus (spinal nerves C1–C4) or pharyngeal plexus/ thyroid	Ears, throat, mouth, jaws, teeth	Issues of faith, expression, responsibility, and related feelings	Higher truths; clairaudience	Blue	G

CHAKRA	BODY REGION IT GOVERNS	IN-BODY LINKS	PHYSICAL ASPECTS IT GOVERNS	PSYCHOLOGICAL PROCESSES IT GOVERNS	MAIN SPIRITUAL ATTRIBUTES & INTUITIVE FUNCTIONS	COLOR	TONE
Sixth	Brow	Carotid plexus/ pituitary	Eyes, nervous system, sinuses, hypothalamus, thalamus, hormonal functions, parts of brain	Vision, perception, feelings about perceptions	Higher vision; clairvoyance	Violet	A
Seventh	Top of head	Cerebral plexus/ pineal	Higher functions of the brain and thinking; skull and cranium bones	Spirituality, purpose, ease versus depression or anxiety	Spiritual purpose; prophecy	White	B
Eighth	An inch over the head	Thymus	Parts of immune system	Issues related to past, alternate present, and possible future lives; mystical interactions	Forgiveness of karma; shamanism	Black or silver	C
Ninth	A foot over the head	Diaphragm	Breathing abilities; holds a set of "correct" or beneficial energy-based genes	Beliefs and feelings creating peace	Oneness; harmonizing	Gold	D
Tenth	A foot under the feet	Bone marrow	Genetic and epigenetic factors; environmental issues; bones problems; parts of the kidneys	Inheritance of emotions and beliefs from ancestors	Attunement to natural world; environmental empathy	Brown	E

CHAKRA	BODY REGION IT GOVERNS	IN-BODY LINKS	PHYSICAL ASPECTS IT GOVERNS	PSYCHOLOGICAL PROCESSES IT GOVERNS	MAIN SPIRITUAL ATTRIBUTES & INTUITIVE FUNCTIONS	COLOR	TONE
Eleventh	Outside the ninth auric field	Muscles and connective tissue	Plays a significant role in many immune and autoimmune disorders; many allergies and addictions; muscle issues	Responses to need for interconnectivity	Ethical relationship with power; commanding	Rose	F
Twelfth	Outside the eleventh auric field	32 secondary points, including many organs and joints	All secondary issues in wake of disease or immune responses	Feelings and beliefs about being unique	Acceptance of uniqueness; gifts are also unique to the self	Trans-lucent	G

Under stress, the chakra or chakras most impacted will respond. Most hard-knock forces naturally attune to a certain chakra and its partnered auric field, which will carry the same numerical label as its chakra kin. For instance, environmental forces most often relate to the tenth chakra, which regulates our relationship with nature. A psychological force that is mainly feelings-based will match the second chakra; one that is chiefly mental will interact with the third chakra.

These associations don't preclude the physical damage afflicted by a force. Imagine you're hit by a tree branch blown by a tornado. Nature-based, the force of the tornado coordinates with the tenth chakra, but the branch injury involves a physical force, which will relate to the first chakra as well as the chakra area physically struck.

The subtle energies carried on a force might most strongly influence the same chakra (and field) affected by the force; then again, those subtle energies might relate to an entirely different chakra. Imagine you're being struck by a physically abusive mate. The first chakra will react to this physical force (sense of personhood, safety and security, physical survival), as might the other subtle structures (such as the meridians) near the blow. If the perpetrator is also thinking cruel thoughts, which comprise subtle energies related to the third chakra, those charges, coming in on the physical force, will also land in the third chakra.

What happens to an impacted chakra? For one, memory of a wounding gets lodged within it. The blow might reduce the chakra's size, making it less functional. If this reduction occurs, any or all of the three major tasks of the chakra can be negatively affected. Bodily areas might weaken, and it could become hard to relate to that chakra's corollary feelings, beliefs, and spiritual truisms.

In an attempt to seize power and authority, a chakra can also become overactive. When overfunctioning bodily areas become hyperaroused, you can experience emotional swings and spiritual arrogance. Over time, the chakra usually deflates, however, leading to exhaustive conditions. As well, the chakras above or below the impacted one might over- or underwork to compensate for their ailing friend, leading to confusing dysfunctions.

Any chakra can also turn into the "house" for the self that gets stuck in a shock bubble when it experienced trauma. In fact, that traumatized self is almost always interjected into, or becomes linked to, a chakra. At the very least, you can intuitively track the traumatized self by focusing on the disturbed chakra; you'll be shown how to do that in chapter 8.

Figuring out the chakra (or chakras) related to a stressor provides an incredible key for healing. In fact, relating symptoms to a chakra can assist you if you're struggling to analyze an issue with your intuition. Simply fit your symptoms to the chakra chart and *voilà!* For instance, imagine that you have osteoporosis. Bones relate to the tenth chakra—therefore, your ancestry and your relationship with the natural world. Knowing this, you will focus on tenth chakra factors for healing. As an example, you can include brown in your décor or meditative visions or even hum the tone E when running errands. By researching physical functions related to the bones, you can figure out if there are particular foods to eat or avoid. Also consider your heritage: Did one of your ancestors have bone issues? Maybe you want to employ a therapist or hypnotherapist to address ancestral (epigenetic) emotions. Finally, spend time in nature, basking in its holy energies.

Knowing the three faces of each chakra can help you pinpoint how they might be affected by a trauma or stressor and what new options for healing they have to offer.

The Three Faces of Your Energy Channels

I introduced you to two types of channels in chapter 2. Now let me tell you about the main functions of each.

The Nadis

The thousands of nadis in the body are chiefly neurological in effect. The following descriptions highlight the functions of the three main nadis and how they respond to stress and trauma.

The Sushumna: This nadi is aligned with your spinal cord and, as such, regulates the health of every chakra, their related bodily areas, and your central nervous system. It is strongly affiliated with the vagus nerve, which picks up subtle energies from the chakras and shares them with the brain and vice versa. Psychologically, the core emotions of the seven in-body chakras are communicated via the sushumna via the chakric nerve plexus. The five out-of-body chakras also communicate through the sushumna via their related physical parts. Spiritually, the sushumna connects you to the earth and the heavens, bolstering the embodiment of your divine self.

The Pingala: Emerging from the right side of the cauda equina, a nerve ganglion in the lumbar vertebrae, the pingala instructs and is altered by your sympathetic nervous system.

The Ida: Emanating from the left side of the cauda equina, the ida informs your parasympathetic nervous system and responds to its marching orders.

Normally, the soul, the main vehicle for consciousness, is centered in the sushumna, which enables an equal distribution of subtle energies between the ida and pingala. The front sides of the chakras regulate our relationship with the future and the back sides with our history. Hence, when the soul aligns with the sushumna, we live in the present. We can draw upon the past for perspective and make reasonable decisions about the future.

An acute stress response, however, can cause the soul to slip forward, shifting its locus of control into the front side of the most shocked chakras. From here, it hyper-accesses the various chakras' intuitive faculties to check for harm that might arise along its life path. The result is energetic anxiety.

The opposite can occur, too: the soul can be knocked into the back side of one or more chakras, where it's surrounded by memories from our past—sometimes even those from previous lifetimes. Mired in these past experiences, like a person with feet trapped in thick mud, the soul has a hard time seeing its present circumstances clearly or seeing future possibilities, both of which make it difficult to decide how to move forward. This is a state of energetic depression.

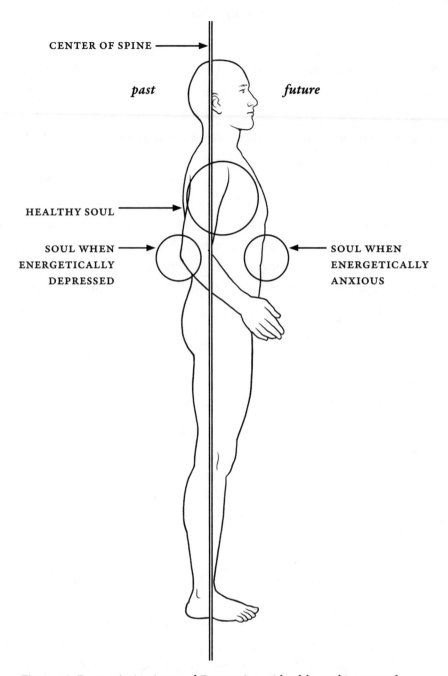

Figure 10: Energetic Anxiety and Depression. *A healthy soul is centered in the middle of the spine, in line with the sushumna nadi. During energetic anxiety, the soul shifts into the front side of at least one chakra, searching the future for answers. Energetic depression occurs when the soul shifts into the back side of at least one chakra, hanging on to the past.*

Making things even more complex is the fact that the soul can be propelled forward in some chakras and at the same time forced backward in others, resulting in concurrent energetic anxiety and depression. In all cases, the soul needs to be brought back into alignment with our energetic plumb line, the sushumna.

Figure 10 will help you glimpse the energetics of anxiety and depression in relation to the nadis and chakras.

I've discovered that embracing the understanding of energetic depression and anxiety as related to the soul's position in relation to the spine can assist us if we're unable to intuitively sense the reason we struggle psychologically. For instance, you can review the chakra chart presented in this chapter and figure out which chakra's issues seem to trigger when you're feeling the most down (depressed) or scared (anxious). From an energetic point of view, you can guess that you might want to further work on that chakra using the applicable techniques offered in chapters 7–10 to address the causal issues.

The Meridians

As illustrated in figure 2 (see chapter 2), every meridian has its own unique task physically, psychologically, and spiritually. They mainly run through the connective tissue and regulate the flow of electromagnetic frequencies through your body.

Under stress, the meridian most affected by related forces and incoming subtle energies bears the brunt of the damage. It might be emptied of necessary energy, which can lead to anything from organ failure to mental dysfunction. It can also become congested as blocks can form along its injury pathway, thereby inhibiting the meridian's function until physical issues eventually ensue.

The fact that meridians carry energy along EMF lines also means that they can be particularly sensitive to modern forces, such as power lines, cell phones, microwaves, and distorted EMF and sound energies. I've worked with many clients who thought they had an autoimmune disorder but were really reacting to, or "allergic to," harmful EMFs. Because of this issue, I've included several methodologies for working with light and sound in chapters 7–10.

Because meridians run through the connective tissue, which is greatly impacted by the immune system such as when chronic inflammation occurs, major meridian problems will eventually feed into chronic illnesses, which can include connective tissue disorders.[62]

---

62   Cedars-Sinai, "Connective Tissue Disorders."

The Three Faces of Your Auric Fields

Basically, each field serves as an external filter system for its cousin chakra, determining what will be expressed from or taken into its collaborative chakra. However, before I briefly discuss what occurs within individual fields in relation to your physicality, psychology, or spirituality, I want to paint a bigger picture: that of the general auric field.

Your summative auric field is your first line of defense when you're being impacted by an incompatible force and any subtle charges carried on it. Imagine being hit by a flying piece of debris—or a power-line EMF field, a spray of sound pollution, or someone's negative thinking. All energies, physical and subtle, enter your space and system through the overarching auric field. Because of this, your auric field is the first subtle structure to be damaged, and it will show the marks and history of your challenges. (That's why, in chapter 7, I'll share a technique devoted solely to working with it.) Incoming missives, concrete or invisible, can inflict terrible punishment in your auric field.

Harm is caused to a specific subtle field and its matched chakra by the physical and subtle energies that resonate with it. Acute or chronic stressors will cause holes, tears, and leaks in the subtle field. In turn, these allow like-minded negative forces or subtle charges into the system.

Even though an illness or injury may, on the surface, seem strictly physical, it has an energetic impact on our subtle fields. Let's say you contract a skin-damaging bacterial infection. Skin relates to the first chakra and field; this means there will be a recording of the infection, your body's reaction to it, and your vulnerability to it within the first chakra and field. If you don't fully flush that microbe out of your system, the chakra will remain disturbed by it, weakening the related bodily organs, and the field will broadcast the message that you can easily catch or trigger the infection again.

Psychological damage, either inflicted on you or resulting from internal self-flagellation, also imprints on a related field. The resulting subtle messaging will be broadcast from the field into the external world, which will draw similarly negative situations to you. For instance, if you grew up being continually shamed, the affected auric fields will reflect that shame and attract blaming people to you.

Spiritually, an impacted auric field can incur a great deal of damage. Under pressure, the field related to an injured chakra can become too weak or overly impenetrable. For instance, imagine that you took on your father's anger through your second chakra when growing up. The second auric field might become prey to others' anger, making you the brunt of significant abuse. Or it could simply ignore others' anger, and subsequently you could fail to respond to others' needs.

It's important to remember that your auric fields can also absorb positive and compatible energies, too, and that is one reason healing is possible.

EMF Pollution: The Invisible Toxic Stressor

The young mom across from me was crying. "I absolutely know that the reason I'm never able to sleep, and the reason my son acts so wild, is EMF. But how are we to exist without Wi-Fi or cell phones?" The dark circles under her eyes proved her point, as did the antics of her three-year-old son, who was running around my office like a puppy.

The "EMF" my client was talking about are electromagnetic fields, invisible areas or waves of energy produced by electricity.[63] Electromagnetic fields are also called electromagnetic radiation, and there are various kinds, including X-rays, infrared, ultraviolet, visible light, radio waves, and gamma waves, each of which operates in a different range of frequency along the overall electromagnetic spectrum.[64] Telecommunications devices, towers, televisions, routers, and wireless local area networks (Wi-Fi) primarily emit radiofrequency (RF) radiation, which is part of a category called low- to mid-frequency EMFs.[65] As use of these telecommunications devices has mushroomed, so has our exposure to RF radiation. We absorb these energy waves through our tissues, which, at the very least, heat the body.[66]

In the scientific community, there is much debate and many studies but no conclusive evidence about how harmful electromagnetic radiation in general and RF radiation specifically is to the human body.[67] Given that heavy cell phone and Wi-Fi use is a relatively recent development and that the technology is changing constantly, it's probably not surprising that there is not yet any solid science on the long-term physical effects of either.

However, given what we know about how electromagnetic and RF radiation affects our bodies and our health—and, just as important, what we don't yet know—many in the

---

63 National Cancer Institute, "Electromagnetic Fields and Cancer."

64 Merriam-Webster Dictionary, definition of "Electromagnetic Wave," and National Cancer Institute, "Electromagnetic Fields and Cancer."

65 National Cancer Institute, "Electromagnetic Fields and Cancer."

66 National Cancer Institute, "Cell Phones and Cancer Risk."

67 Radiation Safety Institute of Canada, "Cell Phones and Radiation: What You Should Know," World Health Organization, "Electromagnetic Fields and Public Health: Mobile Phones," and World Health Organization, "Electromagnetic Fields and Public Health: Electromagnetic Hypersensitivity."

scientific, medical, and public health communities are expressing concern.[68] For example, in 2012 the American Academy of Pediatrics observed that while "short-term exposure to these [electromagnetic/RF] fields in experimental studies have not always shown negative effects...larger studies over longer periods are needed to help understand who is at risk."[69] In 2017 the California Department of Public Health issued guidelines for reducing exposure to RF radiation from cell phones.[70] Organizations such as Physicians for Safe Technology are tracking the data from current scientific studies and evidence and educating the public about digital and wireless technology's impact on health. Meanwhile, the nonprofit Environmental Health Trust is doing its own research on the benefits and hazards of cell phones, Wi-Fi, and similar technology.

Many holistic healers, including me, believe that the EMFs produced by Wi-Fi, cell phones, and cell phone stations are poisonous, at least to some degree. Those of us considered more "sensitive"—meaning our bodies react to unusual environmental energies—know that these and other modern EMFs are challenging our serenity, if not our physical health. My clients frequently report that EMFs cause or contribute to their problems of sleeplessness, agitation, mood swings, headaches, swirling thoughts, sore eyes, and lowered immunity. Some even link or attribute their chronic illnesses, from cancer to heart disease, to EMFs.

I believe that many of these dramatic physical symptoms are the results of these EMFs interacting with our subtle energy systems, including our own personal EMFs, the auric fields. For instance, holding a cell phone to your ear for an extended time period or intermittently but frequently will cause havoc in your fifth chakra. Literally, the EMF vibration will overactivate the chakra. Your clairaudient skills, which are governed by this chakra, can become hyperactivated, making you vulnerable to the negative thoughts of other people or entities. Conversely, your fifth chakra might slam shut in an effort to protect you from the intrusive energies.

EMFs can disrupt the functioning of nearly any chakra, depending on the exact frequency being emitted and what body parts are in contact with them. For instance, when you

---

68 World Health Organization, "What Are the Health Risks Associated with Mobile Phones and Their Base Stations?"

69 American Academy of Pediatrics, "Electromagnetic Fields: A Hazard to Your Health?"

70 California Department of Public Health, "CDPH Issues Guidelines on How to Reduce Exposure to Radio Frequency Energy from Cell Phones."

work on a laptop computer, your fourth chakra will be the most affected, as the emanations usually parallel the heart. These energies can stimulate the negative or repressed feelings in this chakra and cause disruptions in your overall auric field and specifically the heart's field, which is the biggest one on the body. The resulting alterations in these fields, along with alternations in the photons and phonons, can cause commotion throughout the body. Overall, too much exposure to EMFs thins the auric field and depletes your subtle energy bodies, causing affected chakras to absorb other people's energies, which can cause you to become oversensitive to issues that are not your own. These changes can further exacerbate the subtle energy effects of stress and trauma or make us more vulnerable to new stressors.

Now a new EMF toxin has been added to the mix. Since the inception of Wi-Fi, our devices have been operating at 1G, 2G, 3G, and, most recently, 4G power. "G" means *gigahertz* (GHz), a unit of frequency. Radiofrequency (RF) radiation occurs in a broad spectrum that ranges from 3 kilohertz to 300 GHz in frequency.[71] Our current 4G devices operate between 1 and 6 gigahertz, while the newest trend, 5G, will employ between 30 and 300 GHz.[72] As an ultra-high frequency, 5G is very intense and far more perilous to both the physical body and the subtle anatomies of living organisms, including plants, animals, and humans, than its earlier siblings.[73] And as more and more devices begin operating at this frequency, companies will create more sources for 5G emissions.[74]

It's worth noting that 5G also employs what are known as millimeter waves. Studies on millimeter waves suggest that they can affect the skin, corneas, nervous system, and cell structure.[75] Millimeter waves carry larger amounts of data than the electromagnetic waves used for slower-speed data transmissions, but they can't carry it as far. And these waves are easily blocked by buildings, plants, and other objects. So not only do 5G providers need to create a lot more 5G cell towers to deliver the service, but they'll also need to place these towers a lot closer to our homes.[76]

---

71 Fisher, "5G Spectrum and Frequencies."
72 Fisher, "How are 4G and 5G Different?"
73 Davis, "The FCC Needs to Update Its Cellphone Tests for Radiofrequency Radiation."
74 Fisher, "How Are 4G and 5G Different?"
75 Rajiv, "Is 5G Technology and Millimeter Waves Safe?" Moskowitz, "5G Wireless Technology," and Moskowitz et al., "What You Need to Know About 5G Wireless and 'Small' Cells."
76 Fisher, "5G Spectrum and Frequencies," Rajiv, "Is 5G Technology and Millimeter Waves Safe?" and Moskowitz et al., "What You Need To Know About 5G Wireless and 'Small' Cells."

As an energy healer, I've only experienced 5G personally a few times so far, as it is relatively new. Each time I was at an airport that I use frequently. The first time I encountered 5G there, I felt more spacy and confused and much less grounded than I had felt in my last visits. My intuitive sense is that 5G will trigger the same types of reactions in others and also exaggerate the stress—and therefore, related symptoms—of conditions such as ADHD, autism, somatic sensitivities, and even mental health issues. The higher frequencies will disturb our fifth, sixth, and seventh chakras, increasing frenetic activities. I also suspect that the ultra-high frequencies of 5G will muddle our eighth and ninth chakras, cutting them off from the body but also activating internal issues. For instance, you might find yourself dreaming about or acting out past-life events, which are stored in the eighth chakra. You might feel guilty about ways you aren't aligned with ninth chakra values and ideals, regardless of whether or not they're realistic.

What's the solution? How can you protect yourself from the harmful subtle energy effects of both EMFs and 5G? Some people benefit from walking around on the earth barefoot and employing auric field cleansing and protection. For instance, I envision myself sending silver energies through my entire auric field a couple of times a day. Silver deflects negativity and allows for the transmission of positive messages. A friend of mine who is an acupuncturist recommends using acupuncture to clear the meridians of EMF energy. She says stimulating the gallbladder meridian, which flows near the ears, the entrance of much of our cell phone energies, is especially helpful.

If you suspect that electromagnetic toxicity is playing a role in your trauma-related stress and chronic illnesses, I recommend putting the following subtle healing techniques from part 2 on your list of those to try: technique 10, "Cleaning and Strengthening Your Auric Field"; technique 24, "Guided Meditation for a Futuristic Sound and Light Machine"; technique 25, "Recoding Your Phonons and Photons"; technique 26, "Spinning the Mobius Loop"; and technique 27, "Healing Your Meridians." These techniques can also be used as often as you need to counter the everyday effects of EMFs on the subtle anatomy.

On the physical level, we can take practical steps such as eating a healthy diet and spending time in nature, away from our electronics. There are also devices that can be added to our laptops, tablets, cell phones, modems, and routers to protect our bodies from EMFs in general and RF radiation specifically.[77] We can also monitor and minimize our use of RF-radiation-powered devices as much as possible. For example, I use a landline, which isn't Wi-Fi based, for my business instead of a cell phone.

Our cell phones, Wi-Fi, and other devices using EMF technology, including 5G, are here to stay, at least in the foreseeable future. But by understanding how EMFs interact with your subtle anatomy, you can take steps to counter them and keep them from completely disrupting your health and your life.

The Four Essential Selves: Four Aspects of Your Identity

All three parts of our subtle anatomy share a common purpose. Just as they work together to integrate your subtle and physical selves, they cooperate to unify the four essential selves: your spirit, soul, mind, and body.

"Whew," you might be thinking. "Now I have to keep track of *four* parts of me, not only the physical and subtle?" Well, yes. You'll want to grasp the nature of each of these essential selves, as it explains the complexities of our challenges. To clear a challenge, you'll frequently need to pinpoint which aspect of yourself is most affected by a problem or is the cause of a problem.

Your Spirit

Your spirit is your primary essential self. This is your spark, divine self, or immortal flame. Every being has a spirit, the aspect that is always and knowingly connected to the Spirit. Because of this assurance, your spirit can never be injured, damaged, or traumatized. Rather, it is endlessly bathed in healing love, which transforms all concerns. It can also serve as your personal source of accurate information and healing because it carries your original energetic signature, composed of all the energies, ideas, harmonies, and spiritual qualities that make it unique. In my work I frequently use the terms *true self, authentic self, essence,* or *essential self* to describe this first of our four selves, depending on the context and the client. I will teach you how to strengthen your connection with your spirit in technique 12, "Rediscovering Your Original Self and Signature."

---

77   Safespace (safespaceprotection.com) and RadiationHealthRisks.com are two companies that sell EMF protection products. Their websites also offer more information on the physical dangers of EMFs.

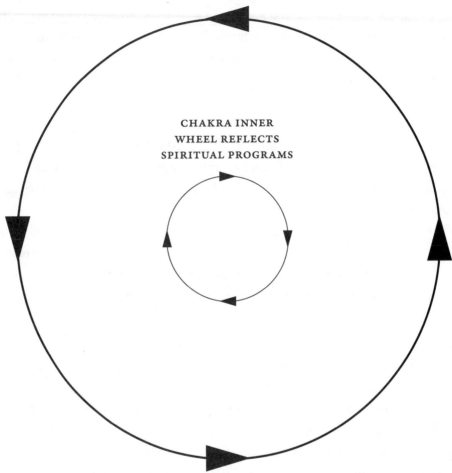

CHAKRA OUTER
WHEEL HOLDS
HUMAN PROGRAMS

CHAKRA INNER
WHEEL REFLECTS
SPIRITUAL PROGRAMS

Figure 11: The Wheels of a Chakra. *Every in-body chakra has an inner and outer wheel, which hold energetic information from a soul's past lives. The inner wheel holds dharmic and spiritual truths, and the outer wheel carries karmic and human programs. The arrows show that energy can flow in both directions along these wheels. The five out-of-body chakras also have inner and outer wheels. The wheels of these chakras operate through the chakras' in-body connection points, as do the chakras themselves.*

Your Soul

Your soul is a slowed-down version of your spirit. Once upon a time, when floating in the sea of oneness, your spirit decided that dwelling in perfection was rather dull. It wanted to accomplish a higher purpose and ultimately create love where there wasn't love, so it encapsulated an aspect of itself as a soul.

Unlike your spirit, which is everywhere at once, your soul travels across the time-space continuum, landing and then locking into specific time periods to experience different lifetimes. As it exchanges energy with other beings and enters scenes that require quick thinking and learning, it makes a lot of mistakes. Therefore, it can be injured, thus incurring emotional, mental, and spiritual damage.

Karma is the Hindu concept referencing the soul's mistaken ideas and errant behaviors. Karma isn't bad. It constitutes teachings still to be gained. The heart of all karma is the soul's belief that it's unworthy of love. This core misperception stimulates a soul to either act cruelly or believe it deserves to be mistreated. However, its experiences—and the truths downloaded by its own spirit—can eventually reveal the higher truths sought by the soul. We are all lovable and loving, and love is our power. These truisms are called dharma, which equals the laws of the Spirit that can make all well.

Many challenges, even those that seem very physically based, such as a virus, are actually soul-based. Basically, souls bring their previous traumas from past or in-between lives into this lifetime. The traumatized aspects of the soul simply transfer into the new body, triggering epigenetic material. This data also programs all related chakras, channels, and auric fields, making them more susceptible to previously incurred mishaps and injuries. This means that if you go through an event similar to one that happened in a past life, your reactions will be extremely strong.

For instance, pretend that you died from a virus in a past life. It was a miserable death. You were alone, no one assisted you, and you faded away in great pain. Most likely, anytime you get a virus in this lifetime, the programming from your soul could make you react with the same intensity. You'll therefore become extremely ill and maybe even frantic. If an ancestor died from a similar virus, your body's responses could be even more extreme.

How does the soul transfer its traumatized issues?

When the soul enters a body during preconception, its karma is loaded into all the outer wheels of the chakras and its dharma into all the inner wheels of a chakra (see figure 11). Your challenges are carried on the karma and your already-gained wisdom in the dharma.

In chapter 7 you'll learn how to clear the outer wheel of a chakra to release karma and also activate the inner wheel, which will awaken dharma. As well, the forgiveness exercise presented in chapter 10 will accomplish the same goals.

Your Mind

Your mind is not your brain. Rather, it is a subsection of your soul that holds the memories of every experience it has undergone, as well as your conclusions about those experiences. These events might have happened in a past life, but they also could have occurred in between lives and even in alternate or concurrent realities. In between lifetimes we dwell on various planes of realities to further our wisdom. Alternative realities are those we might be experiencing simultaneously. As well, we might establish a concurrent reality for a short time, such as within a dream, just to gain a new experience without committing an entire lifetime to it. Essentially, your mind's main job is to make sense of all your soul's experiences. In turn, your brain can draw on the mind to assist it in assessing situations or making decisions.

Some of the philosophies stored in the soul's mind are functional; many are dysfunctional. Conclusions about events from this lifetime are added to the mind and either underscore major beliefs or change them. For instance, an encapsulated child-self from this lifetime might be stuck in a shock bubble because of physical abuse. That self will believe they are unlovable and powerless. If the mind's beliefs mirror these beliefs, the stuck self might not want to disband the trauma bubble. "Why should I come out of here?" the self ponders. "I'm too unlovable and weak to cope with more abuse." Healing will therefore require teaching the mind a new belief system or, if it already holds positive dharma, the unloading of the related truths.

Your Body

Finally, let's focus again on the body. We examined the physical self in depth in the last chapter. I'd like to add another major idea.

If your body is the part of you showing your challenges, you probably think that it is the problem. It isn't. Even if it's the vehicle presenting pain, illness, disease, maladaptive responses, addictions, allergies, or other ongoing stress resulting from trauma, the body is simply the meeting ground of the spirit, soul, and mind. It contains memories of all that has occurred as well as the dreams your soul and spirit nurture for a better future. It holds your karma and the established negative stress patterns as well as memories of the pleasant events you've experienced in past lives. It can even access the positive and powerful knowledge of your ancestors. Basically, your body can access your original energetic signature, which is a mirror of your spiritual essence, and help you more consciously choose events, persons, and even foods that will enable you to align with your spirit's blueprint.

What might happen if your body achieved a 100 percent resonance with your original energetic signature? Well, your life still won't be drama free. You'll still experience sickness, loneliness, and hardships. Reality guarantees constant change. Change brings chaos. However, chaos invites creativity, which allows you to swing, full circle, back to the reason your spirit came to the world in the first place. You are here to create more love! Life is like a blossom, constantly opening to the sun and the skies. It requires the wind and rainstorms to grow. Certainly, the body holds your traumatized selves, whether those are from a past or current life, but it also grounds you in this good earth.

Your Four Selves Work Together

Sometimes clients ask me if there is a logical way to figure out if the origin of an issue might lie within the spirit, soul, mind, or body. My thumbnail response is this:

Spirit: Our spirit is never the source of a dysfunction, as it is knowingly connected to the Spirit at all times. However, it can always be called upon for clarification and aid. Your original energetic signature is embodied within it.

Soul: If you have a sense that the origin of an issue lies in another lifetime or seems historical, off-world, or interdimensional, you are probably dealing with a soul-based issue.

Mind: If the predominant challenge experienced is mental and causes disorder or confusion in your thoughts or perceptions, you might focus on your mind.

Body: If your complaints seem quite physical or can be linked to an event occurring in this lifetime or if they seem connected to an ancestor, your body might be the primary injured vehicle. A wounded inner child will certainly relate to a this-life bodily problem but could also be associated with a similar event from the past, so this could also involve a soul issue.

Our four essential selves often blend to establish a sort of internal authority—an "inner self" or "psyche" that makes deep and sometimes untraceable decisions. I know you've likely experienced this—moments when you might say or think "My inner self took over, and I couldn't help but be mean" or "My internal sage showed me how to deal with the issue."

The effectiveness—or, we could say, karmic or dharmic result of this inner voice—is based on the percentage blend of the four essential selves involved in an event. If our spirit is more in charge of a situation than our other three essential selves, our response will most likely be loving, kind, and reasonable. For instance, we might ignore an offense and actually tend to our "enemy."

However, if a traumatized part of our soul is in charge of a situation, we might make unusual and maybe seriously inaccurate decisions. For instance, we might unconsciously remember that in a past life we were abandoned, and in this life, we have inexplicably strong separation anxiety and difficulty with loss that keeps us from being able to cope with change or taking advantage of opportunities for travel or new work. If an innocent aspect of our body-based inner child is proportionately in charge, we might act sweetly but feebly. We might think that a cruel boss will suddenly be nice, when what we need to do is use more of our mind and report the boss to the human resources department.

Keeping apprised of your inner self, including how much spirit, soul, mind, or body it's operating from at different times, and, especially, accentuating the role of your spirit, can greatly improve your decision-making.

Spiritual Forces: Invisible Sources of Disruptive Energy

As I explained in chapter 2, there are six major types of forces that cause trauma. One type is *spiritual forces*, which include various kinds of nonphysical beings, as well as the subtle energies carried by other beings (physical or nonphysical) or physical objects. I want to give you more information on this particular type of force because it is often the reason that we can't uncover the roots of our trauma or recover from it. Spiritual forces are invisible and inaudible and can be hard to track.

Types of Nonphysical Beings

The following brief sketches portray the various types of beings that can initiate trauma or contribute to stress. I've grouped them into two basic categories: entities and powers.

Entities

These are beings with souls. They can be dead, alive, or dwelling on another plane of existence. There are many different types, including the following:

Ghosts: Ghosts are entities that have been alive and aren't anymore.

Ancestors: Ancestors can impact the living through epigenetic material, which carry their memories, emotions, and illnesses. But ancestors can also appear as ghosts that interact with living people along their lineage.

Angels and demons: Angels are beings that report directly to the Spirit. They deliver messages and assistance. Demons are entities or forces that promote challenges; they might have been angels that turned against the Spirit.

Beings of the natural world: Living and deceased members of the natural world—including animals, plants, and stones—can often communicate psychically. There are also spheres of existence in the natural world that are inhabited by beings like faeries and star beings.

Masters and more: There are high-level beings inhabiting this and other planes available to provide aid and education. A short list includes saints, interdimensional healers, masters, avatars, Christ, the Buddha, gurus, and more.

Powers

These are energies that don't have, or never have had, a soul or a body of any sort. Both souls and bodies are required for incarnation, and powers have never been incarnate. Though they aren't technically "beings," they have consciousness and will. They have a spirit, but some fail to pay attention to the goodness inherent in all spirits. Powers are extremely powerful as they often command invisible or living entities to do their bidding. These strong nonphysical energies are the strength behind a lot of humanity's darkest isms, such as racism, sexism, and elitism.

To my intuitive sight, these dark powers look like dark, semi-opaque clouds. I once worked with a client with a terminal illness. When I looked at his auric field, I detected a racism-related power—specifically, the same power fueling the beliefs of the Ku Klux Klan. We cleared the power from his subtle anatomy. However, as he was leaving my office, the dislodged power caused a bookcase that had been in place for decades to fall right behind him. That's how strong these powers can be. Fortunately, they can be cleared from our subtle anatomy, and we can work with our subtle anatomy to protect ourselves from them. I recommend employing technique 8, "Releasing Others' Energies and Energetic Constructs," to free yourself from a dark power. There are other healing techniques in part 2 that will support your work with technique 8.

Are all powers destructive? Certainly not. I believe that when the dark rises, so does the light, and there are equal if not greater numbers of good powers as compared to evil ones. For example, I once worked with a woman who had been raised in an orphanage in South America. She had certainly suffered many challenges and was sometimes afflicted with a sense of abandonment and overriding fear, but she believed that her inner struggles were outweighed by her keen sense of purpose.

She relayed that even as a small child in the orphanage, she'd been aware of the hardships that she and the other children would most likely face when they were turned out into the world. Many would have to deal with inner wounds, such as the feelings of unlovability and despair, as well as the judgments of a critical and somewhat elitist society. Just as she was about to segue into the "real world" from the orphanage at age sixteen, she sensed the presence of a being that she couldn't fully describe. All she knew was that it filled her with a sense of hope. It also gave her a vision in which all the people in the world were equally valued. It showed her how, from a spiritual perspective, all beings on the planet were considered beloved children of a loving universe. Decades later, my client could still sense this presence around her sometimes, and she often called on it to assist her in creating job opportunities for children who'd lived in orphanages. We could call that presence an angel, but I believe it was a light-filled power because it was indescribable and helped my client in the battle against isms.

You can formally connect to a positive power yourself by using technique 3, "Accessing Guidance Through the Imaginal Realms," found in chapter 7.

"Light" Versus "Dark"

These are code words depicting the motivations of a spiritual being or power. *Light* indicates supportive and loving objectives, and *dark* signifies nefarious and selfish aims. Dark entities or powers often lie behind major challenges as they stir up trouble, whisper negative messages, steal life energy, send nightmares, promote illness and addictions, and worse. These negative beings frequently use or establish energatic attachments, which are described below. I often call these stealthy creatures "interference," as they intrude on the flow of goodness and love that is each person's (or being's) birthright.

In my experience, negative entities and powers are frequently present in people who suffer from severe ongoing stress initiated by a traumatic event or a series of events, as well as chronic illnesses.

You'll learn how to intuitively sense the presence of these types of beings or powers in chapters 7–10. Normally, I suspect the presence of these energies if a problem doesn't respond to several types of treatments or if a client has a sense of a dark presence involved in their concerns.

As noted earlier, light entities or powers can be called upon to help you with healing trauma and challenges. I've included a technique for doing just that—and doing so in a way that keeps you safe from dark or shadowy beings and powers (see technique 3 in chapter 7).

Energies from Others

As I've already made clear, at the root of any challenge are energies that don't match our original energetic signature. Sometimes incompatible and disruptive energies can come from other people. They can include:

- frequencies from another person's body, mind, soul, or spirit.
- frequencies, or subtle charges, emanating from another person's chakras, channels, or fields.
- energies from someone else's past life or from one of your own past lives.
- energies from people one, two, or many more generations back in your lineage.
- frequencies from a variety of unseen spiritual entities.
- energies from any aspect (living or soul-based) of an animal, plant, mineral, or planet.

You can even take in energy from a being that doesn't yet exist, such as a future child or a future self, as well as from groups. In fact, members of a group—whether it consists of people, animals, or entities—often conjoin energy, creating a sort of mass consciousness.

Because the list of potential energy sources is nearly inexhaustible, keep your mind open when looking for the origins of disruptive energies, including when you do the exercises in this book.

Energetic Attachments or Bindings

One reason it's so hard to release others' energies is due to a very specific set of subtle energy constructs. Called attachments or bindings, these subtle energy constructs link one or more people or beings, as well as entities and powers, in unhealthy relationships. They are often established through the subtle anatomy following a trauma or subsequent challenge, but they can also be inherited from ancestors and delivered through the soul. They can impact just about any part of our lives and play crucial roles in our challenges, and knowing about the different types will help you as you address the energetics of a challenge.

Following are descriptions of the main types:

Cords: Energetic tubules, cords appear psychically like garden hoses through which flows an unhealthy exchange of subtle energies. Usually they cause the loss of healthy energy and the acceptance of unhealthy energy. The energy can also flow just one way. Cords can be connected to an organ, chakra, auric field, meridian, or bodily area. For instance, a sexual abuse victim is usually attached by a cord to the perpetrator. The abuser continues to pull positive energy from the victim, most likely from their first or second chakra, and pushes their negative energy into the same area in the victim.

Curses: Made of multiple cords, a curse looks like spaghetti noodles affixed to a part of a person or being. They hold programs that negatively affect the victim. For instance, a poverty issue might be caused by a long-time family curse passed down through the epigenetic lineage.

Holds: Holds are energetic structures that cause repression or oppression of the victim. They are often placed on the victim by the family system, a family member, an angry spouse or "loved one," or a dark entity or power. Someone can also be born into a hold, inheriting it from the family system. From an intuitive point of view, a hold can look like hands or a dark shadow pressing down on a part of a person's subtle or physical anatomy.

Miasms: These are the products of a curse or psychological rules that keep people locked within their family system's dysfunctional beliefs, illnesses, and addictions. It actually occupies the tenth auric field and looks like a distorted matrix, or net. As you'll learn in the next chapter, miasms are behind many longstanding traumatic repercussions and chronic illnesses, as they often mirror the same matrix patterns of the epigenetic material and the mast cells, virtually locking the challenged person into an overwhelming set of problems.

Markers: A marker looks like an "X" on any part of a subtle or physical anatomy and works like a curse. It operates like a beacon that instructs others how to treat the victim in a negative fashion. For instance, a marker can insist that potential employers never hire you. A marker might attract only alcoholics as partners for the victim or insist that the victim assume everyone's shame.

Deflection Shield: This very thin, almost sheer shield lies within one or more auric fields. It deflects positive situations related to the matched auric field. For instance, if it's within the fourth auric field, it will prevent a victim from meeting a healthy mate or making friends. If it's within the second field, it might keep the victim from connecting with emotionally available people.

I can't emphasize enough the power of bindings. For instance, I once worked with a client who was always struggling financially, though her family members were quite wealthy. One of her friends actually gifted her with a session with me, as money was so tight. We discovered that a deflection shield had been unconsciously placed on her by her father. Her father had wanted her to be an engineer; after all, everyone in the family was an engineer, doctor, or scientist. But she was creative. We figured out that he unconsciously didn't want her to succeed, as his own deep, unfulfilled desire was to be a writer. If she became successful as an artist, it would mean that he might have done the same as an author. In other words, he didn't want to feel bad that he hadn't pursued his true spiritual purpose, and so he placed a deflection shield in her first auric field, effectively blocking her flow of prosperity. We removed it, thereby also releasing my client from a shock bubble that kept her in shame and hiding.

My client forgave her father, as she could understand his hidden dream, and galleries started showing her artwork. Interestingly, her father also started writing later in his life and even had a book published. Removing the deflection shield had freed up both of them. Several techniques will assist you with releasing these energetic constructs, including technique 8, "Releasing Others' Energies and Energetic Constructs," in chapter 7.

Just as not all forces will have a negative impact on your auric fields, neither will all energetic attachments. They can be a source of positive energy and love in your life. For instance, I once created a short-term attachment to a friend who was going through a life-endangering surgery, just to send her life energy as an assistance. I didn't give her my own life energy; rather, I sent healing streams of grace from the Spirit through the cord into her. She came out of the surgery unscathed, and I released the connection afterward. (I'll share more about healing streams of grace and how to work with them in chapter 7.)

I've also seen many situations in which a parent or grandparent puts a hold on a very gifted child so that the child's supernatural gifts don't become too powerful too soon. This enables the child to mature like a normal child and gain the wisdom needed to employ strong gifts such as clairvoyance or clairaudience. The hold was removed when the child became an adult and was able to handle their powers.

The Subtle Energy of Microbes

Microbes are physical microorganisms, but they also emanate subtle energy and serve particular energetic purposes.

Viruses: Individual viruses are shadow extensions corded to a greater force that is external to victims. The individual viruses are directed by this outside force, which can be just about anything, such as a dark force, powerful negative entity, family miasm, or ancestral haunting.

Bacteria: These single-cell microorganisms literally have no brain (or nuclei); rather, they store our emotions. The unhealthy bacteria hold our repressed emotions, usually those from an encapsulated self. Healthy bacteria, such as those necessary to our microbiome, distribute our emotions from site to site, ultimately informing the vagus nerve of our state of being, which allows our brains to respond in a healthy way.

Fungi: These organisms interconnect, holding and spreading others' interjected emotions. We can't process emotions that aren't our own, and so we often react against fungi, developing allergic responses and the like.

Protozoa: These intelligent organisms have brains (nuclei) and are parasitic; therefore, they steal our healthy energy to survive and poison us with their off-gas, or waste products.

Worms: Worms are parasites that enter and thrive in the body, steal our energy to multiply, and create blockages in the body. I often find these blockages in a meridian's corresponding area.

How might these microorganisms operate on the subtle level? Let me give you an example.

I recently worked with a client who had Lyme disease. When I uncovered the feelings in the bacteria, she started crying; she remembered that her soul came from a different planet and has always missed her first people. We processed that storyline through her ninth chakra, which allows for harmonizing across time, and the Lyme symptoms disappeared.

A word of caution, however: I've learned that it's very important for individuals with Lyme or any other challenging diseases to use medical treatment whenever it's available. Especially in regard to Lyme, energy work is supplemental to antibiotics, supplements, and even other holistic treatments such as acupuncture. In fact, I once worked with a client in England who had been to doctor after doctor for months, but her symptoms, which included flu-like feelings and weakness in her legs, only worsened. Finally she turned to me to address what might be emotional or subtle causes.

While we were able to accomplish deep work on the emotional and spiritual levels of her being in just a single session, I knew that wasn't going to be enough. She also needed direct medical help to alleviate her condition. I insisted that she go to the emergency room and demand microbial testing, including the test for Lyme. I asked her to take her husband along for moral support. She did what I suggested, and although my client and her husband had to sit in the ER for six hours until a doctor could perform the blood tests, they waited it out. She was diagnosed with Lyme and was finally started on the long protocol required to recover.

Did our subtle energy work make a difference? I suspect that we might have cleared away enough emotional charges that my client, with the assistance and support of her husband, was empowered enough to demand the thorough testing and treatment.

Next let's look at cancer from a microbial and subtle point of view. Cancer can be caused by any number of factors, including microbes.[78] While there's no doubt that chronic illnesses such as cancer require a multifaceted approach that includes sound allopathic medicine, working on the subtle energetic level allows for a depth and breadth of healing that allopathic medicine cannot reach on its own. If I sense the presence of a virus, for example, I know how to start working. I once had a client's stage 1 cancer be easily eradicated by dietary and other alternative treatments because I could intuitively sense that it was caused by a virus. In her case the virus was functioning as a cord connecting her to an ancestor who hated women. My client was the only daughter in the family, and this deceased ancestor

---

78   American Cancer Society, "Infectious Agents and Cancer."

wanted to destroy her. We freed her from this soul bully by removing a virus cord and then connecting her to the Spirit.

Again, many cancers are caused by different microorganisms. At the least, infections leave the body inflamed and susceptible to genetic mutations.[79]

Not all healing occurs subtly, but working the subtle energies can certainly assist with physical healing.

The Subtle Energy of Hormones

Like microbes, the fundamental sexual hormones also carry specific energetic meaning and resonance.

Testosterone: male power, strength, and action

Estrogen: female power, protectiveness, and drive

Progesterone: feminine softness, calm, and serenity

How do I deal with the subtle nature of these hormones? I once worked with an older woman who had no libido, energy, passion, or drive. She was taking bio-identical testosterone, a natural form of the hormone, to no avail. Even though her testosterone counts were technically normal, it seemed the supplements weren't working in her system. Testosterone carries the male oomph necessary for movement and manifesting, and her subtle system was blocking the energy of the testosterone.

When we can't manufacture, access, or use a certain hormone, it's often because the energy of that hormone is internally associated with a stressful trauma. It turns out that my client had been sexually abused by her older brother; she'd also married a series of men who had cheated on her. Her belief that men were abusive was cast onto all men—and male energies, including testosterone. She worked with a therapist and me for several months on the abuse issues while I energetically assisted her first chakra and adrenals, which govern the first chakra. Within about a year, she had plenty of energy. The hormone started to work within her physical body once her subtle programs stopped blocking it.

---

79   Blaser, "Understanding Microbe-Induced Cancers."

The Seven Energetic Imprints of Nutrients

Nutrients are vital to dealing with and recovering from all challenges. The energetics of the seven vital nutrients follow.

Carbohydrates: Represent comfort and safety. Problems with—or cravings for—carbohydrates reflect safety and lovability issues.

Fats: Fats cushion us from others' energies, providing energetic protection. Unfortunately, if we have issues about feeling worthy of love, fats will frequently absorb others' shame, which can be laid down in our physical system and cause inflammation in the areas they land in.

Protein: Represents strength and power. Difficulties with processing or desiring protein often relates to issues of powerlessness.

Fiber: Represents the willingness to release waste, whether it is physical or psychic. An abhorrence to fiber or a lack of response to it indicates problems with letting go.

Minerals: These inorganic elements are crystalline and can carry, attract, or deflect supportive or destructive forces from the earth and cosmos. They are extremely important for maintaining the crystal matrix that organizes the connective tissue, bones, and cardiovascular system. Our ability to metabolize or use minerals is dependent on the energetics of our kidneys; see the "Ming Men Doorway" in the next chapter.

Vitamins: Every vitamin represents something we need to accept, digest, and use. For instance, vitamin B supports our passions, vitamin D allows us to receive light and joy, vitamin C invites strong connections, and vitamin E promotes boundaries and self-organization.

Water: Water molecules form crystalline shapes that mirror our beliefs. Loving thoughts, often spread through the phonons and photons, encourage health; fear-based thoughts do the opposite.

How might I perceive the effects of the subtle energies involved with any of these nutrients? I had a client who was born into severe poverty and sent from one foster home to another. All he owned was the clothing and gear he could carry around in a small backpack, which he had to guard with his life. Later in his life, even after becoming wealthy, he experienced constant constipation. The psychological impact of having to hold onto everything he owned had become programmed in his first and second chakras, which involve excretion and emotions, making it so hard to "let go" that the fiber in his system couldn't unblock his bowels. He worked with a therapist and me, and after about six months, the constipation was gone.

The Subtle Energy of Microchimeric Cells

Like just about any type of issue, microchimeric cells can cause or feed challenges on the subtle level because they emanate subtle energies.

I've explained that your subtle body is composed of energy centers, channels, and fields. Think of cells as having the same makeup. The centers are the organelles; the channels are the EMF, sound, and fluid vessels within and between intercellular structures; and every organelle and cell generates fields. Even though a microchimeric cell is an island—or a clump of them composing an island—they generate subtle frequencies and fields that can either be supportive, harmful, or neutral to the host body.

In the last chapter, I explored how physical organs are negatively or positively affected by these cells. The subtle energies from these cells affect the body in similar ways, except that the most destructive host reactions are caused by strong emotional and spiritual responses. For instance, I worked with a client who was born with a fraternal twin. The twin died at birth. My client suffered from severe emotional issues his entire life and also several chronic illnesses. His connective tissue was also peppered with dozens of benign cysts.

We figured out that he felt guilty about being the surviving twin, an issue reinforced by the fact that his mother insisted the "wrong son" had lived. At an energetic level, my client had absorbed his mother's anger and grief, the subtle energies carried in on the psychological force, which, in turn, caused serious emotional turbulence within himself. The mother's attitude toward him had also hurt and angered him, causing his immune cells to attack the maternal cells within his body in order to "get back" at her.

My client's guilt also caused him to protect the sibling cells by surrounding them with small sacs of fluid, as if providing his twin's microchimeric cells a new womb experience. During the year I worked with him, we performed such techniques as releasing a cord between him and his twin, as well as cords between his cells and the microchimeric cells; sending his twin fully to the Spirit; forgiving himself for surviving; and owning and processing his feelings toward his mother. Eventually the cysts disappeared, as did most of the self-injurious reactions. Exercises such as technique 8, "Releasing Others' Energies and Energetic Constructs," in chapter 7, and several techniques in chapter 10, will help you release, neutralize, or transform microchimeric cells.

Personal Assessment: *Your Challenge and Your Subtle Anatomy*

With this assessment, you'll look at how your challenge affects your subtle energy system and create a chart to record your subtle symptoms. You'll need writing instruments, paper, your physical symptoms chart from chapter 4, and about thirty minutes of uninterrupted time.

1. Look back at the physical symptoms chart you compiled in chapter 3. In the sixth column, on the same row as each physical symptom, write which chakra(s) correlate with that symptom.

   ▸ *Consult the chakra summary chart from page 91—specifically the "body region," "in-body links," and "physical aspects" columns—to help you determine which chakras correspond with each physical symptom.*

   ▸ *If your list of physical symptoms is extensive, start by focusing on just those symptoms you ranked highest in severity or that flare up when you experience high stress.*

2a. On a new piece of paper, create a new chart with four columns, like the sample on page 121. Title this chart "chakra symptoms."

2b. On your new chakra symptoms chart, add your physical symptoms to the second column. (In other words, transfer the applicable information from your physical symptoms chart to your chakra symptoms chart.)

   ▸ *Again, if your list of physical symptoms is extensive, list just those physical symptoms that you ranked highest in severity or that flare up under stress.*

3. Now, looking beyond the body, consider what other symptoms you may be experiencing in connection with your challenge. Look especially at recurring patterns in your life, such as problems that crop up again and again or fears that continue to plague you no matter how or how much you try to resolve them.

   ▸ *Maybe you know that you have a hard time expressing your feelings or expressing particular feelings, such as anger, sorrow, or love. Perhaps a teacher or therapist or trusted friend has suggested that your self-esteem could use a boost. Maybe you often feel lonely, yet find it difficult to make new friends. Or perhaps you're frequently flooded with intuitive information that you can't seem to tune out.*

▸ *Add your nonphysical symptoms to the third and fourth columns of your "chakra symptoms" chart, after the chakra they relate to. If you have many nonphysical symptoms, focus on those that are the most problematic for you.*

▸ *Consult the chakra summary chart on page 91 again—specifically the "psychological processes" and "main spiritual attributes and intuitive functions" columns—to determine which symptoms correspond with which chakras.*

4. Look at your finished chakra symptoms chart. Are there any correlations between your physical and nonphysical symptoms? Are there some chakras for which you listed just a few symptoms? Are there any chakras for which you listed no symptoms at all?

▸ *The chakras for which you listed no symptoms or few symptoms may be healthy and strong—or they may be overworking to make up for the chakras that are compromised by the subtle energies of trauma and trauma-related stress.*

Seeing which chakras are the most affected by your trauma can help you identify which chakra you may want to start with as you work with the chakra-related techniques in part 2. It can help you figure out where to start looking for the wounded part of yourself that's stuck in a shock bubble.

If you have symptoms listed for every chakra, don't be alarmed. As you'll learn in chapter 5, trauma and the stress it triggers can have broad, complex, and far-reaching effects on our subtle anatomy. Part 2 contains a wealth of techniques that will help you address the many layers of your challenge.

Your chakra symptoms chart will play a role in the personal assessments for chapters 5 and 6, so please hang on to it.

Sample Chakra Symptoms Chart

CHAKRA	PHYSICAL SYMPTOMS RELATED TO IT	PSYCHOLOGICAL SYMPTOMS RELATED TO IT	SPIRITUAL AND INTUITIVE SYMPTOMS RELATED TO IT
First			
Second			
Third			
Fourth			
Fifth			
Sixth			
Seventh			
Eighth			
Ninth			
Tenth			
Eleventh			
Twelfth			

Personal Assessment: *Spiritual Forces—Nonphysical Beings,*
Energies from Others, and More

This assessment will help you to identify secondary charges and forces that may be at play in your challenge. You'll need writing instruments, paper, and about twenty minutes of uninterrupted time.

Take a few deep breaths and focus on your trauma or challenge. On a new sheet of paper, respond to these statements:

1. I believe that the following nonphysical forces are or may be involved in my trauma or challenge (you can list more than one):

   ► *entities: ghosts, ancestors, angels, demons, beings of the natural world, masters/teachers, other beings you don't know how to categorize but intuitively sense are involved*

   ► *powers*

2. I believe that the following energies from others are or may be involved in my trauma or challenge (you can list more than one):

   ► *energies from another person (from one of their four essential selves or from part of their subtle anatomy, such as their chakras or auric fields)*

   ► *energies from someone else's past life*

   ► *energies from one of your own past lives*

   ► *energies from your ancestors*

   ► *energies from the future (such as from a future child or a future self)*

   ► *energies from the natural world (can include living beings, such as trees or animals, or environmental, location-based energies)*

   ► *energies from the mass consciousness of a particular group*

   ► *energies you know are not your own but you haven't or can't identify their sources*

3. I believe that the following energetic attachments are or may be involved in my trauma or challenge (you can list more than one):

- *cords*
- *curses*
- *holds*
- *miasms*
- *markers*
- *a deflection shield*

4. I believe that the following microbes/microorganisms are or may be affecting my subtle anatomy in relation to my trauma or challenge (you can list more than one):

- *viruses*
- *bacteria*
- *fungi*
- *protozoa*
- *worms*

5. I believe that hormones (testosterone, estrogen, progesterone) may be energetically involved my trauma or challenge: yes or no

6. I have the following responses to these nutrients:

- *carbohydrates*
- *fats*
- *protein*
- *fiber*
- *minerals*
- *vitamins*
- *water*

7. I believe microchimeric cells are or may be contributing to my trauma or challenge at the cellular level: yes or no

Synopsis

What a beautiful body you occupy—and I mean your subtle body! You've learned that your chakras, nadis, meridians, and auric fields interact with each other, as well as your physical body, to create the life you're living in all of its beauty. You've also learned that these aspects of your subtle anatomy can be impacted by stressors that can lead to or compound other challenges, including chronic illness and other physical-level problems. Three of your four essential selves— your soul, mind, and body—can also contribute to a chronic illness or condition. The fourth of your essential selves, your spirit, connects you to Spirit and holds your original energetic signature. As such, it can support your healing.

Other subtle factors, including spiritual forces such as entities and powers; energies from other beings, such as other humans and natural beings; energetic attachments; and the energies of microbes, hormones, nutrients, and microchimeric cells can also be implicated in chronic illnesses and challenges.

With this newly acquired knowledge of your subtle system and the subtle factors involved in hardships, you're ready to assemble the physical and subtle puzzle pieces to see the full picture of the energies behind your challenges.

CHAPTER 5

Subtle and Physical Together

*All the different elements all come
together in one holistic poem.*
—Matisyahu

Here we're going to put it all together. In this chapter I'll link the puzzle pieces from our physical and subtle anatomical discussions in chapters 3 and 4 to reveal how they interact under stressful disrupters, resulting in trauma and chronic illnesses.

First, I'll introduce Ryan and walk you through a high school trauma he incurred and that was still impacting him when he came to see me. I'll use his story to introduce the three main stages of how a traumatic stressor becomes a chronic challenge. I'll then further detail the subtle and physical events present in both traumatic and chronic illness situations by using the story of another client, Martha.

Finally, I'll return to the trauma and challenges guide presented at the end of chapter 1 and give you short snapshots of the main energetic issues I've often found linked to each challenge. I'll give you an overview of where and how these challenges affect the subtle anatomy so you can begin to look at your own circumstances in a comprehensive way and begin the healing process.

From Trauma to Ongoing Challenges

When my kids were young, they loved the 1995 movie *Toy Story*. One character, a futuristic space toy named Buzz Lightyear, always uttered the same saying: "To infinity and beyond!"

Those afflicted with long-standing reactions to trauma sometimes think they've adopted the same motto. The truth is that stress responses can linger because of the interplay between the subtle and physical anatomies.

To best explain the complications, I'd like you to meet Ryan, who suffered from a youthful football injury and so much more. Ryan's case is particularly helpful because he presented trauma symptoms of every variety—physical, psychological, and spiritual—by the time he came to me. His experience illustrates the three stages in a combined physical and subtle response to a disruptive stressor. After sharing the basics of his brain injury, I'll explain each of his emergent symptoms according to these three stages: (1) the traumatizing stressor, (2) the stress response, and (3) the ongoing challenges.

Ryan's Story and Symptoms

When I met him, Ryan was a middle-aged man who had suffered a concussion when playing football during high school. Soon after taking a blow to the upper right part of his head, he began complaining of mood swings, frequent headaches, insomnia, anxiety, depression, and fatigue. Over time he became overweight, partially because he constantly craved carbohydrates. He also suffered from an inability to concentrate, experienced constant left ear infections, and worried that his husband would divorce him because of his unsteady nature, although his husband said he was there to stay. Ryan was also stricken with nightmares that featured the same repetitive drama, that of being killed in battle. Finally, he couldn't pinpoint a meaningful life goal, and he struggled to contribute financially to his household.

Ryan didn't develop all these symptoms overnight. Instead, they developed over time, as Ryan moved gradually through three stages of response to a disruptive life stressor.

The First Stage: The Traumatizing Stressor

An initial disrupter always sets off a stress response. The question is, can we recover from that stressor or will it lock in?

Ryan's life disrupter was a traumatic brain injury caused by a hit during a high school football game. His head was damaged by a physical force that passed through all levels of his auric field to wound the cranium, which is made out of interlocking cranial bones. This force then continued on to bruise a part of his brain.

Though Ryan's entire auric field had been penetrated, I could see the greatest affliction had occurred to his seventh and first fields, as well as his seventh and first chakras. This meant that the subtle and physical effects were initially borne by his cranium and cranial bones and pineal and adrenal glands, though other chakric areas were also affected because of the body's immediate stress response. The physical blow would have created a subtle entrance wound and pathway and possibly also an exit wound.

The Second Stage: The Stress Response

In this stage, the body reacts to the physical and subtle life disrupters.

As soon as the physical force passed through Ryan's body, his hypothalamus, part of the HPA (hypothalamic-pituitary-adrenal) axis, registered its impact and told the pituitary to stimulate the production of the three main excitatory hormones in the SNS: adrenaline, noradrenaline, and cortisol. These are mainly manufactured by the adrenals.

The polyvagal system, in concert with the thalamus, next sent Ryan's body into shock. Up went Ryan's blood pressure and heartbeat; on turned his sweat glands. Because there was a tangible injury site, the immune system also kicked in, setting off both inflammatory and counter-inflammatory responses. These immune reactions, modulated through the vagus nerve, would have then triggered previous emotional issues and also unsettled the gut's microbiome, temporarily freezing the digestive system and inhibiting communication between the gut and the brain. It is likely that Ryan would have immediately experienced nausea and other gastric disturbances.

So what happened concurrently in the subtle system?

We already know that his first and seventh chakras and fields were stimulated. The triggering of the hypothalamus and thalamus would also have caused reactions in his sixth and seventh chakras. I believe that this triggering occurred as soon as he went into shock, freezing his sixth-chakra-related self-image and seventh-chakra-related sense of his life's meaning at their current level of development. The other after-note was that his bubbled self remained linked to both his sixth and seventh chakras. Indeed, during my appraisal, I could perceive thin energetic lines linking his traumatized self to these chakras.

One other event occurred in relation to these two chakras during the stress response stage: the injury kicked these two chakras, and the first chakra as well, into energetic anxiety.

Science has demonstrated that the physical body reacts to future events between one and ten seconds in advance. In fact, more than forty experiments have measured increased stress reactions in the skin and the pulmonary, cardiac, and neurological systems.[80] Think about

---

80 Walia, "Precognition: Science Shows How Our Body Reacts to Events Up to 10 Seconds Before They Happen."

how much more effectively our soul, versus our brain, can pick up on future possibilities. That's what Ryan's soul was doing as it sat too far in the front side of his chakras. Until it could be brought back to center, his soul, in its effort to protect him, was overstimulating the chakras affected by the disruptive event: the first, sixth, and seventh chakras, which govern physical empathy, clairvoyance, and prophecy, respectively. The energies interjected from all possible—and primarily negative—futures would trigger additional stress responses in his physical body.

As well, any additional subtle charges carried into his system on the initial intruding force would continue to play havoc. Laid down in the entrance and possible exit wounds, and along the pathway in between, these charges were locked into place by the shock dynamics. Any messages they brought in, as well as Ryan's reactions to the event, would have started bouncing around his system through his body's phonons and photons.

The Third Stage: Ongoing Challenges

From both physical and subtle points of view, trauma occurs when the wounded self in the shock bubble gets frozen in time. If assistance is offered from outside of the self, the trauma might not lock in, and recovery can be relatively simple.

But Ryan didn't get any help, except for a couple of bandages and a doctor ordering him to sit out a game, and so his wounded self remained stuck. What were the subsequent effects of this frozen state?

Well, the physical blow to the head had shifted Ryan's cranial bones out of place. The subsequent shock state cemented these bones in the wrong places, putting pressure on certain areas of the brain, especially parts of the limbic system. Besides causing a fear-based response to life to be reiterated, these out-of-place bones threw off the tensigrity of Ryan's entire body.

Tensigrity refers to the interconnectivity of all bodily systems. Basically, if one part of the body shifts position, so do other bodily parts. (The same concept applies to the subtle anatomy.) In Ryan's case the movement of the cranial bones threw Ryan's neck vertebrae out of position, which led to his headaches.

I surmised that much of Ryan's confused state was due to the entrance wound damage and pressure on the brain, but that his earaches and ear infections were because the physical force probably exited through his left ear. This pathway traversed the domains of the sixth and seventh chakras and their related body parts, which pretty much explained why his hypothalamus was in a constant state of overstimulation, resulting in an ongoing stress response, and why he had low self-image, insomnia, and lack of goals.

But what about the nightmares?

When I asked, Ryan relayed that his paternal grandfather had been killed in World War II by a blow to the head. Ryan's injury had been inflicted in the same physical area, thereby triggering epigenetic material linked to his grandfather's injury and death. Ryan had started dreaming about his grandfather's last moments on earth, thus setting off energetic depression in his second chakra and, most likely, his tenth chakra too.

As stated, energetic anxiety occurs when the soul shifts away from the sushumna, the body's energetic plumb line, and into a chakric front side. Energetic depression involves the opposite, the movement of the soul into the back side of at least one chakra. Besides moving his soul into the front sides of his sixth and seventh chakras, Ryan's injury had jolted his soul into the back side of his tenth chakra, which holds ancestral memories. Ryan's grandfather's memories were activated, putting Ryan into a heavy emotional state and trapping him in his grandfather's history.

Ryan's other challenges underscore what's been presented. For example, in chapter 3 I discussed the fact that the head and gut brain often experience opposing states of anxiety and depression. From a physical point of view, this is because our gut will make too much serotonin when the brain stem makes too little and vice versa. When Ryan's seventh chakra became energetically anxious, his brain stem responded by overproducing serotonin, which in turn affects how much (or little) melatonin can be produced by the pineal gland. Melatonin is necessary for sleep. When his second chakra became energetically depressed, the enteric brain responded by underproducing serotonin. Hence, he had anxiety and insomnia because of the head brain and depression and lethargy because of the gut brain. In other words, Ryan's mood fluctuations weren't only subtle or symbolic; they were very real. The long-term disturbance in the gut microbiome, along with the fact that his immune system was constantly running in a stress response, eventually caused leaky gut syndrome, as well as an advanced overgrowth of candida, a fungus. One of the reasons that Ryan craved carbohydrates is that candida requires sugars to thrive. Carbohydrates also promise calm and serenity, so why wouldn't Ryan crave their subtle effects?

Figures 12 and 13 will help you to see how Ryan's subtle anatomy was impacted by the initial trauma, secondary energies and forces, and resulting complications.

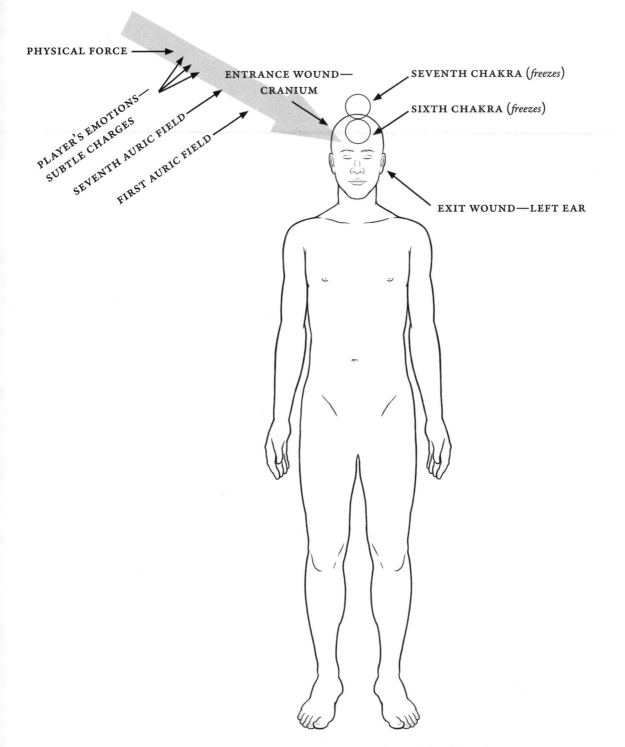

PHYSICAL FORCE

PLAYER'S EMOTIONS—
SUBTLE CHARGES

SEVENTH AURIC FIELD

FIRST AURIC FIELD

ENTRANCE WOUND—
CRANIUM

SEVENTH CHAKRA (*freezes*)

SIXTH CHAKRA (*freezes*)

EXIT WOUND—LEFT EAR

Figure 12: Ryan's Trauma-Induced Condition, Front View.
This figure shows Ryan's trauma from a frontal point of view.

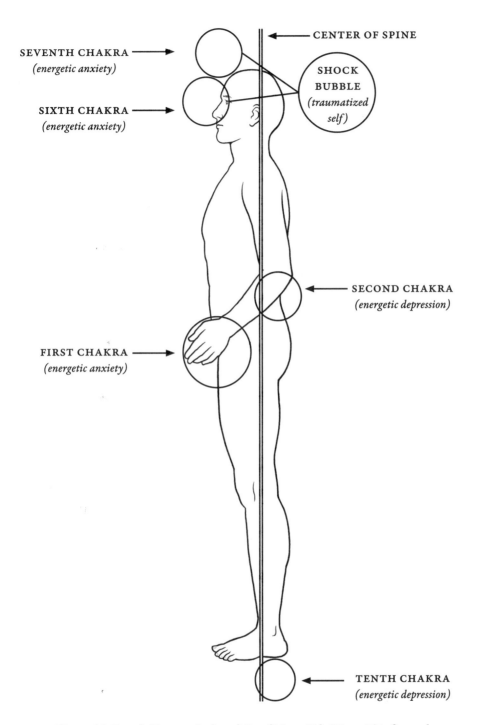

SEVENTH CHAKRA
(energetic anxiety)

SIXTH CHAKRA
(energetic anxiety)

FIRST CHAKRA
(energetic anxiety)

CENTER OF SPINE

SHOCK BUBBLE
(traumatized self)

SECOND CHAKRA
(energetic depression)

TENTH CHAKRA
(energetic depression)

Figure 13: Ryan's Trauma-Induced Condition, Side View. *This figure showcases his injuries from a side view, specifically depicting his energetic anxiety and depression and the shock bubble, which is locked into his sixth and seventh chakras.*

But there's even more to Ryan's case.

When he was sixteen, Ryan's parents were undergoing a bitter divorce. Both were using him as a pawn for determining the amount of child support. Ryan's perception was that both his mother and father only wanted to be the custodial parent because the other parent would then have to pay the support. Ryan's father's family had also just rejected him for coming out as homosexual. Ryan was already dealing with these stressors when he was hit on the football field. The adult Ryan's inability to thrive financially could easily be considered an extension of the push-and-pull of their custodial fight, and being rejected as a homosexual was the event that likely tipped the scales for Ryan. If his own father's family couldn't accept him, how could the world?

Meanwhile, the youth who had injured him in the football game was dealing with his own parents' recent divorce. The subtle charges of the other player's emotions easily traveled to Ryan, who was already sad about his parents' divorce, via the physical force of the football tackle. Funguses hold others' energies, and candida probably started to grow in Ryan's body when he couldn't cleanse the young man's subtle energies from his system.

Helping Ryan

Was I able to help Ryan? Yes, I was, using several of the techniques I'll share with you starting in chapter 7. But it wasn't quick. We had to clear entrance and exit wounds, as well as the trauma pathway; release others' energies; make peace with his grandfather's soul; bring love and care to his traumatized self; enable grieving; correct the energetic anxiety and depression; and deal with soul issues. Ryan also used chiropractic and craniosacral care, changed his diet, and sought spiritual counseling. Over the two years of treatment, however, Ryan's life improved. He began to glow. He lost weight, underwent job training, and learned to accept himself as lovable. His traumatic symptoms disappeared. As Ryan said it, "I finally learned to be my real self." In other words, our most strident work involved awakening his original energetic signature.

I know that analyzing a challenge—or set of challenges—in this manner can seem overwhelming. It can be at first, but it's the most thorough way to get to the root of issues that are often long-standing. And the truth is that the process is worth it because recovery is worth it. You, too, can uncover the roots of trauma and learn to heal and live with—and beyond—them. How do you make this goal easier? You start by examining events for the basics of trauma.

The Basics of Trauma

Based on Ryan's story, we can perceive several events that eventually led to traumatic conditions. During the stress response, a disrupter—an energetic force that doesn't correlate with our original energetic signature—sets off the following responses:

- An entrance wound that's created by the force; also perhaps an exit wound, pathway, and stuck subtle energies.

- Instant injuries to pertinent auric fields and chakras.

- Potential damage to the body.

- Initial development of energetic anxiety and/or depression.

- Establishment of bodily and subtle shock. Besides the triggering of the physical mechanisms causing shock, the subtle anatomy will encapsulate the wounded self within energetic sheaths. This shocked self will be linked to at least one damaged chakra. At this point, immediate assistance can unwrap and release this self.

- The self becomes confused about its original self and signature.

If the stress response isn't healed, trauma sets into the self in these ways:

- The force's dynamics remain in place, stimulating further physical and subtle stress reactions.

- Issues from our soul (such as past lives), epigenetic material (ancestors), and our own lives might stir additional trouble in the damaged chakras, fields, and related bodily areas and functions.

- Energetic anxiety and depression deepen, leading to bodily anxiety and depression.

- The stress reaction keeps looping, further deteriorating bodily systems and causing everything from psychological struggles to microbial infections.

From my point of view, Ryan was lucky: his condition hadn't bumped to the next level, that of a more debilitating chronic illness. As you'll see, however, an unhealed repeating stress reaction frequently leads to chronic conditions and illnesses, including autoimmune disorders, especially if subtle energies are involved.

From Trauma to Chronic Illness

The distinction between a trauma condition and a chronic illness is blurry. Where does one start and another end? The short answer is that chronic illnesses follow in the wake of long-held trauma. The traumatized self remains stuck unless freed, but the stuck state can all too often set off a new anomaly: the development of a secondary internally created force that causes a self-injurious loop or an autoimmune state. For whatever reason, but often because of unresolved grief, the trapped self turns on itself, even as the immune system can turn on the body. Thus is suffering inflicted inside to inside.

The easiest way for me to explain this new challenge is to introduce you to Martha, another client. Martha's situation was very complicated and layered; yours may be, too. I offer Martha's story here not only to give you another excellent example of how the subtle and physical anatomies work together, but to also show you that even challenges as complicated as Martha's can be alleviated and healed.

Martha's Story and Symptoms

Martha was a fifty-year-old woman with one child. She'd been a librarian her entire adult life. She and her husband were distant but "okay," she said, or they had been until about ten years before, at which time she'd started experiencing exhaustion, severe aches and pains, stomach aches, and weight gain, which had recently turned into weight loss.

Martha also complained of feeling increasingly tired and losing her hair. She wondered secretly if she had cancer. She was eating lots of ice cream—actually, she was addicted to it. Lately she continually cried about her mother's death, which had occurred ten years previously. She avoided crowds, as they made her tired. As well, her daughter had recently been diagnosed with Graves' disease, an autoimmune disorder in which the thyroid destroys itself.

To date, the best guess from the medical community was that Martha had chronic fatigue syndrome, a chronic illness that has only recently been linked to problems in the gut microbiome, most likely in the bacterial biome.

Martha's situation was complicated, which is why I feature it.

Tracing the Subtle Stressors

During our first few sessions, I led Martha through several regressions, initially employing technique 5 to categorize the major stressors and the resulting traumas at play in her system. With this recap of Martha's issues I want to show you how several issues—and traumas—can link together even across multiple lifetimes and dimensions of existence.

Martha's Subtle Stressors: An Overview

STRESSOR	TIME PERIOD	RESULTING TRAUMA
Martha leaves the Oneness, with the Spirit telling her to be a healer.	Long, long ago	Her soul feels disconnected from the One; believes the Spirit cast her out; tells herself she must earn the Spirit's love to reconnect.
On earth Martha can't save people from a wave of disease and dark entities.	Previous life, about 2000 BCE	Feeling shameful about not helping the ill or stopping the spread of evil, Martha absorbs others' woes and illnesses. Villagers curse her because she couldn't save them and insist that she will never feel loved again. Her soul decides she is unlovable.
Martha is conceived. Her mother tries to abort her on her own; it doesn't work. Her mother is sick throughout the pregnancy. Martha's mother was also an unwanted child.	This life, about 56 years ago	Martha's inner self has decided she is unlovable, but to earn acceptance and because she is a healer, she forms a cord with her mother to assure her own physical survival. Through the cord she takes on her mother's emotional and physical issues and gives away her own life energy.
Martha's only sense of intimate connection with her emotionally distant mother comes through the experience of being fed. She was fed cow's milk.	This life, infancy	Martha's innate need for the nourishment of mother energy and the sense of security that brings becomes associated with cow's milk.
Martha raised by an alcoholic, angry dad and emotionally absent mother.	This life, early childhood	Martha caretakes her mother; her mother only pays attention to her when she's sick. Martha turns to ice cream instead of milk and unconsciously takes on an established cord between her father and a dark entity. Martha wants to spare her mother the wrath of her father. The cord serves to goad him into addiction. (As I'll explain, addictions are often stirred by entity interference.) By getting between her father and the entity, Martha attempts to lessen her father's hurtful behavior.

STRESSOR	TIME PERIOD	RESULTING TRAUMA
Martha marries Harry, an alcoholic.	Age 30	Dating no one else until Harry, Martha marries him because he is distant and doesn't require her attention—or give any, for that matter.
Martha's daughter nearly dies.	Age 33	Martha's daughter nearly dies during childbirth. Martha stays home for a year to take care of her daughter but feels depressed without her job; she feels guilty for not paying attention when her daughter cries.
Martha's mother becomes sick with cancer.	Age 43	Martha has her mother move in with her. When caring for her mother, she ignores her child.
Martha's mother dies of cancer.	Age 45	Martha's various symptoms worsen. She doesn't want to work, but she forces herself to do so. She is eventually diagnosed with chronic fatigue syndrome.

I've given you only the briefest exploration of Martha's journey across time and only a few of the trauma points. But as you can see, there are multiple moments of trauma that could have either put another part of herself into a new shock bubble or reinforced an existing one.

A Full-On Self-injurious Loop of Chronic Illness: The Subtle and Physical Interactions

So how did Martha's traumas establish the conditioning for chronic illnesses? Let me walk you through them.

Leaving the Oneness

Frequently I discover that a person's traumas, and especially their chronic symptoms and illnesses, originate in what could be called their first soul experience. Think of it: we are united in the Oneness—and then we aren't. Our soul's reactions to the perceived separation settle into it.

Upon leaving the Oneness, Martha's soul immediately decided she'd been rejected, and thus was her first shock bubble created. In this case, Martha's soul established this bubble as she didn't have a body at the time. Her mind, which is related to the soul, carried her mental reactions and perceptions into other lifetimes and bodies from this point on. Ultimately this karmic misperception lingered through the millennia, though the Spirit never actually left her. We could say that Martha inflicted herself with a spiritual force. Spiritual forces make us question the truth of being beloved by the Spirit. You'll learn how to clear forces starting in chapter 7. Healing connections with disruptive spiritual forces is extraordinarily restorative. If we can remember our spirit—the essential self that knows it is and never has been separated from Oneness/the Spirit—we can invite in the healing energies of love.

To compensate for her sense of being unworthy of the Oneness (and, therefore, only deserving to be rejected by it), Martha's soul decided she needed to employ her innate gift as a healer to help others. As we'll see, this decision set her up to absorb others' illnesses, challenges, and problems—in other words, to play God. A decision like this wouldn't affect just a single chakra or auric field; it would comprise a universal dysfunctional belief, therefore affecting all of her essential selves and all of her subtle anatomy.

Past Life

In about 2000 BCE, Martha's soul played out the perceived need to use her healing capabilities to earn love. Dharmically we don't have to earn the Spirit's love, but her soul didn't know this. Hers was a futile endeavor. Not only did she incur a curse—a type of attachment—from members of her community, but the rejection and inability to heal others also solidified the perceptions of being alone and unworthy, thus reinforcing the shock bubble that an aspect of her was already trapped in.

It's at this point that another event might have occurred for Martha. I have found that there is always a primary shock bubble underneath—or causal to—serious traumas. Events in past lives can strengthen this original shock bubble or even form new ones. Think of it in practical terms within a single year of your life. Your subtle system might create one shock bubble if you find that your partner has been cheating on you—and this bubble would be a significant one—and another if you fall and break a bone. However, really deep issues usually involve either the reiteration of a singular, very powerful shock bubble or the establishment of a new one that hooks into or builds upon the most causal of bubbles.

Initial and secondary shock bubbles, along with curses, cords, holds, and other attachments, don't release until they are addressed. As I've shared, they can all pass from lifetime to lifetime. The attachments constitute spiritual forces. The first spiritual force that Martha's soul inflicted on itself made her vulnerable to entity associations, but shame was the real culprit. Shame is always present within chronic illnesses, especially autoimmune diseases, as it represents the belief that there is something wrong with us and that to become "right," we must self-sacrifice, allow ourselves to be hurt, and even turn on ourselves.

Conception/In Utero

In her current lifetime, Martha's soul immediately experienced the trauma of an abortion attempt. This event might have initiated a new shock bubble, but I believe that it mainly reinforced the one already existing from her separation from the Oneness. My sense was intuitive and also logical. After all, the main negative components of Martha's experience were comparable across time.

My professional knowledge of the energetics of spontaneous and deliberate abortions is that a soul doesn't enter the new body until the fetus is at least five months along. Sometimes a soul doesn't come in until the birthing. Nonetheless, the physical body is affected by all early experiences that either don't match its signature or that trigger previous karmic shock bubbles. In this case, the physical force of the abortion attempt was a physical stressor and caused a stress response. Because there wasn't anyone to assist Martha's soul, and because Martha's mother had herself been an unwanted child, the physical violation also delivered a psychological force. Martha was already predisposed to try to earn love and survival through being a healer, and so a cord was established between her first chakra and her mother's. Through it, her mother gained life energy and Martha took on her mother's physical and psychological woes.

Life energy is electrical energy. We must have this electrical energy pulsing up the spine from the first chakra to animate the entire physical and subtle anatomies. Electricity manufactures EMF, the basis for our physical and subtle boundaries. Losing so much electricity compromised the entirety of Martha's physical and subtle systems, including everything from the vagus nerve to auric fields. The vagus nerve—which helps the body to monitor and discern the health of the microbiome, as well as protect itself—has anti-inflammatory properties. If the vagus nerve is stressed, it's vulnerable, as its ability to respond appropriately to the microbiome in the gut (determining whether all is healthy or not healthy) is compromised. This can lead to depression, anxiety, irritable bowel syndrome (IBS), and other challenges.[81] As well, some of Martha's chakras become either energetically depressed or anxious.

Martha was truly traumatized, but she hadn't yet developed a chronic illness.

---

81   Bonaz et al., "The Vagus Nerve at the Interface," and Breit et al, "Vagus Nerve as Modulator of the
       Brain-Cut Axis."

Infancy

As a baby, Martha was fed formula made of cow's milk. For some, cow's milk is an allergen that can often lead to leaky gut syndrome, food allergies, and the resulting inflammation. Food reactivity is a common factor in chronic illnesses, as I'll explain.

As shown in chapter 10's chakra-based foods and substances chart, every form of nourishment holds a positive energetic charge that supports a specific chakra. This energetic charge represents how food can energetically support or help us. If a food carries charges that don't match a person's original energetic signature, it will create detrimental, even self-injurious, effects.

Food cravings aren't bad by and of themselves. We might crave a food that we need. If the craving is overwhelming and doesn't disappear, however, it's because that food or substance is bringing in subtle energies not conducive to our original energetic signature. Usually it's because that food's subtle charge is associated with a harmful or missing force.

Instead of being showered with unconditional maternal love—heck, even given hugs—Martha was given cow's milk, a first chakra substance. Cow's milk, in the form of ice cream, became her go-to substitute for love—a significant force that should have been her birthright, but that was missing from her childhood. Unfortunately, as she grew into adulthood, her wounded self, recognizing that no amount of milk or ice cream was an adequate substitute for love, triggered her immune system to develop antibodies against the subtle energies of ice cream, which were transformed into an allergen. This threw off her gut microbiome, the HPA axis, the vagus nerve, and just about everything else.

Early Childhood

Alcoholic and rageful father, absent mother—here alone are causal factors for a shock bubble or two (or three). Martha was already entrapped in an unhealthy energetic attachment with her mother. Now she added a new one: an attachment with her father's rage, a psychological force of great magnitude. Martha, with her soul's healing prowess, would have felt compelled to protect her mother.

As a side note, many addictions involve the presence of interference. Entities encourage addictions. Why? Because when the addict is engaged in an addictive process, an entity can steal the addict's life energy. And when the addict falls into the inevitable soup of shame that follows acting out, the entity can steal their light, or spiritual energy. To promote addictions, entities or forces often cord to the addict. (I'll further explain this in chapter 10.)

Martha already carried a soul curse and a mother cord, making it relatively easy for an entity to promote a father-Martha cord. The cord was established into Martha's third chakra, a common site for cords between an alcoholic and another person, because the liver, a part of the third chakra, is greatly influenced by alcohol.

Age 30

Martha's marriage to Harry is the culmination of her relationship with an emotionally absent mother and alcoholic father; Harry's personality and pathology matched elements of both. Life partners frequently connect into an individual's already existing cords. Although he was an unwitting accomplice, Harry's soul connected with the cords in Martha's first and third chakras, thereby maintaining her unhealthy energetic relationships with her parents.

Age 33

The near death of Martha's daughter during birth immediately reactivated Martha's first chakra traumas from this and earlier lives, also inflicting trauma in her second chakra, in which lies the uterus. Whatever emotional solvency Martha had formulated during this life would have now been lost with this intensely traumatic experience, debilitating her enteric nervous system, which is associated with the first, second, and third chakras.

Age 43

Martha's mother gets cancer, and Martha, already preprogrammed as a healer/caretaker, focuses solely on her mother, ignoring her daughter's needs. She eats more ice cream. While she doesn't assume the cancerous condition from her mother, she later worries that she has done so. After all, she takes on nearly everything else from her mother!

Age 45

Death doesn't eliminate cords. Martha's mother's soul passes, and the cord between it and Martha's soul simply stretches. Martha spins into a ten-year crisis, as if trying to bring her mother back to life by sending life energy through the ethers. The dark entity in her third chakra claps for joy as Martha almost doesn't have enough energy to perform the one activity she likes: being a librarian.

Age 55

By this point, Martha is afflicted with chronic fatigue syndrome, and her daughter is afflicted with Graves' disease, an autoimmune disorder affecting the thyroid. In fact, I'm going to start with the daughter, as I want to emphasize the effects of microchimerism on chronic illnesses.

Martha's body held her daughter's fetal cells, and her daughter's body carried mother cells. When Martha ignored her infant daughter's cries, a missing force was established for the daughter. Because Martha didn't attend to her daughter's fifth chakra screams, the daughter's immune system angrily attacked the mother cells in her thyroid. But all they did was injure the healthy cells, setting her up for the autoimmune disorder that eventually developed.

The development of Martha's chronic fatigue syndrome also wasn't surprising, although she could have developed a different chronic illness or several of them. As explained earlier, chronic fatigue syndrome is often associated with debilitating gut bacteria. Bacteria hold our own emotions. Think about how many unexpressed emotions were held within Martha's various shock bubbles—enough to create an overpopulation of unhealthy bacteria.

Martha's hormones were also off. Her hyperactive thyroid might very well have been an attempt to counteract her daughter's thyroid condition—to essentially take the problem into herself. But what about Martha's low estrogen and testosterone? The low estrogen reflected the lack of protection from Martha's mother and also her own lack of connectivity with her daughter. Her low testosterone reflected her fear of her father and her husband.

By the time someone has a full-blown chronic illness, another energetic event will have occurred. It involves a networking between the epigenetic material, mast cells, and a miasm in the tenth auric field, all of which start to mirror each other. The networking unfolds like this:

1. Epigenetic material turns on genes and emotional and physical disease processes that are similar to those of at least one ancestor. Energetic lines develop between the activated genes, forming a subtle and chemical pattern.

2. Mast cells flood the body. They are joined together by subtle and chemical energies that form a matrix pattern similar to that found in the activated genes.

3. These mast cells will continue to overproduce histones, which in turn cause allergic responses, and the over-release of cytokines, which stimulate more inflammation, especially in the connective tissue, meridians, and eleventh chakra and field.

4. Miasmic patterns fully activate: A miasm is made of familial events that we feel bound to duplicate. The energies of these events, held within the tenth auric field, turn on and formulate a matrix pattern that mirrors that already present in the epigenetic material and the mast cells.

We are now fully caught in a chronic, self-injurious loop of disease ("dis-ease") and illness. Figure 14 shows how the matrix patterns of these three aspects mirror each other.

For Martha, this networking between the epigenetic material, mast cells, and miasms didn't happen until she was forty-five. For others, the networking can occur in the womb or later in life, but this networking occurs in all cases of chronic illnesses.

Figures 15 and 16 offer a comprehensive view of Martha's condition on the subtle anatomy level. Let these images, and the ones you saw of Ryan's condition, help you to understand and visualize your own challenges with your subtle anatomy.

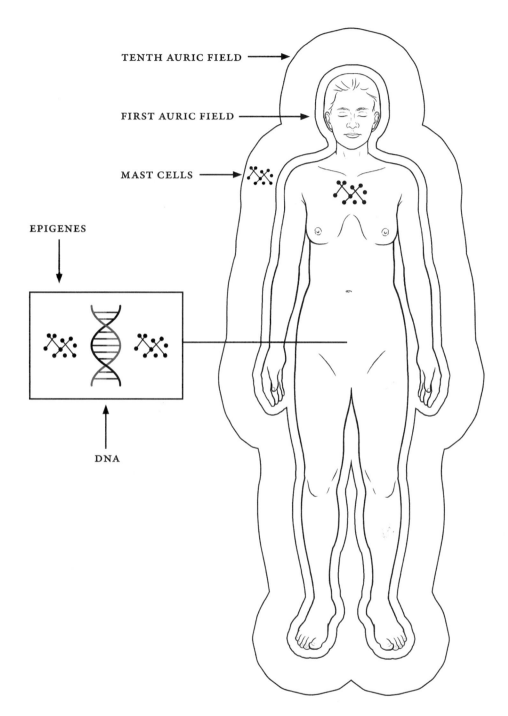

Figure 14: The Matrix Patterns of the Epigenetic Material, Mast Cells, and Miasms. *In chronic illnesses, the matrix patterns formed within epigenetic material, mast cells, and miasms often mirror each other.*

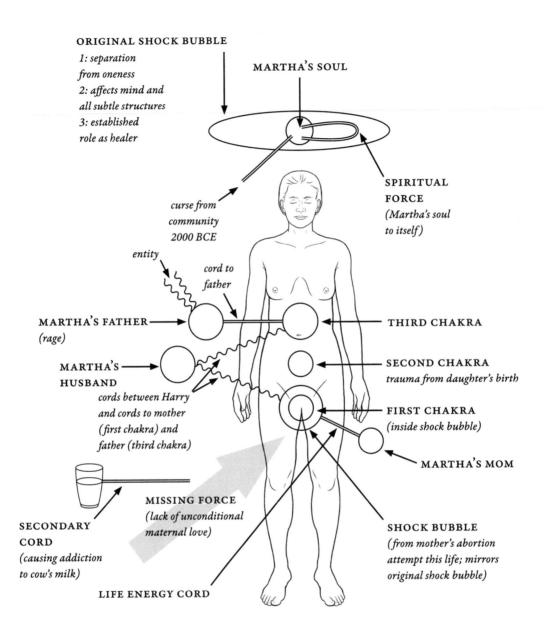

ORIGINAL SHOCK BUBBLE
1: separation from oneness
2: affects mind and all subtle structures
3: established role as healer

MARTHA'S SOUL

SPIRITUAL FORCE
(Martha's soul to itself)

curse from community 2000 BCE

entity

cord to father

MARTHA'S FATHER
(rage)

THIRD CHAKRA

MARTHA'S HUSBAND
cords between Harry and cords to mother (first chakra) and father (third chakra)

SECOND CHAKRA
trauma from daughter's birth

FIRST CHAKRA
(inside shock bubble)

MARTHA'S MOM

SECONDARY CORD
(causing addiction to cow's milk)

MISSING FORCE
(lack of unconditional maternal love)

SHOCK BUBBLE
(from mother's abortion attempt this life; mirrors original shock bubble)

LIFE ENERGY CORD

Figure 15: Martha's Autoimmune Condition Before Age 45. *Martha suffered dozens of traumas after her soul separated from Spirit and incurred her original soul wound. The development of a chronic illness in the form of an autoimmune disorder took several incarnations and played out as she entered middle age. Figure 15 shows Martha's traumas from her original soul wound through age 45.*

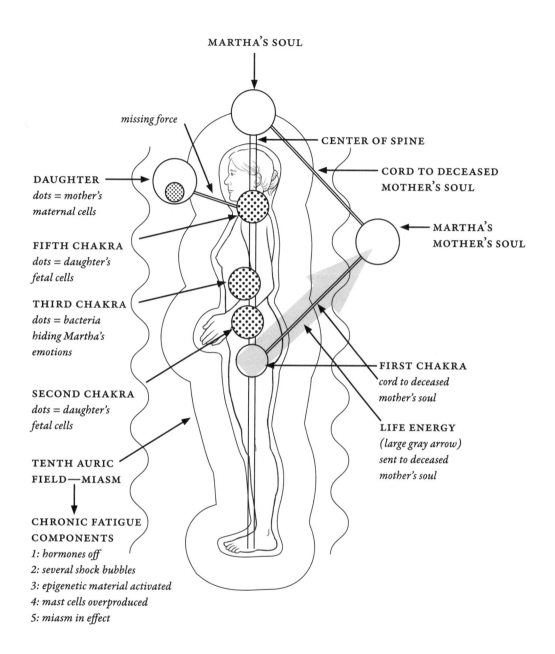

MARTHA'S SOUL

missing force

CENTER OF SPINE

CORD TO DECEASED
MOTHER'S SOUL

DAUGHTER
*dots = mother's
maternal cells*

MARTHA'S
MOTHER'S SOUL

FIFTH CHAKRA
*dots = daughter's
fetal cells*

THIRD CHAKRA
*dots = bacteria
hiding Martha's
emotions*

FIRST CHAKRA
*cord to deceased
mother's soul*

SECOND CHAKRA
*dots = daughter's
fetal cells*

LIFE ENERGY
*(large gray arrow)
sent to deceased
mother's soul*

TENTH AURIC
FIELD—MIASM

CHRONIC FATIGUE
COMPONENTS
*1: hormones off
2: several shock bubbles
3: epigenetic material activated
4: mast cells overproduced
5: miasm in effect*

Figure 16: Martha's Autoimmune Condition After Age 45. *This figure depicts
her wounds from age 45 to when she came to see me. The wavy lines up and
down the front and back of the body indicate several energetically anxious
chakras (in front) and several energetically depressed chakras (in back).*

Helping Martha

Assisting Martha wasn't nearly as complicated a process as you might think, although I also had her work with other practitioners to assist her on the emotional and physical levels. Our main work was spread out over several sessions, during which I assisted regressing Martha back in time. We began with the inception of her major shock bubble way back when her soul separated from her spirit and the Oneness. During our first session, she became aware of her pain, but also of the conclusions she stored in her soul (and mind) about being unworthy of the love of the Spirit. In our second session, she allowed herself to reconnect with the Spirit, as well as her own spirit, and to open to the Spirit's reassuring love and care.

Martha's life began to immediately change. She became willing to work with a holistic doctor to balance her hormones and alter her diet, including cutting out cow dairy and gluten. (You'll discover more about the subtle energies related to these food products in chapter 10.) A third regression into the traumatic past life allowed her to address the spiritual forces she incurred because of the so-called sin of being imperfect. From there, she continued working with me, and also a trauma therapist, on her this-life childhood issues, including the attempted abortion and her trying relationship with her mother.

At this point, my main interactions with Martha involved subtle energy work, including clearing pathways and helping her release the selves (and letting the Spirit help free her) from shock bubbles. The more therapeutic sessions Martha underwent, the more she was able to grieve the traumas she'd encountered throughout her lifetimes and the more willing she was to release energetic constructs. I frequently find this is the case; as you'll find out in chapter 6, grieving is often a necessary part of healing from trauma and resulting chronic illnesses.

Eventually, Martha became psychologically strong enough to insist that her husband enter treatment for alcoholism. During the family part of this involved process, Martha and her daughter received loving assistance, and Martha's daughter entered therapy as well. Though the marriage was still difficult, it started on a new track, as did Martha's relationship with her daughter. And Martha began enjoying her work as a librarian more than ever. She still struggled with some fatigue, but a new exercise and diet program, as well as infrequent sessions with me to dissolve secondary forces, established her as happier and healthier than ever before.

The energetic components of a chronic illness or illnesses are complicated, but—as Martha's case demonstrates—they can be systematically addressed and healed. To make the complex picture a little clearer, let me summarize the factors involved in specific chronic illnesses.

The Basics of Chronic Illness

Chronic illnesses are an extension of established trauma. As such, their development begins with the sequence of events outlined in "the basics of trauma" section earlier in this chapter. Then any number of other factors can compound the unhealed trauma and exacerbate the stress response cycle, which just keeps repeating if left unaddressed.

These factors often include the following:

- Past-life soul issues that, when triggered by the trauma, reinforce current-life traumas and stress.

- Predominance of shame and unworthiness issues.

- Bindings to dark entities and powers, other living people, ancestors, and other spiritual sources.

- Multiple selves trapped in multiple shock bubbles.

- Creation of at least one secondary force that links the self-injurious self with a harmful person, entity, pattern, addiction, or the like.

- Microbial infections.

- Hormonal imbalances.

- Microchimeric effects.

- Networking between epigenetic material, a tenth chakra miasm, and mast cells, which causes a full-blown chronic illness.

- The emergence of sensitivities, allergies, and addictions.

Traumas and Challenges Guide, Part 2
Subtle Energy Insights for
Common Chronic Illnesses and Problems

In this chapter I shared the stories of two clients, laying out the many specific physical and subtle indications of their issues. As you've seen, the energetics of unaddressed trauma and its effects can be very complex. The following guide lists types of trauma, common diagnoses, and issues, along with directions on what to look for and assess regarding your subtle anatomy. It will help you to better see and make stronger connections between your physical and subtle anatomies and their relation to initial and secondary forces and charges.

As a special note, attachments can be part of any of the following conditions. If you know or suspect that you're dealing with past-life issues, I suggest you interact with your eighth chakra and field. You can assess an issue for eighth chakra problems using technique 4 in chapter 7 and then use a variety of tools to address the challenges, including technique 13 in chapter 8 for healing purposes.

Environmental Trauma

If you've been affected by an environmental trauma, I recommend the following starting places:

▸ *Environmental, Natural:* Address the tenth chakra/field, bones, repetitive soul issues, and epigenetics; also the first chakra/field, emphasizing the adrenals if possessions or lives were lost.

▸ *Environmental, Human-Caused:* Focus on the fourth chakra/field, especially the following:

Airborne Toxicity: Lungs.

Geo-Pollution: Tenth chakra/field, emphasizing the bones and epigenetic material.

Sound Toxicity: Phonons; fifth chakra/field, especially the throat, neck, and thyroid.

Electromagnetic Toxicity: Sixth chakra/field, checking the pituitary; third chakra/field, specifically working the gallbladder and liver.

Physical Trauma

For all physical trauma, you'll want to make sure you do the following:

- Check the entirety of the auric field, most specifically the first chakra/field.
- Clear and balance the adrenals and the polyvagal system.
- Analyze the force's entrance and exit wounds and pathway for interjected subtle charges.
- Find out if the first chakra's electrical energy is flowing up the spine/sushumna or not.
- Evaluate gut microbiome; figure out nutritional cravings. (You can do the latter in chapter 10.)
- Analyze for hormonal imbalances and their subtle meanings.
- Evaluate for microbes and their subtle meanings.
- See if microchimeric cells are triggered.
- Compare and address the matrix patterns between the miasmic tenth field, mast cells, and epigenetic material.

Psychological Trauma

You must always track a psychological issue to its initial psychological force and, from there, to the most damaged chakras/fields. At least one wounded and encapsulated self will always be present.

Also evaluate the tenth chakra/field and epigenetics, as psychological injuries often activate ancestral issues. I usually check the eighth chakra as well, as the soul's karma might have

GUIDE 3

been triggered by psychological damage. Finally, I review the eleventh chakra/field if the harm has caused extreme issues of shame and powerlessness.

The following are condition-specific recommendations.

▶ *Emotional Abuse:* Focus on the second chakra/field, the enteric nervous system, and the sixth chakra/field, especially self-image issues.

▶ *Verbal Abuse:* Include the fifth chakra/field and third chakra/field; the latter holds the negative beliefs related to psychological disturbances.

▶ *Psychological Abuse:* This abuse is caused by conjoined emotional and verbal forces and necessitates working with related areas, as well as with the seventh chakra/field if the abuse was spiritual and sixth chakra/field if the hardship strongly affected one's self-image.

▶ *Moral Trauma:* If forced to act against your value system, analyze the seventh and first chakras/fields. Also evaluate the ninth chakra/field, as these allow harmonization with the world, an ability that is compromised under immoral pressures. Moral challenges will probably debilitate the pineal gland and executive brain functions.

▶ *Digital Abuse:* This relatively new source of challenges, which includes digital bullying, dating manipulation, fast news cycles, and hyperavailability, spans the physical and subtle anatomies. Always work with the fourth chakra/field, as digital abuse impacts our relationship patterns, as well as the first chakra/field, as it causes an overstimulation of the SNS.

The EMFs involved will injure the third chakra/field, and negative social media posts, extreme criticism, and the expectations of meeting others' needs in a blink will negatively impact the third and sixth chakras/fields. An inability to manage what others are doing or thinking will injure the eleventh chakra/field and one's sense of power, as well as connective tissue and the flow of energy in the meridians.

▶ *Learning Issues:* There are dozens, if not hundreds, of potential physical and subtle causes for and energetic factors involved in learning issues. The following is an energetic exploration to assist you in dealing with any related traumas.

GUIDE 3

Attention Deficit Hyperactivity Disorder (ADHD). With attention deficit disorder (ADD), which causes an inability to focus, the front of the third chakra is too open and the back side too closed. The third auric field will be collecting subtly charged cognitive data from others, which it will send to the front side third chakra. In turn, the front side passes this intuitive data into the brain, which struggles, as the brain's organizational abilities can't keep up with the needed categorizing; hence, the difficulty in focusing.

The hyperactive element (the "H" in ADHD) involves ADD challenges and a too-open front side first chakra, along with a relatively closed back side first chakra. Basically, the first auric field will be absorbing others' physical energies and overloading the first chakra. To discharge this extra energy, the body becomes hyperactive.

With ADD and ADHD, the enteric nervous system becomes hypersensitive to genetically modified grains (GMOs), cow dairy, and food dyes and chemicals, mainly because the SNS is hyperattuned through the tenth chakra/field to unhealthy environmental disturbances, such as geo-pollution and sun spots. ADHD individuals usually have a highly developed seventh chakra/field and many past-life spiritual gifts encapsulated in the eighth chakra.

Autism Spectrum. The souls of those on the autism spectrum are very sensitive and often stuck replaying a past-life trauma via a cord connecting their current incarnated self to a past-life self. The auric fields are frequently stacked in the wrong order; usually, the first through third are on the outside of the overall field, and the other fields are underneath, causing extreme sensitivities within the enteric nervous system and an unbalanced microbiome. Typically, there is both energetic anxiety and depression present in the system. The vagus nerve is often hyperstimulated, leading to social anxiety, and there are usually allergic conditions that, stimulated in utero, continue to cause problems in the microbiome.

Somatic (Body) Sensitivities. These always involve the first chakra and auric field and an erratic polyvagal system. The first auric layer might be on the very outside of the auric field, causing some of the oversensitivity. Survival issues are paramount and often carried in from past lives or caused by in utero experiences. The first chakra is highly developed and quite attuned to others' physicality, to the point of triggering microbes in one's own body that are in play in others' bodies.

Dyslexia and Similar Challenges. Various auric fields are often laid down in an atypical order, making it hard for the higher brain to make sense of situations and also causing reading or math problems. For instance, the third auric field might be switched with the sixth auric field. This means that the information coming in through the eyes (sixth chakra/field) could enter the third chakra instead of the sixth chakra. The third chakra isn't visual, so it can't process the incoming data in a logical fashion.

As implied, dyslexia is almost always a sixth chakra/field visual inadequacy. Normally the eyes form an inverted image on the retina and the brain must reverse it. This doesn't happen correctly with these types of learning issues, in part because of physical or subtle optic challenges. The second (creative) chakra tends to be very developed, as is the related emotional empathy gift.

► *Psychological Illnesses and Conditions:* These are quite complicated, so I've only included the bare-bones clues—just enough to give you a heads-up when treating trauma using the techniques in chapter 8.

Depression: Look for energetic depression, inflammatory conditions, and the assumption of others' subtle energies, as well as the repression of one's own feelings, which can lead to microbial imbalances and seventh chakra issues. In particular, postpartum depression can occur because of energetic hormonal issues and a frayed connection between mother and child through an energetic umbilical cord that connects the two until about four years of age. Frequently the mother takes on her child's grief about "missing heaven" (perceived as the unification with the Oneness and/or the nonphysical state in between lifetimes) and can't process those feelings.

Anxiety: Examine energetic anxiety, the assumption of others' energies in one's own body, and past-life experiences that are triggering epigenetics and selves in shock bubbles.

Post-Traumatic Stress Disorder (PTSD). Post-traumatic stress disorder (or post-traumatic stress syndrome) is the clinical name for the mental health condition that can develop as the result of witnessing a terrifying, frightening, or dangerous event.[82] It is characterized by vivid flashbacks or nightmares. Other symptoms include emotional numbness, increased emotional arousal, and difficulty sleeping or concentrating. These symptoms are usually so severe that they disrupt everyday life.[83] PTSD is the result of the ongoing stress cycle and must be tracked to its origin to be healed. I have worked with countless individuals over the years who are suffering with PTSD, and I admire the people who are committed to their PTSD recovery. Most of the techniques in this book will assist with this process, and I have found them instrumental supplements to traditional therapies.

It's worth noting that PTSD is different than post-traumatic stress (PTS). The latter term is sometimes used to describe how, after a traumatic event has passed, people may re-experience the same fight-flight-freeze response that happened during the event, including all or some of its physical symptoms, such as increased heart rate, increased breathing, and muscle tension. PTS is typically considered to be a natural response and frequently subsides with time.[84]

GUIDE 3

Codependency. Mainly discussed in the next chapter, with a healing process presented in chapter 9.

Additional Mental Illnesses. In general, always look for abuse issues, past-life soul issues, very early childhood disrupters, dark entities and forces, and disturbances in the polyvagal system caused by or leading to microbiome imbalances. I've included a smattering of particular subtle factors and, when appropriate, discussed the role of codependency in particular conditions.

- *Bipolar Disorder.* There are many types of bipolar disorder. Overall, I believe there is usually a history of abuse. (The abuse could have

---

82 National Institute of Mental Health, "Post-Traumatic Stress Disorder."
83 Anxiety and Depression Association of America, "Symptoms of PTSD."
84 Bender, "What Are the Differences Between PTS and PTSD?"

occurred in a past life.) The bipolar person "splits" into a highly creative, "good" self and a depressed, angry, "bad" self. There will almost always be a seventh chakra issue involved in this split; in other words, the "good" part makes an ethical judgment about the "bad" part.

- *Borderline Personality Disorder (BPD).* I see this as a third chakra condition and categorize two types of BPD from an energetic point of view. As you'll learn in chapter 7, the third chakra develops between ages 2½ and 4½. If a child figures out that they can get their way by throwing tantrums, along with blaming others for their problems, they will use bullying, the major characteristic of BPD, to assert their personal authority. The other type of BPD is really a codependent issue. It is distinguished by individuals who assume others' feelings or thoughts in order to create peace. When a true BPD person pushes them, they will blow up. For instance, a BPD person might ignore their own rage and anger. The codependent BPD person feels these energies to the point of absorbing them. Finally, the codependent BPD person erupts in an attempt to get the BPD person to own their own emotions. That won't occur, and now the codependent looks crazy.

- *Narcissism.* From a subtle anatomy point of view, narcissism is initiated in the first chakra. As you'll discover in chapter 7, the first chakra develops in the womb through the sixth month of age. During this time period, we're supposed to be the apple of another's eye. We should have at least one person devoted to us and seeking to meet all our needs. When this doesn't happen, some individuals unconsciously decide they are "due." They use their innate intuition and charm to convince others to dote on them. If someone fails to do this, the narcissist becomes really angry, projecting their rage from childhood at the current "offender." Another set of individuals, those whose needs aren't met during this time period, become codependents to narcissists. They adopt the belief that to meet another's needs is the path to being loved. Often the narcissist codependent ends up in relationships with narcissists.

- *Schizophrenia.* This condition is characterized by a break with reality. I consider it to be, at least partially, a psychic wound. Either a part of the soul or the inner self has fragmented and leaves the body, leaving the remaining parts of the self susceptible to invasion.

Addictions and Allergies

These were introduced earlier in this chapter and will be a focus of chapter 10. In general, look for missing forces, reactions against subtle charges carried into the system in this or earlier lifetimes, attachments, epigenetic triggers that cause the self to act out ancestral issues, and microbiome imbalances. The gut-brain axis is almost always distorted.

Aging

Aging is a normal part of life, but our reactions to it might not be. Advanced aging difficulties usually involve the tenth chakra/field and epigenetic triggers; first chakra challenges such as hyperactive adrenals, hormone-related difficulties, and a stressed out SNS; a debilitated vagus nerve; the assumption of others' energies; loss of life energy due to too many selves in trauma bubbles; incomplete grieving, which I'll cover in the next chapter; or an eighth chakra issue in the soul, which doesn't want to be incarnated anymore.

Financial Problems

These always involve the first chakra/field and deep issues of unworthiness, as well as the assumption of others' judgments and energies. It can be helpful to address the tenth chakra epigenetics, looking for ancestral trauma. Also frequently involved are one to several deflection shields, which keep out abundance, and sometimes shame in the soul from karma, addressed through the eighth chakra/field.

Insights on specific financial issues:

- ▶ **Being the Piggy Bank:** Are you always paying for everyone else? There will be a cord going into others' first chakras—hence, an energy leak in your first chakra. A karmic issue might cause you to believe you owe a debt to others.

- *Being the Poor Relation:* Is everyone else in your family well-off? You are their gas station in that they are siphoning off the supply of gas (energy) that was meant to be yours, leaving you depleted and having to continuously work to refuel instead of being able to act upon your own vision or desires. Cords established between you and other family members, or the presence of a miasm, will be costing you your gain.

- *Debt:* Search for the cause of a depletion in the first chakra/field. The back side of this chakra will also be closed, not open to receiving abundance.

- *Failure to Keep a Job:* In addition to examining the first chakra for issues, search the energetic field for an energy marker, which will be "telling" others to not hire you.

- *Greed:* A belief in lack will be impacting your first and third chakras. This thinking might be inherited through the tenth chakra, as ancestors' greed might have resulted in wealth.

Relationship Problems

These are best understood by examining codependency issues, the topic in the next chapter, and often involve patterns asserted by the selves in the shock bubbles.

Spiritual and Psychic Problems

These always involve the eight chakra and field, which encompass the soul and past lives; the seventh chakra and field, which are vulnerable to spiritual issues; and any chakras that have attachments and are under- or over-psychic because of their challenges. In particular, the tenth chakra/field will be affected by the spiritual issues and entities associated with one's ancestors.

Complications of Grieving

See the next chapter.

Specific chronic illnesses will be examined in chapter 9.

Personal Assessment: *Tracing the Origin of Your Challenge*

When and how did your challenge begin? That's the question this assessment will help you answer (or at least help you begin to answer). You'll need writing instruments, paper, your physical symptoms chart from chapter 3, your chakra symptoms chart from chapter 4, and about thirty minutes of uninterrupted time. You may choose to enlist the help of trusted family members, friends, or your health practitioners as you're doing this assessment.

1. Take a few deep breaths and focus on your challenge. Now respond yes or no to this statement: I believe this challenge originated with a single traumatic event.

   ▸ *If you answered yes, continue with step 2.*
   If you answered no, skip to step 3.

2. Respond to the following statements about the traumatic event:

   • I would describe this traumatic event in the following way:

   • I was this age when the traumatic event occurred:

   • This trauma impacted my body in the following ways:

      Consult your physical symptoms chart from chapter 3 as you respond. Which of the symptoms you listed arose immediately after the initial trauma or as a direct result of it?

   • I believe this trauma immediately impacted my subtle anatomy in the following ways:

      Consult your chakra symptoms chart from chapter 4 as you respond. Which of the symptoms you listed there occurred immediately after the initial trauma or as a direct result of it?

   • I believe the following physical and subtle symptoms are secondary, or second-stage, responses to the initial trauma:

      Consult your physical symptoms and chakra symptoms charts as you respond. Which of the symptoms you listed on these charts developed in the months or few years immediately after the trauma?

- I believe the following symptoms are long-term/ongoing effects that have developed as a result of the unresolved factors from initial trauma and/or the secondary stressors that followed:

  ▸ *You may or may not link all or most of the symptoms on your physical symptoms and chakra symptoms charts to one of the three stages of the stress response. If there are outstanding symptoms on either list, continue with step 3, which may shed some light on their origins.*

3. Take another few deep breaths. Now respond to the following statements:

   - When I think back on my childhood, the following experiences stand out as being traumatic, stressful, difficult, or otherwise significant:

   - When I think back on my adult life to date, the following experiences stand out as being traumatic, stressful, difficult, or otherwise significant:

   - The last time I felt completely free from or unaffected by any symptoms was:

4. Finally, consult your physical symptoms and chakra symptoms lists again. For each of the symptoms on your list, write down what age you first experienced it and where you were at that time.

   ▸ *If your symptoms lists are long, focus on those symptoms that you ranked as the most problematic, then record what origin details that you know of about any other symptoms on your list.*

   ▸ *Be as specific as you can, but don't worry if you can't remember the exact details.* Why does it matter *where* you were when a particular symptom began? Because environmental forces, spiritual forces, or the energies of other people who were in that place at that time may be contributing to the symptom.

When doing this assessment, you might discover that some symptoms have been affecting you throughout your life or that you have no idea how or when they originated. This lack of information is just as helpful as what you *do* know. If you can't pinpoint when specific problems began in your life or you can't remember a time a symptom wasn't affecting you, those problems/symptoms may have their origins in the earliest part of your life that you can't consciously remember, in a past lifetime, or in your ancestors' lives.

· · · · ·

Synopsis

In this chapter, we delved into the specifics of how the physical and subtle anatomies interact in response to traumatic stressors and how the stress response, left unhealed, can lead to chronic illness. Listed were the main physical and subtle anatomical factors involved in these challenges.

Now that you understand the complicated dance of physical and subtle factors contributing to your challenges, it's time to focus on two softer issues: grieving and codependency, along with the parts they play in our challenges.

CHAPTER 6

The Grieving Heart and Codependency

The psyche cannot tolerate a vacuum of love.
—Sam Keen, *The Passionate Life: Stages of Loving*

A major reason that a traumatized self remains trapped in a shock bubble, whether some-one's condition has progressed to a state of chronic illness or not, is a failure to grieve. Too many of us lack an outlet for the grief that naturally follows in the wake of stressors, so our stress locks in and turns into trauma. Incomplete grief is also the main reason we become codependent.

In this vital chapter, I'll first define grief and explain why grieving can create a new state of wellness after we've been felled. I'll describe how inadequate grieving impairs the immune system and can underlie a host of additional physical and psychological problems. I'll show how incomplete grieving creates dysfunctional relationships and additional hardships that I call "energetic codependency," a form of codependency that includes the standard type and also implicates subtle energies. A plethora of examples will help you perceive the intercon-nections between grieving, energetic codependency, and life's ongoing challenges.

The Need to Grieve

My client Ethel was more than uptight. Her mother had continually shamed her when growing up. Since she was young, she'd struggled with asthma and chronic bronchitis. Now, at age seventy-five, she'd added heart and knee problems, arthritis, and diabetes to her list of hardships.

When we met, Ethel's main concern was the fact she was being mistreated by several friends. She wondered what she was doing wrong.

It didn't take a brain surgeon to perceive the parallel between the cruelty of her mother and that of her friends. The psychological forces she experienced in childhood had locked Ethel in a shock bubble from which she'd never escaped. Neither had she grieved, which was one of the reasons she was experiencing physical hardships, as well as codependent relationships.

What Is Grief?

Grief is a multifaceted response to loss. Though we usually limit the concept to the experience of losing a person, relationship, or job, grief is very personal. We might grieve our health or youth, the death of a dream, or the shattering of innocence. We might grieve having a learning disorder or even all the time spent on work.

We usually think of grieving as an emotional process. The standard model for grieving explains the emotional stages involved, as presented decades ago by Elisabeth Kübler-Ross. These five stages are denial, anger, bargaining, depression, and acceptance.[85] The model says that, psychologically, we must visit each stage to deal with a loss. Sometimes, though, we cycle through them in no particular order. And regardless of how we encounter these stages (or not), grief is usually full-on and *gritty*.

Grief often alters our behavior, causing isolation, intolerance, restlessness, and tearfulness. Mentally, it can cause confusion, hallucinations, and the sense of disconnection. It can result in appetite changes, insomnia, tiredness, and physical ailments, as well as difficult feelings like guilt, fear, regret, and resentment. Most typically, it also compels us to question life's meaning or our faith.[86] In other words, stress triggers grief, but grief also causes stress.

This statement is especially true if we perceive the loss as dangerous. For instance, if the family breadwinner dies, we'll become frightened about survival. If a child dies, we'll wonder about the existence of goodness. In really tough cases, our body triggers the same emergency-mobilizing chemicals that all stressors do, altering our chemistry right down to the microbiome and immune system. In fact, the trauma of grieving has been shown to cause the

---

85   Kübler-Ross and Kessler, *On Grief and Grieving*.
86   Beyond Blue Support Service, "What Is Grief?"

appearance of illnesses, including cardiovascular disorders, cancer, lymphoma, lupus, influenza, chronic itching, rheumatoid arthritis, alcoholism, chronic depression, and more.[87]

I showcase these symptoms to emphasize my point. Locked-in bodily trauma and chronic illnesses are intimately interconnected with the grieving process—in particular with what is often called "complicated grief."

The Complications of Grief

When my boys were young, they endured lots of scrapes and bruises during recess at school. They didn't cry right away. Upon arriving home, they would tear up and tell me how much their knee/elbow/chin hurt. I'd clean up the owie, put on an action figure bandage, and they'd run off to play. The injury wasn't hurting when they saw me; they simply needed to share their feelings with someone who cared. It was the unwrapping of their feelings that convinced them they were being healed. As with any stressor or trauma, healing required receiving outside-to-inside assistance.

How much more grieving is needed for a traumatized self still stuck in a bubble? When very little grieving has taken place, that grief becomes complicated.

Complicated grief occurs when the grief of the shocked self goes unexpressed or is incompletely processed. There are several negative effects of complicated grief, and they're easiest to explain when you can visualize the subtle energies involved.

Picture the traumatized self trapped in a shock bubble. Most likely there are several layers of trauma surrounding the original wounded self. That self is its own mini person, with the energy layers around it forming a set of subtle boundaries; in fact, these boundaries could be considered a sort of auric field. The self in the bubble, frozen in the trauma, continually re-experiences the trauma, even while the subtle energies associated with the trauma, including the forces, the subtle charges transferred in, and the traumatized self's feelings and reactions, are programmed into the mini auric field. In turn, this combined group of energies—the totality of initial incompatible energies and the subsequent responses to that wounding—is reflected in the related chakra(s) and mirrored within the external auric fields.

Grieving is the means for healing post-trauma. The self in the bubble can't start or finish their grieving process, however, without outside help. Until then, the trauma's energies are

---

87   Neeld, "The Physical Stress of Grieving."

broadcast into the world as a cry for that help, like radio transmissions announcing, "Look, I'm sad! I've been abused! I think I'm unworthy!" The hope is that someone will pay heed. That doesn't always happen.

Energy attracts like energy. Too often, the broadcast for attention, which travels through the surrounding compromised aspects of our subtle anatomy, attracts people, situations, and experiences that match the original trauma, further inculcating the traumatized self. Thus, the body activates additional signs of the trauma. If these signs recur unabated, symptoms of chronic illnesses arise as the captured self forms self-injurious activities in an attempt to get further attention as it continues, compulsively, to reenact the trauma internally.

Meanwhile, no matter if we're dealing with trauma or a self-injurious situation, the caught self continually replays the wounding. Added to the emotional drama are new feelings: hopelessness about the inability to heal. Shame about not becoming free—or, at a certain point, not even wanting to. The energetic field starts to feel comfortable, like home. Ultimately, the entrenched self feels sad about the deepest of pains: the inability to express the original self.

This was the case with Ethel. Her trauma started with her mother's intense shaming, which transferred destructive subtle messages into her subtle anatomy through a psychological force. During her childhood, Ethel embalmed her wounded self in a shock bubble to self-protect, but the shaming kept occurring. No one recognized what was happening deep inside of her protective casing. She simply smiled into the world and became a well-known psychiatrist.

Unfortunately, the self in the bubble—or rather, the subtle messages being sent from its energetic sheathing—attracted people like her mother. Though Ethel also appealed to loving personalities, the ones that affected her most were the mean and nasty ones. They intuitively and energetically sensed they could be dishonorable because Ethel was vulnerable and because her injured self agreed with their negative assessments of her. After all, what her mother had said of her must have been true, right? Because no one could perceive what Ethel was going through, no one helped her.

Eventually, Ethel's body turned on itself. She developed complicated grief. In an attempt to clean out the traumatizing energies, as well as to incite the grieving process, her physical body began to injure itself. The subtle anatomy participated in this process, too, attempting to rid itself of the congested energies. Eventually, Ethel developed physically diagnosable conditions.

When working with Ethel, I addressed only one physical aspect of her chronic illnesses, suggesting that she was afflicted with a microbe. In particular, I intuitively sensed that she had contracted chlamydia pneumoniae (a respiratory tract infection) early in her childhood. This airborne bacterium enters the lungs but operates atypically. As I further explain in chapter 9, it functions like both a bacteria and a virus. I'd worked with this bacterium before. It gravitates toward weak organs and underlies many chronic illnesses, including those exhibited by Ethel. I also knew that on the subtle level, the bacterial component would hold Ethel's grief and the virus would be attached to her family system. And guess what? When she was tested, Ethel was found to have the microbe.

The other part of my work involved helping Ethel recognize that on the energetic level, her issues came down to the trauma of being shamed and the fact that her "friends" kept retriggering her mother's cruelty. When I shared this with her, Ethel's face lit up. Her life— and struggles—all made sense. I suggested that the path to freedom was to feel her feelings, detach from her mother's family system, and grieve.

Ethel grieved mainly by keeping a journal. In it, she wrote about every time she'd been shamed and how that behavior had made her feel. She was able to link the most severe of shaming experiences to the appearance of various bodily disorders. And then, to free herself from the self-injurious pattern, she owned that she had participated in the patterns by failing to comprehend her worth and value. After unpacking the emotional events, grieving the mistreatment, and undergoing medical care for the microbe, she felt good enough that, after consulting with her doctor, they decided to actually cancel an upcoming heart surgery.

I can't emphasize enough the need to grieve a trauma we've experienced. It is the key to unlocking the door of the shock bubble. Afterward, our life might just return to what it was pre-trauma. Then again, it might not. Though a lost limb won't reappear, we can learn to walk with a prosthetic. Though a broken marriage might not be restored, we can learn how to love again. Though our bodies may not be able to shed all of the extra pounds we may have gained, we can live our days with renewed vitality. So important is grieving that I must underline this point: if you can't unearth grief on your own, or through subtle energy means, confer with a professional. We are worthy of having a loving and trained professional walk the walk with us.

Grieving is key to another important healing process, and that is the release from co-dependent patterns that can result from trauma. I believe that one of the reasons we develop codependency, which we'll explore next, is complicated grieving.

CHAPTER 6

The Causes of Codependency

What does codependency have to do with the need to grieve? Moreover, what is energetic codependency, the specific type of codependency I want to introduce you to?

Classically, codependency involves participation in an unhealthy relationship pattern. Often, the codependent suffers from an excessively emotional or psychological reliance on a partner who is stuck in their own dysfunctional energetic or behavioral pattern because of illness, addiction, or some other challenge. Codependency is often considered a relationship addiction because the codependent becomes addicted to the partner. They focus on controlling the partner's moods and behaviors instead of caring for themselves. The codependent ignores their own needs, feelings, and thoughts and often becomes resentful and angry as a result.

In my studies of codependency, I've learned that there are three standard causes for codependency: exposure to abuse, addictions, and mistreatment that causes a fear of people or perhaps even of the world. Note that each variety results in trauma.

Abuse-caused codependency strikes those who have been abused or witnessed abuse. The resulting powerlessness instigates distorted relationships with abusers or participation in events mirroring the abuse. In addiction-related codependency, an addictive substance/behavior/activity turns into the addict's "god" or "mate," and the codependent must provide for the addict in order to feel loved and needed. The self-sacrifice is demanding and demeaning. In fear-based codependency, the codependent has learned to value others' opinions more than their own—perhaps even more than their spiritual beliefs. The resulting insecurities leave the codependent vulnerable to others' influence.

I'm a big believer in receiving professional help for codependency. I've done so myself, including participating in the twelve-step Al-Anon program, which assists codependents of alcoholics. Even then, I also worked in the subtle realms, as there is more to the codependency story than the standard causes. In fact, I've determined that subtle energies can create a state of energetic codependency.

The Ill Under Our Ills: Energetic Codependency

To define energetic codependency and its relationship with grief, trauma-induced challenges, and chronic illnesses, I'm going to return to Ethel.

As explained, Ethel's challenges all can be seen as the result of a traumatized self trapped within a shock bubble. Within that bubble, the trapped self, who wasn't invited to grieve, was compelled to form negative relationships. Each of these relationships accomplished very specific goals, although they weren't healthy. In line with the causes of codependency (abuse, addiction-related, fear-based), these objectives could be characterized in these ways:

Abuse-Related: By forming a relationship with unloving friends, Ethel's traumatized self kept alive the abuse she'd suffered from her mother. This guaranteed that her traumatized self wouldn't forget or be forgotten. In fact, the traumatized self could count herself as important enough to recall the horror she'd lived through.

Addiction-Related: In a way, the relationships with the cruel friends could be seen as an addiction. The traumatized self would have felt she "needed" the way these friends treated her, as it was all she'd known growing up. The retriggering of the inner shame, fear, and low self-esteem had defined the wounded self when Ethel was growing up; at some level it still did, no matter how accomplished Ethel became in her other relationships and her profession. In short, we get used to the way we've been treated, and it provides a strange comfort. On the other hand, the existence of negative bonds also retriggers the wounded self, which is also a plus: it's impossible to completely forget mistreatment if it still occurs, and that thought offers hope for healing.

Fear-Based: Trauma is a rigid teacher. It tells us, or an aspect of us, exactly what we deserve by having us experience the opposite of what is in alignment with our original energetic signature. Ethel's experience with her mother forced Ethel to believe that she wasn't worthy of love, goodness, and kindness. The wounded aspect of Ethel agreed, and she felt compelled to remain in her bubble and re-create the negative patterns. Why even try a new pattern when it might merely reinforce the "truth" of the shame-based one? Consequently, Ethel developed a fear of intimacy.

On an energetic level, a new event occurred inside Ethel's subtle anatomy: the mini auric field around Ethel's traumatized self evolved.

During my initial session with Ethel, I could still see her traumatized self wrapped within a trauma bubble. But there was also another wave of energy, one I call a secondary force (*not* a secondary charge), that encircled this self and also surrounded another subject—or, in Ethel's case, a set of subjects. This beam of brackish energy came off her original trauma bubble and reached outside of her body to encompass the evil friends. This is exactly the type of pattern I perceive when someone has developed a full-blown chronic condition or illness. But in this case, the self-injurious loop connected Ethel in codependent relationships with people who mirrored the abuse from her mother.

At no time had Ethel been able to grieve the abuse, nor had she had a moment in which to address and grieve the negative relationships. Stuck within her history, she was experiencing what I call energetic codependency. (It was not just codependency because in addition to relationship patterns, subtle energetics were involved.) At the very least, the secondary loop constituted a subtle energetic stressor.

This is not to say that energetic codependency doesn't have a physical side. It does. Physically, the brain and other bodily systems are wired to replicate known relationships. As we briefly explored in chapter 3, the vagus nerve, programmed with our social beliefs, operates within the polyvagal system to cause and deal with stress reactions. Our traumatic memories are locked into the cells by the neurotransmitter GABA (gamma-aminobutyric acid) and are also programmed into our infra-low brain waves.

There are many brain waves, including alpha, which keep us alert in daily life, and delta, which helps us sleep and dream. Cycling slower and longer than delta waves, infra-low waves oscillate at a rhythm that is only .5 hertz (Hz) per second. Infra-low waves are cortical brain rhythms, which means they store and echo our trauma and negative programs. They operate through our unconscious, so they stimulate codependent actions that we're not aware of. I consider them part of the energetics promoting codependency. Because of this, you'll learn how to assess and clear them in chapter 8. Bottom line, they reinforce our stress reactions and keep trauma locked in, as well as recycling through, the body.

Healing from energetic codependency involves shifting ingrained and self-injurious patterns on the subtle and physical levels, and you'll learn several techniques enabling both in the chapters 7, 8, and 9.

Ethel was able to be freed from her loop of energetic codependency. How about a different client example?

Sam was a middle-aged man whose parents withheld money or resources from him every time they were unhappy with him. If Sam failed to please his emotionally demanding mother, such as by not listening to her endless complaints against his father, she would refuse to give him his allowance. If his father was mad that his son didn't pitch perfectly during a baseball game, he wouldn't buy Sam baseball equipment, such as much-needed cleats.

This wounding established a trauma bubble connected to Sam's first chakra. No one in his immediate family noticed or cared what was happening within Sam, and so Sam's inner self remained locked into place, unable to grieve or even speak to the damage. Eventually, Sam married a woman who was a gambling addict. Interestingly, he had been dating another loving woman, who was emotionally healthy, before he met his new wife. But he was smitten with the person that matched his parents, and Sam felt compelled to marry her instead, actually turning away a healthy relationship in order to enter a dysfunctional one.

On the energetic level, Sam's original energetic signature had actually allowed him to attract a dharmic path toward restoration—the nice woman. But his wounded child self, still held within a shock bubble, was stuck in the fiscally punishing program. The gambling addiction comprised the subject of a new secondary force (self-created but injurious in nature through the wounded self's further effort to bring attention to itself), which looped around Sam's already traumatized self and also his wife, who was simply a stand-in for his parents. Hence, he was trapped in an energetically codependent relationship.

In order to earn his wife's love, Sam enabled her addiction, covering her expenses but feeling unlovable all the while. Over time, he actually started taking risks as a stock investor. Eventually, he lost more money than he made. He had developed his own form of a monetary addiction in order to uphold his codependent energetic pattern.

There were many additional challenges complicating Sam's situation, including cords between his father, mother, and himself, and the presence of a dark entity linked to his wife. We had to address them all. The keys to freeing Sam were to find the traumatized self in both bubbles (the shock bubble and the secondary force wrapped around it), support the release of this self, and free him from his codependent patterns. In both cases, Sam had to grieve—grieve through his loneliness, the pattern, and his pain. Only then could he start making different relationship decisions, which inevitably resulted in him leaving the marriage when his wife wouldn't deal with her addiction. Sam joined an Al-Anon program for

Gamblers Anonymous and gradually stopped playing the stock market himself. Last I heard from him, he was dating a "perfectly lovely *and* loving person."

Like both Ethel and Sam, you, too, can alter any energetic codependent patterns you find yourself in.

Trauma and Challenges Guide, Part 3
The Influence of Codependency and Unresolved Grief

When it's time, how might you start working on energetic codependency themes? Following are a few tips for you to work with. Know, too, that if you discover codependent relationships carried over from past lives or that attachments are implicated, you'll also interact with the eighth chakra and field.

Environmental Trauma

These challenges always include an environmental force and often the following:

▸ *Environmental, Natural:* Repetitive tenth chakra/field issues, such as patterns from the ancestors and cords and holds formed under duress. Codependent bonds can also exist with natural beings, such as an animal saved during a climactic disaster.

▸ *Environmental, Human-Caused:* Focus on the first and fourth chakras/fields that were traumatized during the environmental disaster and any relationship patterns that developed following it. For instance, if your entire family survived a crisis except for your father, you might have taken on your father's role to compensate.

Physical Trauma

For all physical trauma, check for these relationship patterns, which might involve not only a traumatized self but also a secondary loop:

• A traumatized self who is scared about survival and stuck in the first chakra/field and subsequent insecure relationships.

- Subtle energies absorbed from the abusive, addictive, or frightening parties.
- Cords between the first chakra/field and the harmful parties.
- Cravings for foods that might energetically nourish the traumatized self but also repress grief. For instance, a desire for protein might serve to strengthen the abused self but can also be overeaten to squelch the feelings of powerlessness.
- Out-of-balance hormones. For instance, a woman abused by a man might repress her testosterone because she's scared of male energy.
- Attachments to subtle forces and entities promoting disastrous patterns and also behaviors such as addictions. In turn, the addictions stir up the shame about having been traumatized. For instance, someone sexually abused by their father could attract partners that are sexually violent, while an entity might promote overt sexual activity to keep the shame alive.
- Cords to microchimeric cells if the codependent subject was part of an abuse cycle.

GUIDE 4

Psychological Trauma

You must always track the psychological force initiating the trauma, and there you will find the traumatized self attached to a primary chakra/field. This self will be acting in a repetitive, codependent manner. Check for tenth chakra/field and microchimeric patterns and evaluate the eighth chakra/field, as codependent relationships often start in—or are underscored by—past lives. I also examine the eleventh chakra/field if the psychological damage included shame and intense powerlessness or, conversely, an authoritarian attitude. Specific recommendations follow.

> *Emotional Abuse:* Check on the second chakra/field and examine for a codependent exchange of emotions and unexpressed creativity—creativity unexpressed so as to caretake someone else. You'll find the inaccurate self-image and its effects in the sixth chakra, which is projected through the sixth field to attract unhealthy relationships.

- *Verbal Abuse:* Dive into the fifth and third chakras/fields to discover the inaccurate beliefs causing low-functioning relationships.

- *Psychological Abuse:* This abuse is caused by both emotional and verbal forces, so you must examine the same issues as those involved in emotional and verbal abuse. If the abuse also incorporated a spiritual force, evaluate for an unhealthy approach to religion or spirituality through the seventh chakra/field. Also check the tenth chakra/field for epigenetic iterations.

- *Moral Trauma:* Codependency nearly always creates a moral challenge. When we sacrifice ourselves for another, we lose our self-integrity, furthering feelings of unworthiness and shame. We might then become an addict ourselves to "prove" that we aren't good. Always help the morally bankrupt self through the first, seventh, and ninth chakras/fields. If the person is involved with an unhealthy or fundamentalist religion or spiritual group, examine these same chakras for a secondary force including that religion or group.

- *Digital Abuse:* When we're victims of digital abuse or we inflict it upon others, we must assess our codependent patterns. Are we repeating a psychological drama? If so, we'll want to examine any number of chakras/fields, but especially the second or third. Are we attempting to fit in with peers by bullying others? Then we'll have to probe our third and fourth chakras/fields. Do we feel powerless and believe we must respond to others' demands? If so, take a look at the eleventh chakra/field. Has your identity been stolen and you believe you must pay to restore it? Dig into your first chakra/field.

- *Learning Issues:* Having a learning issue can serve as a precursor to acting in certain codependent ways. I'll give you a few examples.

   Attention Deficit Hyperactivity Disorder (ADHD). Shame about having auditory processing issues can cause you to absorb others' thoughts and beliefs through your third chakra/field, especially if you tell yourself you're stupid. You could dampen your third chakra power, avoid positions of power, ignore conflict, or people-please as a means to gain approval.

If you are also hyperactive, you might be running others' physical disorders, pains, and illnesses through your own first chakra/field. You could also feed into others' addictions or develop your own to feel needed or secure.

Autism Spectrum. Autism often involves cords connecting someone to past-life relationships, so always examine the eighth chakra. Social programs can also be indoctrinated through the tenth chakra into the epigenes and the vagus nerve. Others' energies can also be frequently absorbed through the reversed fields; remember, in guide 3 I discussed the idea that the auric fields in autistic individuals are often stacked in the wrong order. Frequently, the fine souls of these individuals are very codependent and constantly process others' issues for them. As well, their systems often mirror the allergies in their loved ones, and so their bone marrow (tenth chakra) can create the same allergens.

Somatic (Body) Sensitivities. Double-check the tenth and first chakras/fields for codependent patterns and attachments. Given that the first auric field is sometimes on the very outside of the other auric fields, it's important to check for the reasons that the somatic sensitive take on others' first chakra issues.

Dyslexia and Similar Challenges. Very frequently the sixth chakra/field is busily processing others' low self-esteem issues. There can also be a codependent relationship involving the third chakra/field that creates an addled mind.

▸ *Psychological Illnesses and Conditions:* These are quite complicated, so I've only included enough bare-bones clues to get you started.

Depression. Making this distinction is important: Who is actually depressed or stuck in the past? Are you depressed or are you feeling another's grief? Ask yourself if you've become depressed in order to take care of others' histories.

Anxiety. Anxiety often occurs if we have absorbed others' energies into our own physical or subtle bodies. Energies that aren't our own frighten the body, which seeks to get rid of them; sometimes, this alone can cause the body to initiate what become the self-injurious responses that underlie chronic illnesses. We can also be taking care of others' fears, perhaps in an attempt to avoid our own.

Post-Traumatic Stress Disorder (PTSD). Everyone I've worked with who had been diagnosed with PTSD has had energetically codependent patterns. The question is, who or what are we enabling? Consider all possibilities. I once worked with a veteran who had taken on all the physical and emotional pains of his fellow soldiers who died during an IED explosion. Because of his survivor guilt, he kept re-experiencing their life issues and death pains, thinking he could help them "get to heaven" this way. Most of his issues went away after he addressed this first and fourth chakra/field "decision."

Additional Mental Illnesses: Personality Disorders. If you are energetically codependent with someone who has a personality disorder, I'd like to alert you to a specific challenge you face. I'll feature codependency in regard to narcissism and to borderline personality disorder (BPD) to make my point.

As I covered at the end of guide 3, narcissists are afflicted in the first chakra. From the time they were in utero to six months of age, they weren't the apple of someone's eye. Hence, they subconsciously decided to be the center of attention for the rest of their lives in order to make up for that. People with BPD are usually stymied in the third chakra, having learned that they can get their needs met by bullying others. In addition, the person with BPD projects their feelings onto others in an attempt to not feel their own deeper feelings.

Both narcissism and BPD affect the related energetic field and encourage energetic codependency. The strongest energy field in a narcissist is their first auric field; in a person with BPD, it's their third auric field. To meet their needs, the narcissist spreads their first auric field energy throughout the entirety of their entire field; the person with BPD does the same with the energy of their third auric field. Thus do both narcissists and people with BPD invite others to occupy their field and enter an energetically codependent bonding.

If you are or have been in a codependent relationship with either of these personality types, know that the key to releasing yourself is understanding that, inadvertently, you are ensconced in their primary field. You might not know it, but if you've become entangled with someone with either personality disorder, you not only occupy a seat within their primary field, but also have been handed, and are playing out, a stage role. In other words, in the relationship, you are a prop in their psychological drama, not a person in your own right.

I once worked with a man whose mother was a narcissist. She kept accusing him of cheating on his wife, which he wasn't doing. She would then break down in tears and he would feel guilty, even though he wasn't complicit in any wrongdoing. I pointed out that he was occupying a role in her first auric field: he'd been cast as his mother's father, who had cheated on his wife. Unwilling to actually deal with her own childhood feelings, the narcissistic mother turned her son into her father and kept at him until he acted the part of her father, even to the point of absorbing the feelings she *wanted* her father to express.

I also worked with a woman whose wife had BPD. My client was constantly felled by her wife's bursts of rage and would end up sad, despairing, and lonely. It turned out that my client was simply occupying a role within the third energy field of her wife, who was using my client as a placeholder for herself. The wife had grown up with an abusive father and as a child had been constantly sad, despairing, and lonely when around him. She was now projecting her feelings onto—and into—my client, who was so shocked that she took on her wife's personal feelings and felt them for her.

If you are in an energetically codependent relationship with anyone with a personality disorder and certain types of mental illnesses, such as bipolar disorder, I would recommend that you use technique 30 in chapter 10 to assure the correct energetic boundaries between you and the other person.

Addictions and Allergies

We'll identify these issues in chapter 10, including the codependent factors.

Aging

How can codependency make us struggle with aging? Here are a few of the many possibilities.

- We are in a codependent connection with a living or deceased ancestor, taking on their aging issues and fears through our tenth or first chakras/fields.

- Through our sixth chakra/field, we are assuming—and trying to fulfill—cultural norms. If we fail to match the air-brushed images or other ridiculous societal standards presented by the world, we might feel ugly and embarrassed.

- We might be adopting beliefs about aging from people around us. Do we want to look quite youthful for ourselves or to please our life partner? Various chakras/fields might be involved, depending on the motivation. For instance, if we think we'll be divorced and thrown "out on the street" unless we are handsome or pretty, our first chakra/field is implicated.

- We can absorb another's emotions about aging, mainly through our second chakra/field. I used to feel my mother's challenges with aging even as a young child. I felt old when I was only ten years old, and I worried about wrinkles I didn't have.

Financial Problems

These always involve the first chakra/field and the role we assume to assist the family. Financial problems—such as never making enough money, paying for everyone else, or having to be rich—can also be carried in from a past life, therefore involving the eighth chakra/field. They might also come from our tenth chakra/field, thereby constituting an epigenetic pattern. Or maybe your dead ancestor's soul is compelling you to take on the financial role they played in the family system.

Nearly any other chakra can also be complicit in a financial pattern. For instance, I worked with a client who was continually destitute because her mother had told her that God only rewarded the poor. My client was in a codependent connection with her mother's spiritual opinion through her seventh chakra. Literally, a secondary force looped through her seventh chakra into her mother's belief system; I could see this force loop as a dark blob outside of her head. Once she rejected that lie, her earnings soared.

Relationship Problems

These are always some rendering of a codependent pattern. Your best way to deal with them is to track a trauma to the causative chakra and self in the shock bubble, begin healing that wounded self, and then search for a secondary loop, as you'll be shown to do in chapter 9.

Spiritual and Psychic Problems

These nearly always involve some sort of codependent issue, which should be traced to the appropriate chakra/field. You can be codependent to an entity or a force with which you might be connected to through not only a primary loop but also a secondary loop. For instance, I worked with a client who was diagnosed with dissociative identity disorder (formerly known as multiple personality disorder). In a session that also included her therapist, we discovered that she was corded to a "missing twin," a child that had been spontaneously aborted. Through the microchimeric sibling cells, as well as a secondary loop, my client kept taking on the missing twin's emotions and personality because she felt so guilty about surviving when her twin died. Once we used the techniques found in chapter 7, all her symptoms disappeared.

GUIDE 4   Specific chronic illnesses, including autoimmune disorders, will be examined in chapter 8.

Personal Assessment: *Unresolved Grief*

In this assessment you'll identify which events or areas of your life you have yet to grieve. Grieving is the key to unlocking shock bubbles. Identifying unresolved grief can give you clues about where to look for shock bubbles, as well as help you release secondary energies. You'll need writing instruments, paper, the results of your personal assessment from chapter 5, and perhaps your chakra symptoms chart from chapter 4 as well. You'll also need about thirty minutes of uninterrupted time.

You may feel grief rising as you answer the questions. Please be compassionate with yourself and take your time if it does.

On a new sheet of paper, respond to the following questions:

1. Do you feel unexpressed grief inside you or do you suspect some grief is locked or trapped within you, unable to be expressed?

2. Have you ever felt a strong sense of grief arise seemingly out of the blue (meaning, grief not connected to people or situations around you at the time)?

3. Looking at your answers to the personal history assessment in chapter 5, do you notice events or situations, or people involved in them, that you have not been able to grieve or grieve in full?

   ▸ *If you have trouble gaining insight from your chapter 5 assessment, employ the chakra symptoms chart you made in chapter 4. Which chakras feel blocked or do you feel a resistance to?*

   ——————————————

Grieving is an essential part of healing. It can also be very deep and emotional work. Please contact a mental health professional, a spiritual counselor, or other sources of support if you need it.

Personal Assessment: *Energetic Codependency*

In this assessment you'll explore which of your relationships, if any, are energetically codependent. You'll need writing instruments, paper, your physical symptoms chart and chakra symptoms chart from previous personal assessments, and about thirty minutes of uninterrupted time.

Remember that energetic codependency is a result of trauma, so it's important to be compassionate with yourself as you do this assessment.

On a new sheet of paper, respond to the following questions:

1. Do any current relationships mirror challenging relationships you've had in the past? If so, how?

2. Do any of your symptoms flare when you are around certain people? If so, which symptoms and which people?

   ▸ *Consult your physical symptoms chart and chakra symptoms chart as needed for this step.*

3. What nonphysical characteristics or patterns seem to always present themselves when you're around a particular person? For example, do you always question your own value or purpose after you've been with a certain friend or your boss?

4. Write down which people, past or present, you suspect you may have or have had energetic codependent relationships with. Then write down what patterns you notice coming up with each person.

Releasing yourself from codependent relationships is necessary and doable. It can also be very deep and emotional work. Please contact a mental health professional, a spiritual counselor, or other sources of support if you need it.

Synopsis

The way out of the shock bubble can be summarized in a single word: *grieving.* To grieve is to allow ourselves to unwind our feelings as well as our physical and spiritual reactions to a life disrupter. If we don't grieve, we'll remain stuck in a shock bubble and might eventually develop symptoms of chronic conditions, if not a full-on manifestation of an illness. We can also become codependent or engage in dysfunctional relationships. Moreover, we can develop energetic codependency, in which we attract situations and people like those that caused the challenges in the first place, thus furthering our trauma, and eventually turn on ourselves, becoming vulnerable to chronic illnesses. The good news is that, despite all of the potential complexity of your health situation and its challenges, you're ready to acquire the tools you'll need to heal into a full life.

Part 2
Breaking Free

Techniques for Recovering & Healing the Self

It's time to ready, set, and *heal*!

Part 1 painted the picture of your complex self. Physical and subtle, you are a being of great beauty. The next part of the journey is learning self-healing exercises for transforming your health and your life so you can fully express and *enjoy* this dance of life.

To create your healing toolkit, you'll first be shown ten basic healing techniques, all of which can be applied to address trauma, stress, and chronic illnesses, including autoimmune disorders. Then, in the following chapters, you'll concentrate on different aspects of these concerns and gain more guidance for furthering your recovery. At the end, these activities are all aimed at one higher goal: to support your dreams—your dreams for yourself, your life, and the world.

CHAPTER 7

Addressing Your Challenges:
Ten Techniques for Your Subtle Energy Toolkit

*There is no one giant step that does
it. It's a lot of little steps.*
—Peter A. Cohen

This chapter will present ten powerful and fantastic energy tools that will help you heal and recover from trauma and chronic illnesses. In subsequent chapters you'll customize and apply these techniques to get your life flowing; you might even experience some initial healing while learning these processes.

A few of the techniques include connecting with the Spirit, applying a universal healing process, aligning with spiritual guides, finding the wounded self in a shock bubble self, and releasing others' energies—and there are so many more. As a note, if you feel encouraged to put a technique into practice right away, you can always apply it to the symptoms or challenges you isolated as you worked through the personal assessment questions in the first part of this book.

Technique 1
Spirit-to-Spirit: Your Main Technique

Spirit-to-Spirit is an all-inclusive technique for engaging intuitively. You'll employ it before conducting any of the other subtle energy techniques in this book.

Spirit-to-Spirit guarantees the provision of accurate information, strong energetic boundaries to ensure your safety, and the ability to send and receive healing. Its three steps and their goals are as follows:

1: Affirm Your Personal Spirit. As shared in chapters 2 and 4, your spirit is your true and original self. When you decide to act from this essential self, you are acknowledging that only your spirit, your highest self, will function in any undertaking.

To perform this step, you can affirm in words, said internally or externally, that your spirit is in charge; visualize a picture that describes your spirit—such as an angel, star, light, flame, or flower—or simply feel into your essential light.

2: Affirm Others' Spirits. This step sets an incredible intention: you will interact with only the highest aspect of someone or something else. This list can include your own traumatized selves, other people or their traumatized selves, and natural and otherworldly beings, such as dark or light entities and spiritual guides.

Simply acknowledge your decision or visualize the others as angels, saints, or another iconic form.

3: Call Upon the Spirit. This step allows you to surrender the entirety of an activity to the Spirit, thereby inviting the Spirit to do the following:

- provide accurate intuitive insights
- contribute spot-on interpretations of intuitive and physical information
- send messages to whomever or whatever needs them, such as a traumatized self
- guarantee protection for yourself and all others involved in a process, specifically to protect you and others from interference while allowing you to perceive intrusive forces so you can deal with them
- send healing and manifest new outcomes

Acknowledge the Spirit in the way you desire. You can sense its unconditional love, state a personal affirmation silently or aloud, or imagine a picture of a white flame, a dove, the sun, the Christ, Mary, Ganesh, the Buddha, or another iconographic image.

Technique 2
Healing Streams of Grace: The All-Purpose Process

Healing Streams of Grace is an all-purpose technique for activating healing; releasing traumatized selves from shock bubbles; creating new opportunities; clearing negative attachments, holds, entities, harmful cells, and the like; and formulating best-case outcomes. To fully embrace this technique, it's important to understand the meaning of grace.

Grace is love that enables powerful change. Healing streams of grace, which I also call "the streams," "healing streams," and "streams of grace," are continually generated by the Spirit. To visualize them, think of the Spirit as a sun with beams of loving light constantly emerging from its center. Always available, these streams need only be bidden for you, a part of you, or someone or something else to be linked to them. Once attached, they will remain in place, changing form as needed, until their job is complete. You don't even need to request their removal. Just as the Spirit provides and customizes them, so does the Spirit release them.

In the next technique, you'll use both Spirit-to-Spirit and Healing Streams of Grace together to conduct an important process.

Technique 3
Accessing Guidance Through the Imaginal Realms

Most subtle energy practitioners acknowledge the existence of spiritual helpers or guides that can be called upon to provide information, inspiration, healing, and assistance with manifesting and healing. Technically, connecting with invisible assistance is a part of step 2 of Spirit-to-Spirit, but connecting with particular spiritual guides is actually done after you've conducted step 3, calling upon the Spirit. Ultimately, asking the Spirit to select particular spiritual help for you ensures you obtain only the safest and most powerful help.

The caveat, which has already been addressed in chapter 4, is that there are shadowy or dark otherworldly beings, as well as beneficial ones. For instance, one ancestral soul might be more than willing to promote wellness; another might be invested in keeping you sick. To guarantee security, I want to introduce you to the imaginal realms.

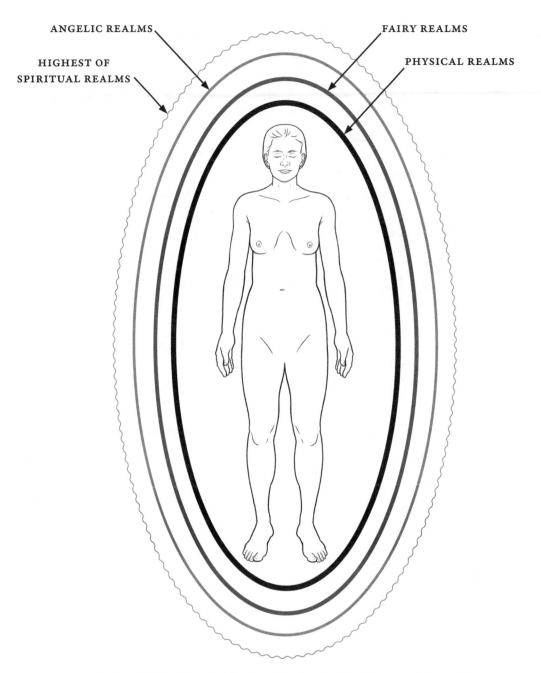

ANGELIC REALMS

HIGHEST OF
SPIRITUAL REALMS

FAIRY REALMS

PHYSICAL REALMS

Figure 17: The Imaginal Realms. *The imaginal realms are subtle worlds of existence that can be reached intuitively. They can be pictured like concentric spheres surrounding the body. The densest realms are the ones closest to the physical realm, and the more etheral ones are farther away.*

The imaginal theory was first shared by Ibn Arabi, a mystic who lived in the 1200s. Employing the Arabic term *Alam al-Mithal,* Ibn Arabi, now revered amongst Sufis, described the imaginals as a series of subtle realms every bit as real as the physical world. When connected to these planes of existence, you could interact with spirit animals, angels, spiritual masters, and more.

During the 1900s, Henry Corbin, an Islamic scholar, further explained these realms. He described the imaginals as a series of maps or terrains through which we can subtly travel to develop our soul and enhance our lives. I teach my students how to remain located in their body consciousness and use Spirit-to-Spirit to usher in guidance from these realms. Basically, the Spirit will engineer the correct connection, bring a spiritual helper into your awareness, and allow a secure interaction, thereby intertwining spiritual and corporeal realities.

Figure 17 shows my image of the imaginal realms. I visualize them as a series of concentric spheres rippling around you. They can be accessed by your inner self. Close to the body are the more physical realms, such as those that house living humans and natural beings. Just farther out are the fairy worlds, then the angelic realms, and finally the highest spiritual realms. There are infinite numbers of other realms besides these, however.

Here's what to do to practice making a connection:

1: Focus On a Challenge. Select a challenge for which you'd like to receive insight or healing.

2: Settle Quietly. Find a quiet spot in which to settle and make sure you won't be disturbed for several minutes. Have a pen and paper available to take notes.

3: Conduct Spirit-to-Spirit. Affirm your essential spirit, the spirits associated with the challenge, and the Spirit.

4: Make Your Request. Think about or write down your request regarding the challenge. Would you like information? Inspiration? Explanations? Remembrances? Healing energies? You can set your intention as broadly or specifically as you like.

5: Imagine the Realms. In your mind, picture the imaginal realms as a series of concentric spheres around you. Sense and feel yourself as securely cocooned within them.

6: Turn It Over. Request that the Spirit choose which realm is best suited for your intention and to unseal a gateway or line of communication between the chosen realm and yourself. Then ask the Spirit to connect you with the appropriate being that can help you with the challenge you have in mind.

7: Connect. Spend a few minutes associating with the being that the Spirit has connected you with. If you want, write down any details you become aware of. What do they look like? What type of being are they? Do they have a particular job within their realm? Is there a name they would like you to use for them? Moreover, what would they like to offer you in regard to your intention? Continue with your interaction until you feel fulfilled.

8: Offer Gratitude. Thank the being for its help, and the Spirit for its help. If you think you'd like to connect with this being again in the future, ask it if you may do so. Lovingly release the being, which will return to its home.

9: Close. Review what you've learned and breathe deeply, requesting that the Spirit lovingly close any open gateways or lines of communication with the imaginal realms until contact needs to be made again. When you're ready, return to your everyday life.

Technique 4
Locating a Causal Chakra

When performing subtle energy work, it's helpful to find the causal chakra(s) affected by a life challenge. This is the chakra most severely affected by an original trauma, which, in turn, spawned challenges. Pinpointing a specific chakra will assist you with tracking a traumatizing force's pathway, finding a wounded self, and conducting healing.

There are several ways to locate a causal chakra. Six methods are presented for this technique. The best way to learn these methods is to try out each of them and see how it works for you.

The purpose of this technique isn't to completely understand or clear a life challenge; that will happen through applying the techniques in the next chapters. Rather, your goal here is to simply locate the causal chakra.

1: Perform Spirit-to-Spirit. Acknowledge your own essential spirits, the spirits of all others that were—or are—involved in a particular challenge, and the Spirit.

2: Think of a particular life challenge.

3: Use one of the following six methods for identifying the causal chakra.

Method 1: Use Logic

Logic is an acceptable process for isolating a causal chakra. In the personal assessment at the end of chapter 4, you created a chakra symptoms chart to help you track the physical, psychological, and spiritual components of your challenge. Reviewing this chart will point you toward the most likely causal chakra.

For instance, if you have heart pain and are often involved in strained relationships, you would select the fourth chakra. If you lack purpose, you would choose the seventh chakra. If you have symptoms that match more than three chakras, concentrate on the fourth chakra, which integrates all other chakras, unless you sense the existence of many negative spiritual presences, in which case you should concentrate on the eighth chakra.

Method 2: Select an Age

Every chakra activates and is most affected by events that occur during a certain age range. Evaluate the chakra activation by age chart provided right after this technique. If you can remember when an originating stressor occurred, work with the related chakra.

Method 3: Use Your Intuition

There are four main intuitive styles. Try employing each of the following to locate your causal chakra:

Veer Toward Verbal: Focus your consciousness on your fifth chakra and breathe deeply. Ask the Spirit for an auditory message to indicate the causal chakra. This answer can be relayed as a song, a word, or even a statement. You might hear it with your inner ears or regular ears. Just trust.

Vie for Visual: Bring your awareness to your sixth chakra, which is also called the third eye. Be still and request that the Spirit illuminate an image revealing the causal chakra. This vision might be metaphorical or literal. It could also show the color or location of the chakra and might even explore the original traumatic event.

Sense the Spirit: Fix your attention on your fourth or seventh chakra, whichever you feel most drawn to. Then ask the Spirit to serve as your messenger and help you recognize the causal chakras through a spiritual knowing.

Bode Your Body: Our body reveals answers through physical sensations or emotions. Hold your hands on your abdomen and breathe into your belly. Then ask the Spirit to attune your physical self to allow you to feel the causal chakra. What part of your body responds? Where do your feelings direct you? Follow the impressions until you locate the causal chakra.

Method 4: Follow the Course of the Force

If you sense which type of force delivered a challenge, track the force to a chakra. You can also use technique 8, found in this chapter, to do so. Include the following chakras as indicated.

Environmental: tenth chakra

Physical: first chakra

Psychological: second and third chakras, but also explore and include the following:

- mainly verbal abuse: the fifth chakra
- mainly emotional abuse: the second chakra
- mainly mental abuse: the third chakra
- accompanied by physical abuse: the first chakra
- if the abuse was implemented by a really close person: the fourth chakra

Modern: Can be any chakra. For instance, the fifth chakra might be involved if you are assailed by emails; the fourth chakra if you are being catfished, or being deceived by someone pretending to be someone they aren't; or the third chakra if you are affected by digital bullying.

Spiritual: It's always safe to focus on the seventh chakra when spiritual abuse has been present. If you never feel connected to others, you could also focus on or include the ninth. If you are overbearing or seem completely lacking in leadership skills, consider the eleventh chakra as well.

Missing: Use one of the previously covered methods to figure out which chakra was most affected by a missing force.

Method 5: Ask a Friend

Sometimes a loved one knows us better than we know ourselves. Ask a friend, trusted relative, therapist, or another close person where they would start.

Method 6: Analyze an External Chakra Wheel

If you need further information about the origin of a challenge, employ technique 6, "Analyzing an External Chakra Wheel," to obtain that data.

What if you identify more than one causal chakra? This can happen, especially when you're coping with multiple chronic illnesses or related conditions. (See Martha's story in chapter 5 for an example of a complex situation involving more than one challenge.) Select the one that seems the most likely to have suffered the original damage. You can always work on additional chakras in subsequent sessions.

Chakras and Age Activations

Every chakra activates during a specific age range. Trauma that locks in during these time periods will be recorded in that chakra, which will also link to a bubble-self injured during that stage. The chakra-linked trauma will send ripples of negative energy throughout all related chakra and auric field functions, potentially causing a widespread affect.

To help you pinpoint a challenged chakra and also understand the effects of trauma on your life, the following chart outlines each chakra, its activation period, and main themes.

Some chakras are instigated at more than a single time period. For instance, your eighth chakra houses past-life traumas and also spans a specific age range. Your tenth chakra stores ancestral memories but also awakens during two stages of your current lifetime.

As a note, once we reach the seventh-chakra activation at age 14, the chakras begin to cycle every seven years. During each seven-chakra period, we retrigger chakras one through seven, one year at a time. This revisiting allows us to clear old issues and establish new patterns. For instance, between ages 14 and 15, we work on the theme of the seventh chakra, which includes spirituality, and also revisit our first chakra, dipping back into our safety and security issues. This same looping occurs from this point onward. I've shown the cycle under chakra seven so you can see what I mean.

Why is the tenth chakra on the top of the list? Because as the chakra activated just before we're conceived, it is technically the first chakra affecting a lifetime.

Chakra Activation By Age

CHAKRA	AGES/TIME PERIODS	THEME
Tenth	Preconception; 35 to 42 years	Environment, lineage, nature connections
First	In utero to 6 months	Safety, security, physical health
Second	6 months to 2½ years	Feelings, creativity, emotional health
Third	2½ to 4½ years	Personal power, structure, mental health
Fourth	4½ to 6½ years	Love, healing, relational health
Fifth	6½ to 8½ years	Communication, guidance, verbal ability
Sixth	8½ to 14 years	Vision, self-image, ideas about the future
Seventh	14 to 21 years	Purpose, prophecy, spiritual health
	Age 14 to 15	Revisit first chakra
	Age 15 to 16	Revisit second chakra
	Age 16 to 17	Revisit third chakra
	Age 17 to 18	Revisit fourth chakra
	Age 18 to 19	Revisit fifth chakra
	Age 19 to 20	Revisit sixth chakra
	Age 20 to 21	Revisit seventh chakra
Eighth	21 to 28 years; past lives	Mysticism, karmic pursuits, health
Ninth	28 to 35 years	Idealism, harmony, sense of unity
Eleventh	42 to 49 years	Leadership, natural and supernatural power
Twelfth	49 to 56 years	Individual to us

After age 56, we start over again with the tenth chakra, revisiting each chakra for seven years at a time, but our goal is to spiritualize the themes. Basically, we are invited to examine our lives through spiritual eyeglasses.

Technique 5

Tracking a Force's Pathway and the Traumatized Self

As shared, the pathway of a force can inflict multiple problems. From a mechanical point of view, we need to examine for, and potentially repair, the entrance point, exit site, and pathway. In this process, we can also uncover the traumatized self, who has been left in a shock bubble linked to at least one causal chakra. While a traumatized self might be found inside a causal chakra, that self can also be located in another vicinity altogether. Maybe it will be just outside of this chakra, either in the body proper or a specific organ. It could also be found within an energetic field or even another time period; the latter may be the case if the original injury occurred in a past life.

I've even spotted the cocooned selves in others' bodies. For instance, I once worked with a woman who'd been in love with her teenage sweetheart for thirty years, although he'd broken up with her abruptly and hurtfully. She continually pined for him. I discovered her traumatized self trapped within the heart chakra of her ex, still attached to her with a cord. She hadn't taken back this aspect of herself upon breaking up, nor had he released it. If I hadn't searched for her bubble self in an open-minded way, I might not have found her!

Do you want to know how to find a traumatized self while assessing for a force's entry and exit wounds and pathway? This exercise will help you do so. Because I don't want to leave an injured part of you dangling, I'll also help you send healing to that self and along the pathway. That activity will give you further practice with healing streams of grace.

1: Prepare. Find an isolated space. You can follow the steps of this exercise as a guided meditation or employ a paper and pencil to note your observations.

2: Select Your Focus. Concentrate on your trauma site or experience and affirm your willingness to let the Spirit operate through your intuition to give you guidance.

3: Conduct Spirit-to-Spirit. Affirm your spirit and then others' spirits. While acknowledging the Spirit, give permission for the Spirit to link you with helpful beings from the imaginal realms.

4: Sense Into the Force. Ask the Spirit to help you label the major force(s) that impacted you. You'll check for a physical, psychological, modern, spiritual, missing, or environmental force, or a combination of these.

5: Uncover the Entry Point. Request that the Spirit clarify the original entry point of the traumatizing force. You might visualize it, hear a message that describes it, or sense into a bodily area or emotion. Mull over the long-term challenges you've experienced at the site of this entrance wound.

6: Flow Through the Pathway. Intuitively track the pathway left by the invading force. Check to see if any of the following has occurred.

- *Pathway empty.* The pathway might be devoid of energy, which means certain related subtle and physical tasks in its vicinity aren't being accomplished.

- *Lodged forces.* Some forces get stuck, locking into a part of the body or subtle anatomy. These stuck forces often create congestion and physical or emotional pain. They can also attract attachments and stir up microchimeric cells, in addition to attracting microbial infections.

- *Pathway filled.* The pathway can be filled with mismatched energies, which can include others' or your own subtle energies.

- *Charges are active.* Subtle charges from the harmful force can remain in the pathway and might be attracting like-trauma.

- *Pathway healed or partially healed.* Sometimes a pathway fills with beneficial energies that enable healing.

7: Pinpoint Any Exit Wounds. Discern if there is an exit point or multiple exit points, which can sometimes occur, such as when someone is shot with a scatter bullet. What is happening with, or at, the exit site(s)?

8: Find the Wounded Self. Ask the Spirit to help you perceive the wounded self, who is held within a shock bubble. Also sense which causal chakra and related field that wounded self is most affiliated with. You might psychically perceive lines of subtle energies, or a band of energy, connecting this self to the chakra. The self could also be contained with the chakra. Relate to this self, spending as much time as you need to sense its feelings, desires, experiences, and more. Ask the Spirit to fully attend to this self's needs, even while it's in the bubble.

9: Request Healing. Ask that the Spirit provide healing streams of grace to clean, fill, and smooth the force's entrance point, pathway, and any exit sites. Know that the streams required will remain linked as long as necessary and will also attend to the wounded self.

10: Request Additional Insight. Ask the Spirit to provide you any additional insight or knowledge about how to further assist the wounded self and improve your life. If you feel like you need additional information, employ technique 6 (below) to obtain it.

11: Close. Take a few deep breaths, thank the Spirit for the help, and return to your everyday life.

Technique 6
Analyzing an External Chakra Wheel

The outside wheel of a chakra holds all karmic programs, whether they are inherited, absorbed, or based on personal experience. Basically, imprinted and empowered on these wheels is the sum total of perceptions, feelings, and memories carried over from past lives, plus those reflecting ancestral events, family programs, personal dramas, and applicable cultural, religious, gender, and socio-economic influences.

I want you to know how to read an external chakra wheel so you'll be able to more fully understand a traumatized self and the event(s) that injured it. Sometimes we don't need a lot of data. Other times, we do. The latter occurs if the traumatized self will only heal if they get to "speak," or share their story. When communicating, that self will need someone to listen. The witness can be another person, such as a therapist. Your own healthy self can also serve as this observer, as long as this aspect of you is providing care to the traumatized self.

1: Prepare. Grab a paper and pencil to keep track of your findings. Find a quiet place and focus on a challenge.

2: Perform Spirit-to-Spirit. Acknowledge the brilliance of your spirit, all spirits involved with this challenge, and the Spirit.

3: Track the Causal Chakra. Focus on a challenge and track it to its causal chakra, as you were taught to do in technique 4. If there are multiple chakras involved, choose the most obvious one. You can always work with another chakra later.

4: Assess for Events and Programs. Request that the Spirit help you perceive the outer wheel of the causal chakra as if it's a computer screen. Visualize yourself sitting in front of this screen while you intuitively see, sense, or hear the information needed to fully understand the underpinnings of your challenge. Then all you have to do is focus on each of the questions listed next and note what you perceive.

1: What is the event that caused the underlying trauma?

2: When did it occur?

3: Whom did the event mainly affect?

4: How did this experience involve you?

5: What force(s) was/were involved in this event?

6: What were the trajectory and long-term effect(s) of the force?

7: How did this event influence you . . .

- physically?

- psychologically?

- socially?

- spiritually?

- in other ways?

8: What was the major misperception formulated from this experience?

9: What feelings became locked in, repressed, or overbearing?

10: What energies from others did you internalize?

11: How have the energies from others been affecting you?

12: Where is the traumatized self in relation to this chakra?
Possibilities can include the following:

- part/entirety of the body

- part/entirety of the auric field

- part/entirety of the chakra

- outside of the body proper

- in a different time period, place, or dimension altogether

13: How does the traumatized self appear?

14: Are any of the following affecting the traumatized self or chakra, and if so, how?

- attachment(s): cords, curses, holds, miasms, markers, deflection shields
- dark entity/force
- microchimeric cells

15: Are any of the following impacting this wheel and, therefore, the traumatized self?

- cultural or societal influences
- socioeconomic factors
- gender or sexual issues
- religious or spiritual affects
- peer pressures
- past lives (if this hasn't already been presented)
- ancestral memories/epigenetics; if these are present, are any of these other influences also interactive:

    —ancestral actions or memories

    —ancestral illnesses, wounds, or other injuries

    —ancestral-related microbes

    —food or other substance cravings related to ancestors

    —behaviors related to ancestors

    —allergies or addictions related to ancestors

16: What is the overall impact of the issues affecting this outer chakra wheel?

5: Review. Summarize all that you have found and then ask for healing streams of grace (see technique 2) to assist you at every level. You can return to this information at any point or continue basking in the healing streams.

6: Close. Thank the Spirit and all spirits involved for this undertaking.

Technique 7
Illuminating the Internal Chakric Wheel

As discussed in chapter 4, the inner wheel of a chakra holds our dharmic understandings, yet so much more. Dwelling within every chakra is our own spirit, which exists in concert with the Spirit. This internalized spirit also holds our original energetic signature, the codes and qualities of our unique self. Within the center of each chakra, our spirit merges with the Spirit's energy to produce the healing streams of grace required to transform the outer wheel, transform negative energetic programs into those matching our original ones, and subsequently provide immense healing and manifesting assistance.

One of the easiest healing techniques involves activating the inner wheel of a chakra in order to wash the outside of the chakra with a sea of liquid light. This generated energy can also help you better understand the nature of a trauma, find a traumatized self, release others' energies, and more. I suggest you practice this technique's easy steps now so you will be proficient with them. You'll be employing this process at points during the next chapters to clear nadis and meridians, as well as the vagus nerve.

1: Prepare. Find a quiet spot. Focus on a particular challenge and the primary chakra involved.

2: Conduct Spirit-to-Spirit. Affirm your personal spirit, which occupies the center of the influential chakra. Acknowledge that all needed help is being provided by the Spirit, which, in turn, calls upon the appropriate beings in the imaginal realms for you.

3: Light the Inner Wheel. Open your intuitive faculties—your ability to sense, feel, hear, and see truth—as you perceive the Spirit lighting the inside of the focus chakra. Just like that, healing streams emanate from this inner well and wash over and around the outer rim of the related chakra. This same energy will now bathe the entire bodily area, as well as the partnered auric layer and any traumatized selves that may be located here.

4: Surrender. Give permission for the Spirit to manage this entire process now and as you move forward.

5: Close. Breathe deeply and go about your life. All is well and will be made even better through the power of grace.

Technique 8
Releasing Others' Energies and Energetic Constructs

Addressing challenges often requires releasing energies that are not our own. This list includes subtle charges brought in by a force or harmful interaction; ancestor's memories or feelings, usually shared from the epigenetic material; past-life issues; and attachments. As well, we might need to let go of the charges emanating from or stuck in a traumatized self or those negatively impacting us from microchimeric cells. Whew! Is there really a simple way to accomplish all of these goals?

Yes—we need only use healing streams of grace; it can also be helpful to employ the energies from a chakric inner wheel (see technique 7). You might still need to actually process and grieve an event. The clearing technique offered here will enable that clearing to be truly transformative, however.

1: Prepare. Select a challenge that you believe involves the induction of others' issues or energetic constructs. Then find a quiet place in which to work for a few minutes.

2: Perform Spirit-to-Spirit. Acknowledge your spirit, others' spirits, and the Spirit. You might become aware of spiritual assistants that arrive from one of the imaginal realms.

3: Ask for Insight. Request that the Spirit assists you in locating an area that needs to be cleansed of interfering energies. You might be led to a causal chakra, bodily area, the auric field or part of it, or some other focus point. Now let the Spirit provide the perceptions you need to understand what interfering subtle charges have been causing challenges. You might intuitively sense the answer, feel into the emotions involved, receive a visual picture, or hear a response. Remain in this process as long as required.

4: Perform Healing Streams of Grace. Ask the Spirit to send healing streams to and through the area of concern to cleanse you of the undesirable energies. Some of these streams might emanate from the center of a causal chakra. These streams deliver healthy and benevolent energies to replace those being released or transformed. The Spirit brings all unneeded energies to a safe place or space with grace in mind, even as it informs you of whatever information you need to know about this process. Breathe deeply and remain in this place of cleansing as long as required.

5: Close. When you feel ready, breathe deeply. Stand and stretch, trusting that the Spirit will continue to reinforce this healing.

Technique 9
Uncovering, Moving, and Adding
Generative and Degenerative Forces

I frequently find that trauma remains, as do chronic illnesses, because of the unconscious mismanagement of two very particular forces: generative and degenerative forces.

Everywhere around and within us are subtle energy forces that can stimulate either growth or destruction. For instance, the generative force of creativity compels innovation. The degenerative force of deterioration will trigger dissipation. We often don't know that we're connected to these forces or what they are doing because we aren't aware of them. They can, however, become attached to us because of karmic beliefs and dharmic needs, as well as through disruptive attachments.

A difficult condition is nearly always held in place by misplaced generative or degenerative forces. For instance, I often find a degenerative force on the healthy cells surrounding a malignant tumor and a generative force on the cancer cells. When money is lacking, the first chakra, which governs security, is often afflicted with a degenerative force, while shame issues are accelerated by a generative force.

You don't need to know the specific names of degenerate or generative forces to uncover them and attach the desired type to the right places. Rather, let the Spirit do the thinking and the fixing, using healing streams to set things right.

1: Prepare. Focus on an issue that you'd like to shift. I recommend you select one that you've worked on as hard as possible, to little or no avail.

2: Conduct Spirit-to-Spirit. Affirm your own spirit, all involved spirits, and the Spirit.

3: Focus. Ask the Spirit to help you focus on the related trauma area, tracking the trauma to a bodily part, chakra, or auric field.

4: Check On Forces. Request that the Spirit enable you to sense the existence of one or more generative or degenerative forces and to know how they are either supporting the traumatic experience or preventing it from clearing.

5: Ask for a Shift. Now ask the Spirit to use healing streams to deliver the generative or degenerative forces that would help clean and clear the trauma. The Spirit will also shift the forces around, if beneficial. Ask if there is any follow-up you need to perform.

6: Close. Sense the difference in your body, chakras, and demeanor. Thank the Spirit and return to your world.

Technique 10
Cleaning and Strengthening Your Auric Field

Safety is paramount in recovering from—and transforming through—life's challenges. This quick technique will clear and boost your subtle energy boundaries—in other words, your auric field. You can employ this practice anytime you feel unsafe or desire stronger parameters. It's also helpful to perform after any other healing activity.

1: Perform Spirit-to-Spirit. Affirm your personal spirit, others' spirits, and the Spirit.

2: Request a Cleansing. Ask that the Spirit pour healing streams of grace through each of your auric layers. If you desire, picture the colors of these streams in the order of the fields, from the closest to farthest away from the body. Their hues are red, brown, orange, yellow, green, blue, violet, white, black or silver, gold, rose, and opalescent. Then watch as the bright white light of the Spirit infuses the overall field. Fully cleansed of others' energies, as well as personal energies you're ready to let go of, affirm the sparkling brilliance of your auric field.

3: Switch Any Out-of-Place Boundaries. Some challenges are characterized by switched boundaries (see the discussion about learning issues in chapter 5 for more). For instance, your first auric field might lie on the outside of your auric field, thus causing somatic challenges. Ask the Spirit to move your auric fields into the right places and spaces for your own well-being, if this needs to be done. Then feel the rightness of that switch.

4: Strengthen Your Boundaries. Finally, knowing that you're lovingly encapsulated in a cocoon of grace, ask the Spirit to fortify your entire auric field. Sense the healing streams filling in every weak spot or vulnerability.

5: Close. Content and secure, thank the Spirit and return to your everyday awareness.

• • • • •

Synopsis

In this chapter you learned ten techniques and immediately put them to good use. Spirit-to-Spirit and Healing Streams of Grace, in particular, will show up frequently. But you also practiced techniques to help you access the imaginal realms, locate a causal chakra, track and clear a force-created pathway, and perform any number of other powerful activities.

You'll now employ these processes and learn others in order to recover from—and transform through—trauma.

CHAPTER 8

Recovering from Trauma:
Techniques for Assisting a Traumatized Self

Then again, he supposed the healing process,
in contrast to trauma, was gentle and slow...
The soft closing of a door, rather than a slam.
—J. R. Ward, *Lover Reborn*

In this chapter you'll be presented with several processes for assisting a traumatized self. You might have several wounded selves, each cocooned within individual bubbles of shock, and some of them may not even be from your current lifetime. Not every one of these injured selves must be ferreted out and aided, but the most challenged should be. If you free the most deeply hurt self, the lesser injured selves can slide out of their protective bubbles and resume the journey of life.

However, healing is seldom an overnight process. First we have to locate a hidden traumatized self. Obtain trust. Clear pathways. Support grieving. Address codependency tendencies. Make life changes, such as to your diet, as covered in chapter 10. But each step is a step forward in the slow walk toward the sunrise, when you'll be ready to greet the world with newfound hope.

As I've explained throughout this book, because trauma was delivered outside to inside, healing must be delivered the same way. You qualify as one of those external healers, as do friends, professionals, beings of the imaginal realms, and, of course, the Spirit. Don't limit the list; just know that you can ask for help when needed.

In order to assist you, this chapter's techniques will build on techniques outlined in the last chapter and concepts presented throughout this book. First, you'll create a safe healing haven in which to conduct your transformational interactions. You'll use this healing haven as part of other techniques throughout the remainder of the book. Then you'll become joyfully acquainted with your genuine self, which reflects your original energetic signature. Next, you'll be ushered through additional techniques, each aimed at assisting your traumatized selves.

Techniques 11, 12, and 13 are best conducted in sequential order. Techniques 14–19 may be useful or not in this moment. However, they can be integrated into techniques 11–13 or conducted anytime a traumatized self requires help.

Ready to open the door and free your traumatized selves? It's time to do so.

Technique 11
Creating a Safe Healing Space

Your first trauma-releasing task should be establishing a safe space in which to perform trauma recovery. The more often you undertake healing in this setting, the more likely a traumatized self will trust a therapeutic process conducted within it and enable transformation.

There are two main types of functional healing environments: physical and subtle. You can create one or both kinds. If you have to select only one type, however, I'd focus on sculpting a subtle energy haven. This is because a traumatized self, especially when you begin interacting with it, can pop up at any time—at night, during a meeting, when you're meditating, even when you're cleaning the house. It can be useful to have a sacred space that can be immediately accessed from anywhere.

The following tips will help you establish external and internal healing havens.

Develop an External Sacred Space
There are two steps for establishing a safe physical zone for your inner work.

1: Formulate Guidelines. Grab a writing instrument and respond to these questions:

- How do I want to feel in this space? For clues, list adjectives such as comforted, fortressed, held, contained, supported, natural, or cozy.

- What might I name my place? For instance, label it with your name, such as "Cyndi's Healing Haven," or pick a label that is descriptive, such as "The Healing Haven."

- Am I comfortable with giving others access to this space? If you are, decide what that means. Can a spouse or child enter? A pet? If you'd rather others not enter, figure out what physical area will guarantee a boundary.

- Do I want to tell others about my space? It's always okay to be private; then again, you might want to tell others about your area so they stay out.

2: Set Up the Tangible Space. Conduct Spirit-to-Spirit and then design and inaugurate your space based on responses to these questions:

- Shall my space be inside or outside?

- If outside, do I need to weatherproof it?

- If inside, what actual room or physical area will suffice?

- How can I ensure silence? For example, you might choose a space with a door, put up a curtain or screen, or hang up a "do not disturb" sign.

- What colors will support my need for security and trust? How might I bring these colors into the space? You might do so with a pillow, altar cloth, or blanket.

- How else might I decorate my space so a traumatized self will feel protected and beloved? Examples include incorporating candles, stones, religious icons, journals, pictures, stuffed toys, or posters.

You can update this space on an ongoing basis.

Design Your Inner Healing Space

An inner space can be built using visualization, which is also the tool you'll use for accessing this sacred ground. The following steps will guide you through the creation process. If it's helpful, use paper and writing instruments to keep track of the details of your space.

1: Conduct Spirit-to-Spirit. Acknowledge your own essential spirit, the Spirit, and the spirits of any beings from the imaginal realm you and the Spirit may call upon to assist you in this endeavor.

2: Visualize an Outdoor or Indoor Setting. Picture all the basics of the environment.

3: Construct Safe Parameters. If your healing refuge is an outdoor setting, forge a shelter under a tree or inside a bank of clouds. If it's indoors, imagine the exact room and location. Maybe it's in a room you slept in at your grandparents' house as a child; if you love books, you can craft a space in a library.

4: Decorate Your Creation. Select items and colors that will remain constant through all visits. I recommend that you insert two to three set pieces into your inner space that convey messages like "I am secure" or that can be used for healing. Examples include a comfortable couch, a mirror for obtaining answers, or a crystal wand that can transport healing streams.

5: Select a Guard. If you want a guardian, ask the Spirit to appoint a gatekeeper that will filter harmful from helpful beings and energies.

6: Plan for Healing Streams. Request that healing streams surround your private area to protect it, maintain it, and also be ushered in to help with healing when required.

7: Name Your Haven. Do you need a name for your special bit of heaven? Select one, such as "Recovery Sanctuary" or "The Transformation Room."

8: Practice Using It. Play in this space! Get to know it. Does it feel good for wounded selves and also your adult self? Make changes accordingly. Then, when a traumatized self or your conscious self needs to enter, the space will be instantly available.

Anytime you need to, you can invite your traumatized self to occupy this inner shelter. Depending on the healing process, you can also invite your adult self, beings from the imaginal realm, and the Spirit.

Technique 12
Rediscovering Your Original Self and Signature

A few years ago, a client asked me a vital question. "How do you embrace your 'true self' if you haven't been in touch with him or her?"

Perhaps you're already aware of your authentic self—your spirit, essence, or immortal being-ness. And if you're not, that's okay. The main purpose of this technique is to initiate a relationship with *or* become better acquainted with your true self, your spirit—the essential self that carries and holds your original energetic signature. As I explained in chapter 2, it is the aspect of you that is knowingly and unceasingly connected to the Spirit. The corollary goal of this technique is to comprehend how this unique self can best transfer into your everyday world. While it can seem that understanding your spirit self is a little like trying to describe the ineffable—the aroma of the moon, the color of love, or the sound of bliss—converting these understandings into practicalities will assist you in assessing and transforming your traumatized selves.

The following process can take awhile; then again, it's okay to undertake it in one fell swoop. Either way, our spirit self is constantly unfolding; because of this truth, I suggest you accept the adventure of learning about this essential self on an ongoing basis. And since our fundamental nature is creative, I've designed this process of defining your essential self and original energetic signature so it is equally creative. Hence, I'm going to walk you through a story in which you'll fill in the gaps.

To prepare, bring a writing instrument or recording device into your healing space. Set aside a good hour, and then, after conducting Spirit-to-Spirit, fill in the spaces in this story. You can always stop and return to the process at a later time.

———————————

Once upon a time, I dwelled in union with the Creator and all other spirits. I was unique among the many, displaying these special traits: _____.

I also filled a vital role in the unity, which was to _____. And, unlike any other being, I knew the following essential truth: _____.

One day, the Creator asked me to join the manifesting reality, or earth plane. The Creator said it was because I had to share the following type of instruction or love with others: _____. Only I could take on this job because I was able to do the following: _____. I felt _____ about leaving unity with the Creator and _____ about joining the earth plane.

Before I departed, the Creator pulled me aside and infused me with a special energy, which I can best describe as _____. The Creator told me that it would enable me to _____, and in order to reflect and wield this energy, as well as my already present gifts, I had to do the following: _____. In this particular body, that has meant that I must consider the following factors, among others:

- *the type of spiritual qualities to concentrate on (such as faith, truth, hope, healing, joy, love): _____*

- *the types of movement or exercise that express my spirit and how frequently to perform them: _____*

- *the types of environments to enjoy (mountains, lakes, oceans, forests, deserts, for example) and how often to visit them: _____*

- *the sorts of foods supportive of my spirit: _____*

- *the types of beverages and non-food substances beneficial to my spirit: _____*

- *the balance—and types of—introverted and extroverted activities that would support my spirit: _____*

- *the kind of work purpose and functions revealing of my spirit: _____*

- *the personality traits and characteristics that showcase my spirit: _____*

- *the types of groups I need to participate in to uphold my essential self: _____*

- *the issues I must constantly delve into to keep my spirit active: _____*

- *the qualities that should be present in various styles of relationships (romantic, life partner, relatives, friends) to maintain my true self: _____*

- *the colors, flowers, natural beings, tones, songs, and symbols that characterize my essential nature: _____*

- *The place within my body that I can focus on to intuitively sense, perceive, feel, smell, see, relate to, or hear the sum total of all these factors, which comprise my original energetic signature: _____*

There are other factors you can consider that might be unique to you. Please add these to your assessment.

Technique 13
The Five Stages to Healing a Traumatized Self

This technique is quite lengthy. That's because there are actually five stages involved in healing the traumatized self from outside to inside:

- *Stage 1.* Tracking the traumatized self
- *Stage 2.* Typifying the traumatized self
- *Stage 3.* Freeing (at least, partially freeing) the traumatized self while clearing the pathway
- *Stage 4.* Supporting a grieving process
- *Stage 5.* Integrating

The need to address codependency issues will be discussed in chapter 9.

The reason I'm weaving all five stages into a single technique is that each is vital to the transforming of a traumatized self. You might not need to conduct every stage. You might find yourself skipping around. No matter what, it's helpful to perceive the flow of activities involved in healing from trauma. You are *more* than worth all the time and attention these processes might take.

If you undertake all five stages in one sitting, simply ignore the first and second stages at the beginning of a follow-on step.

Stage 1: Tracking the Traumatized Self

You already practiced a version of this process in the last chapter (see technique 5). Here I'll walk you through an abbreviated version.

1: Prepare. Gather writing instruments, enter your healing space, and focus on the challenge you'd like to address. This challenge might be a long-term one but could also be a contemporary issue you're struggling to resolve. In case of the latter, you might discover a newly stress-traumatized self in a fresh trauma bubble or that you've retriggered an injured self from the past.

2: Conduct Spirit-to-Spirit. Affirm your personal spirit, which reflects your original energetic signature; the Spirit; and, finally, all guiding spirits, including those involved with the trauma.

3: Track the Traumatized Self. There are two ways to locate the traumatized self. You can employ technique 4, "Locating a Causal Chakra," which you learned in chapter 7, to find the causal chakra. From there, employ your intuitive skills to sense, see, or listen for the traumatized self. This self might be found within the actual chakra, but you might also perceive a beam of energy emanating from the causal chakra to the traumatized self. (Think of following a spider's thread to a web.)

You can also use technique 5, "Tracking a Force's Pathway and the Traumatized Self," also found in the last chapter, to find an encapsulated self.

If employing either technique, you'll begin a healing process but will return to more thoroughly complete it in stage 3 of this technique.

4: Be Gentle. Simply let your consciousness hover over the traumatized self. Ask the Spirit to help that self recognize your presence and absorb your intense love and compassion. Healing begins with a connection.

5: Close (Optional). If you sense that this process was enough for the moment, ask the Spirit to send a constant flow of healing streams around and into the traumatized self. Your love will also continue to linger.

Stage 2: Typifying the Traumatized Self

During this stage you'll assess the traumatized self without removing it from the shock bubble. This self has become used to its protective sheath, even if it's not beneficial. We want to avoid undue stress by initiating healing before we begin to slip the traumatized self out of its cocoon. We do this by figuring out which of three trauma states the injured self presents.

Trauma states are the stages related to an entrenched trauma. While reading through my descriptions, you'll notice that they build on each other. For instance, the first state, the Refugee, is usually the most fundamental of injured selves. After a while, an aspect of the Refugee often splinters and turns into a Protector; still later, either the Refugee or the Protector might divide again, forming a Distractor. In fact, a single challenge can create all three traumatized selves, which relate to the trauma like spokes on a wheel.

Work on the most obvious of trauma stages, such as the one that appeared in the last stage. Then, as time goes on, check if a sub-aspect emerges.

The three trauma states are as follows:

Trauma State One: Refugee

This distressed self is still caught up in the shock, pain, and hurt from the original wound. It is probably also disturbed by pathway injuries and the energetics involved in the initial trauma, preferring to hide rather than let itself be seen. Within the traumatized self are extreme emotions and unexpressed grief. Often, our Refugees are child selves, though they might also be past-life selves. Their emotions can trigger easily, and they can frequently send up flashbacks as cries for help.

Trauma State Two: Protector

This agitated self knows that there is a wounding and is determined to prevent further injury. Most frequently, a Protector guards a Refugee; consequently, it is often very rigid, warrior-like, controlling, and demanding. Unfortunately, Protectors are usually aspects that had to grow up or develop adult-like characteristics before their time; hence, they are often gripped in terror and fear, embarrassed about the fact that they don't really know what they are doing.

Trauma State Three: Distractor

This oft-creative self is grittily untiring in its commitment to a single goal: it doesn't want its related Refugee to be seen or freed. The Distractor "knows" that if the outside world were to peer through the shock bubble or, worse, if the self were to be presented to the world, the result would be judgment, disbelief, shaming, and further abuse. To the Distractor, emotional vulnerability is dangerous, hence the need to create distractions that often involve self-harm, addiction, codependency, and even physical and mental issues—in other words, chronic self-injurious challenges. We'll address Distractor healing more thoroughly in the next two chapters; specifically, in chapter 9 we'll examine the codependency factors, and in chapter 10 the addiction, craving, and allergy issues.

How will you figure out what trauma state you're working with, the one depicted in stage 1? Follow this process.

1: Prepare. Continue your work from stage 1 or ensconce yourself in your healing haven with writing instruments if you want. Conduct Spirit-to-Spirit if you haven't already done so. The Spirit can connect you with appropriate helpers from the imaginal realms, if needed.

2: Activate Healing Streams. The traumatized self needs to feel secure enough to offer up information. Remember, trauma is only repairable when assistance is provided outside to inside. With this in mind, ask that the Spirit surround you with healing streams; these streams will help you appear compassionate and loving to the traumatized self. Then request that healing streams encase the traumatized self to provide safety and security.

3: Request Information. Connect with the traumatized self at a deeper level and allow the self, the Spirit, or a spiritual guide to help you understand whatever the traumatized self wants to share at this time. You can always analyze the related chakra wheel by employing technique 6. Then ask for clarity to typify the traumatized self and figure out what trauma state they are in. Return to the earlier description of the states if needed.

4: Close (Optional). Release yourself from this process by acknowledging your conclusions to the Spirit and requesting grace for all. You'll perform additional work with the information about trauma states in stage 4.

Stage 3: Freeing the Traumatized Self While Clearing the Pathway

You can use many of the processes you learned in the last chapter to accomplish this stage. I'll name these activities, but basically you're continuing the healing you initiated in stage 1 of this technique.

1: Prepare. As needed, resume the process completed in stage 2 or start anew, gathering your writing instruments and entering your sacred space. Conduct Spirit-to-Spirit if required.

2: Clear the Pathway. Return to technique 5, "Tracking a Force's Pathway and the Traumatized Self," from chapter 7. You might have run through this process in stage 1 of this technique, and it's time to complete it. Pick up the process at "Sense into the Force" and enable a full healing for the traumatized self.

If the Spirit directs you, also employ the applicable sections of technique 7, "Illuminating the Internal Chakra Wheel," technique 8, "Releasing Others' Energies and Energetic Constructs," technique 9, "Uncovering, Moving, and Adding Generative and Degenerative Forces," and technique 10, "Cleaning and Strengthening Your Auric Field."

3: Free the traumatized self. The purpose of this step is to further free the traumatized self to whatever level is safe *in this moment*. This process can take days, months, and, honestly, sometimes years, but don't lose heart. As you learned from Martha and Ryan's stories, the stages of healing can be palpably felt. The full integration, which involves stage 5 in this technique, can take equally long. However, it's essential that at this time you invite the traumatized self into the greater self.

Do your part by sharing your heartfelt love for this traumatized self. Let yourself send feelings of love from your heart chakra to its heart chakra, along with psychic images and words of understanding and welcome. Let yourself receive whatever it is going through, from concern to excitement, and ask the Spirit to bless both you and the traumatized self with healing streams.

Ask too for streams to surround this traumatized self and to disintegrate whatever negative energies have been surrounding it before forming a riverway it can flow along into the greater self. The traumatized self can begin this process right now or when ready. Simply let it move as far along as is comfortable.

4: Close (Optional). Thank the Spirit and all imaginal helpers for the assistance. Also express gratitude to the traumatized self for being willing to so courageously participate in this process.

Stage 4: Supporting a Grieving Process

Usually you must initiate grieving before the traumatized self is willing to fully leave the shock bubble. Other times it is willing to be unwrapped but must grieve before it is able to integrate. Much of the time, grieving is an ongoing process.

This process necessitates allowing that self to move through the five feelings related to grieving, which are denial, anger, bargaining, sadness, and acceptance. The traumatized self must receive permission to feel *all* its feelings and to also share memories, disappointments, needs, and desires.

As already covered in chapter 6, grieving is complicated. It can also lead to codependency, which is why you might need to use technique 22 in chapter 9 to invite the full range of grieving in relation to codependency. However, for right now, you'll assist your traumatized self according to its trauma state.

1: Prepare. Continue the healing process completed in stage 3 or begin this stage right now, contained in your healing space and having writing instruments at hand if desired. Conduct Spirit-to-Spirit if needed.

2: Assist with Grieving. You'll help your traumatized self to grieve in the following ways, according to its trauma state:

- *Refugee*

Make sure that the Refugee is surrounded by healing streams. See if it requires comforting props, which might be held by your concrete self or given to its energetic self. For instance, if the Refugee is young, hand it a teddy bear. If it is from a past life, imagine it in a safe setting in the historical time period.

Breathe deeply and allow the Spirit to assist the Refugee in doing the same. Now connect to your physical body—in particular, to your legs and feet and your tenth chakra, which lies under the ground. Picture a gold line of love streaming from your ninth chakra down through the top of your head into your sushumna and then following the sushumna downward to your tenth chakra. Ask that the Spirit establish this same energy flow in the Refugee. Both of you are now held in a supportive beam of godly power.

A Refugee self must be brought back from numbness and then guided to feel angry, confused, and sad before it can then be brought into the acceptance process, which is furthered in stage 5 of this technique. Accomplish this goal by acknowledging what the Refugee has lost. Ask for the Spirit and imaginal helpers to do the same. As you did in the last few stages of this technique, invite the Refugee to share memories. Stir within it the sense of what it has lost by remaining trapped in a trauma bubble. Acknowledge aloud or quietly what life can offer if it shifts from apathy to aliveness.

Ask what it would like to do or accomplish. What heart's desires does it hold? Make a list of its dreams, from small to great, and then attune to each part of its grief process. Know that you might need to include a professional therapist in this process, and you can use whatever tools leap out for you in the next two chapters, as well as those in the latter part of this chapter.

- *Protector*

This particular self will feel raw, angry, and quite disturbed at being found. The most important part of addressing the Protector's needs is to first assure it that it hasn't done anything wrong. Rather, it's been attempting to help in the absence of real assistance. And so, in a meditative state either within your mind or in writing, ask them questions.

What authority figure was it missing? What did it wish someone or something would have done for it? What spiritual qualities would a concrete or spiritual protector have provided? Ask whatever questions you'd like to.

Then guide the Protector through the various feelings it's never been given permission to have. The shock it felt about how the Refugee was treated. The unfair way that it's been perceived. How angry it is about how both it and the Refugee were treated. How hard it's been to believe that the trauma was real and how sad it feels about the lost time and opportunities. Finally, compliment its vital qualities and then let it daydream about what it wants for its future. How can its strength be used to develop a gift or power, rather than caretake the Refugee? What fun activities can it undertake with its free time?

You might need to more fully address or heal the Refugee to complete the freeing of the Protector. However, you can also ask the Spirit to grant the Protector a spiritual or true-life mentor that can free up its own future.

- *Distractor*

Sometimes the Distractor is the most difficult trauma state to find or assist. After all, the Distractor doesn't want you to find the Refugee. Upon discovering the Distractor, the most important action to take is to figure out how to start protecting it from itself. Surround it with healing streams; find a twelve-step program related to its behaviors; and ask the Spirit to appoint it a spiritual guide to deal with its fear and shame.

Then start to work with the Refugee associated with the Distractor. You'll usually find the Refugee in a shock bubble underneath or on the other side of the Distractor, from a subtle point of view. You can return to the beginning of this technique to assist the Refugee and use the material in the next chapter. However, you can also assure the Distractor that it need not feel any shame for what it has done to cope with an unfair reality. Let it feel loved, and never, ever shame it.

Because the Distractor can commonly form an unhealthy relationship with a substance, person, entity, or the like, I recommend performing further work with it in the next two chapters. Distractors are the most common trauma type to develop self-injurious dysfunctions that can lead to everything from illnesses to addictions.

3: Close (Optional). In a way, you can't really close this stage. Grieving—and rebirth—is ongoing. For the moment, though, give thanks to anything and everyone that has assisted you and your traumatized self.

Stage 5: Integrating

To be honest, returning from a challenge—integrating after trauma—is an ongoing process, but it is one in which you can always move forward. You'll want to use applicable techniques from the next two chapters and personalize your integration process. However, I can provide tips to be used right now.

1: Prepare. You might be moving into this stage having just completed stage 4 or you might be starting this stage anew, having worked through the previous four stages in separate healing sessions. If you are beginning it now, entrench yourself in your healing haven, with writing instruments at hand if desired, and then conduct Spirit-to-Spirit.

2: Integration Tips. Consider the following integration techniques specifically for the traumatized self:

- *Continually Befriend the Traumatized Self.* No matter where the traumatized self is in its recovery process, know that your conscious current self must be its friend, parent, and guardian. Within your mind or aloud, suggest what it can do to help itself or, conversely, ask what it needs from you. Ask about its feelings or memories. Above all, be patient.

- *Send Healing Streams.* After conducting Spirit-to-Spirit, bathe your traumatized self in healing streams as many times a day as needed. Visualize it flowing along streams of grace into the greater you, making sure it knows that integration can be that easy.

- *Compliment and Express Gratitude for It.* Tell it how brave it has been and how important it was that it coped with life's challenges, even in unhealthy ways, in order to survive. It did what it had to, and you—and it—are alive because of it.

- *Call On Concrete and Imaginal Mentors.* The traumatized self wasn't given helpful advice or protection its first time through life (this or a past life.) You can serve as a mentor, but if you're lacking the needed knowledge or skills, find a real person or a great book. Or ask the Spirit to send imaginal mentors, and encourage the traumatized self to use them. You might even do the same yourself!

- *Transform Your Inner and/or Outer Environment.* As your traumatized self grows, it will become important to make adjustments to its internal environment and perhaps also your external environment. For the inside self, select positive reading material. Start catching and changing negative thoughts. Take meditation classes. Label feelings and find new ways to act them out. For instance, if a traumatized self learned to deal with anger by yelling, teach it a new way—and model the new behavior yourself. Allow challenging emotions to only arise at a certain time each day or perhaps with a trusted therapist or mentor.

Externally, declutter and tidy your environment and become creative with color and décor. Why? Your traumatized self has been burdened with an overwhelming onslaught of hard and confusing feelings, thoughts, and memories. Putting the external environment in order helps the traumatized self do the same internally. And think about it: if grief and trauma could be described on a color wheel, they might be pictured as gray and black (maybe with a little red pain thrown in). By beautifying the environment, you exchange dull and painful hues for colors, signaling a rebirth.

- **Try New Activities.** Slowly add new and vital activities. What would your traumatized self be doing now if it hadn't been traumatized? Try it! Find the next best thing if it's not possible to start over again.

- **Slowly Make Plans.** While maintaining your focus on your everyday life, plan for tomorrow. Is it time to plan for a trip? To write a book? Begin to spread your wings while making space for any leftover grief.

Know that you don't need your newly emerging self to integrate all at once. After all, you have the rest of your life to explore and soar, no matter what your age. Remember that you were born with an original energetic signature, and your spirit can never be damaged; trust in your own intrinsic ability to heal and ability to be yourself.

Technique 14
Cleansing and Transforming the Vagus Nerve

As explored in multiple chapters, your vagus nerve is key to the physical and subtle anatomies. Stanley Rosenberg, a well-known craniosacral therapist and Rolfer, says that the key to release from all stress states is the activation of the ventral branch of the vagus nerve, which governs social engagement. This release ensures peaceful responses and well-being. It also assists with dampening the fight-or-flight response of the sympathetic nervous system, as well as the defensive, fear-based responses of the dorsal branch of the vague nerve.[88]

---

88   Rosenberg, *Accessing the Healing Power of the Vagus Nerve*, 52.

The following activities are partially based on Rosenberg's work and also my own. They are very simple, and I heartily recommend them for any stage of trauma recovery.

Simple Touch. When receiving a massage or if touching yourself, focus on the skin's sensations. Tune everything else out of your mind and simply feel. Every time the hand is moved, follow the change with your consciousness and sink into all reactions. Bodily awareness assists with grounding the self in the present reality.

Stroke Your Face. As pointed out by Rosenberg, lightly stroking the face calms us and relieves stress.[89] I recommend that you do so with your thumb, which in many traditional Chinese medicine systems is a powerful digit for alleviating grief.

Diaphragmatic Breathing. To breathe in a healthy manner, you want your diaphragm to move up and down, allowing the abdomen and chest to expand and contract simultaneously. I find that we can kick into correct breathing by using our index finger to block one nostril for three breathing cycles and then doing the same with the other nostril. Then breathe through both nostrils for ten breaths, repeating the process if your breathing hasn't become rhythmic.

Perform Rosenberg's Basic Exercise. Rosenberg recommends a very easy exercise to reactivate social engagement abilities. It repositions your atlas and axis cervical vertebrae (vertebrae C1 and C2) and boosts blood flow to the brain stem in order to positively affect the ventral branch of the vagus nerve, as well as the cranial nerves.

First, comfortably rotate your head to the right. Return to center, wait a moment, and then comfortably rotate it to the left. Notice how far you're able to turn your head with ease.

- Lie on your back. Interweave the fingers of one hand with those of the other hand.

- Put your interlaced hands behind the back of your head and rest your head on them. (You can use just one hand if your shoulders are really stiff.)

- Remaining in this position, keep your head in place and look to the right, but only move your eyes. Don't strain. After thirty to sixty seconds, you should find that you will yawn, sigh, or swallow. This will

---

89   Rosenberg, *Accessing the Healing Power of the Vagus Nerve*, 63.

relax your autonomic nervous system. Bring your eyes straight ahead again.

- Now move your eyes to the left and repeat the previous step, ending by looking forward again.

- Remove your hands and sit or stand up. Pause and go slow if you become dizzy.

- Sit up and reevaluate your neck's mobility, as you did before undertaking this exercise. You should find yourself with less pain and more movement.[90]

Track Your Chakric Path. As you can see on figure 7, the vagus nerve taps into every in-body chakra. Using figure 1 as a guide to the locations of these seven chakras, conduct Spirit-to-Spirit and perform diaphragmatic breathing while focusing on the general area related to your first chakra. Ask the Spirit to tap you into the inner wheel of that chakra. Focus here for ten seconds as healing streams are generated from the center of that chakra and wash around the outside of it. Then shift your focus to the inner wheel of the second chakra area and perform the same cleansing with healing streams. Repeat with each in-body chakra until you reach the seventh chakra region on the top of the head.

Now deliberately ask the Spirit to link you with your ninth chakra, which is about an arm's length over the head. Request that the gold energy from this chakra stream into the inner and outer wheel of the seventh chakra, first passing through the eighth chakra right below it, and then down through all in-body chakras. This golden stream flows through both legs and out your feet and then, finally, through your tenth chakra, to anchor in the center of the earth. At this point, this waterfall of energy expands until it interconnects and bolsters every single chakra, every part of your body, and your entire auric field. Take a couple of deep breaths and know that this beam of energy will continue to hold you in safety and love as long as needed, also repairing your vagus nerve as it does so.

---

90   Ibid., 186–190.

Technique 15
Soothing the Nadis

As we explored in chapter 2, the nadis chiefly equate with the nerves. While it's clearly help-ful to repair and smooth your vagus nerve, it's also useful to pacify the nadis and, therefore, your nervous system. It's easy to do this. You'll simply activate the inner wheel of your first chakra and allow that energy to cleanse and awaken the remainder of your chakras' inner wheels. You'll then work with the core lumbar vertebrae that serve as the origin of the nadis.

The spinal house of the first chakra is called the *kanda*. This junction equates with the cauda equina, a bundle of nerves located at the lower end of the spinal cord, around the first and second lumbar vertebrae. This physical area, the mouth of the nadis, collects and directs all the energy that circulates through about 72,000-plus nadis—in other words, the entirety of the body. By sending healing energies through the kanda, you can create peace for the entire nervous system.

Here's the step-by-step process:

1: Prepare. Find a peaceful place, such as your healing haven, and make sure you'll have at least fifteen minutes of quiet time.

2: Perform Spirit-to-Spirit. Confirm your personal spirit, the Spirit, and any helping spirits you or the Spirit call in to assist you.

3: Concentrate on the Chakras. Focus on your first chakra and ask the Spirit to acti-vate healing streams within the center of this chakra. Spend a few minutes enjoying the angelic, blissful energy promoted from within until the Spirit courses this liquid light around the outside of the first chakra and then into the first auric field. Finally, this bounti-ful love leaps to the inside of every chakra, which shares the love with their corresponding external wheels and fields.

4: Move to the Nadi's Mouth. Focus on the kanda, located around lumber vertebrae one and two. Give permission for the Spirit to begin trickling streams of grace from the internal first chakra wheel into this area. You'll sense the mouth of the nadis becoming sat-urated with beautiful, stress-relieving energy.

5: Feel the Flow. Simply sense this spread of energy, which will be slowly distributed throughout the body in every direction. This energy will course gently through your physi-cal and subtle systems as long as needed.

6: Close. When complete, return your focus to your everyday life.

Technique 16
Harmonizing the Infra-Low Brain Wave

Brain waves are electrical impulses in the brain. They are measured in cycles per second, or hertz (Hz), which depict the average measurement of frequencies produced by the neurons in the brain. While our various brain-wave rhythms change constantly, there is one wave that's particularly important to address during trauma recovery. This is the infra-low brain wave, which operates on the slowest and lowest of all waves, even lower than delta, the sleep wave.

As explained in chapter 6, infra-low brain waves are under .5 Hz. They are known as modulators and stabilizers, and they also reveal our cortical rhythms, the control networks of the nervous system. These waves contain the chemical codes of our deep stressors, such as PTSD. In fact, I believe these waves mirror the stressful memories encoded in our free GABA receptors, which are mentioned in the section "The Next Level of Stress: Trauma" in chapter 3. We want to clear these repressed memories from these GABA storage vessels or they can easily retrigger. The good news is that if we energetically cleanse and harmonize our infra-low brain waves, we can soothe away all hidden stressors.

I'll enable you to smooth these rhythms through your heart chakra, which will enable a clearing of the cortical rhythms and GABA receptors throughout the body.

1: Prepare. You can conduct this exercise lying down, when you have time to rest.

2: Accept Your Stress. Before you can heal your infra-low brain waves, it's beneficial to accept everything that has caused and is causing you stress. Take a few deep breaths and simply be. Accept any bodily, mental, or emotional tensions.

3: Perform Spirit-to-Spirit. Affirm your personal spirit, the Spirit, and any imaginal spirits attending you. Settle deeper into your body.

4: Center in Your Heart. Rest your mind within the inner wheel of your heart chakra, letting the Spirit activate streams of grace within this space. Love and serenity flow into and through you, cleansing the outer wheel of this particular chakra before cascading through all chakric inner and outer wheels, as well as through the sushumna and other nadis.

5: Clear and Suffuse the Infra-Low Brain Waves. Even as the Spirit washes your entire system, the healing streams infiltrate the infra-low brainwaves. You might recognize them as slow pulses or oscillations laced with jagged and ragged energies. These waves match the stress locked into the free-range GABA receptors that hold our traumas and impact all traumatized selves. The healing streams fill all tense areas with calming waves that soothe and repair on a chemical basis and also a subtle basis. Your body might tingle. You might also perceive chilly areas, which indicate the release of old energies, or warm areas, revealing the influx of healing energies.

Under the Spirit's direction, energies not yours, including others' energies, attachments, microchimeric programs, epigenetic programs, and the like, are swiftly washed away to be tended by the Spirit. Remain in this state until your body grows calm and peaceful.

6: Ask for Continual Healing. Request that the Spirit continue to bathe you with healing streams over the next few days and nights.

7: Close. When you feel energized and renewed, thank the Spirit for the assistance and return to your life.

Technique 17
Coloring Your Chakras

Filling a disturbed chakra with its corresponding color is an easy and natural way to assist a related traumatized self while also restoring balance to the chakra and related bodily areas. Simply follow these steps:

1: Prepare. Decide which chakra is linked to a particular trauma (and traumatized self) using technique 4 or 5 from the last chapter. Then settle into your healing space.

2: Conduct Spirit-to-Spirit. Acknowledge your personal essence, the Spirit, and any helping spirits.

3: Infuse the Chakra. Focus on the pinpointed chakra and ask the Spirit to send healing streams into it with the appropriate color hue, selecting from the following list. If the Spirit indicates through your intuition, you can also ask for a generative force to be added, which will supercharge the healing streams.

First chakra—red—passion, excitement, energizing

Second chakra—orange—innovation, sensuality, enthusiasm

Third chakra—yellow—clarity, optimism, focus

Fourth chakra—green—healing, love, connectivity

Fifth chakra—blue—knowledge, calm, wisdom

Sixth chakra—purple—vision, strategy, mystical guidance

Seventh chakra—white—purity, spirituality, bliss

Eighth chakra—if black, provides mystery, karmic healing, and soul healing; if silver, grants deflection of negativity and transmission of higher ideals

Ninth chakra—gold—harmony, peace, and activation of soul's special abilities

Tenth chakra—brown—grounding, stability, clearing of ancestral issues, connection to earth and cosmos

Eleventh chakra—rose—activation of environmental and spiritual powers, as well as leadership abilities

Twelfth chakra—translucent—awakening of aptitudes that are unique to you; will also activate the traumatized self's hidden gifts

4: Flow with the Process. You'll sense, feel, or see the color as, held within healing streams, it emerges from the center of the associated chakra's inner wheel and is brought into that chakra's external wheel and bodily area. Notice how this wave of energy permeates the auric field around the traumatized self and is expressed into the chakra's related auric layer. Enjoy this easy flow of color and beauty as long as you desire.

5: Close. When finished, ask the Spirit or your spirit to rebalance all your chakras. When you feel restored, breathe deeply and return to your normal life.

Technique 18
Hindu Chakra Sounds for Healing Your Traumatized Self

Every in-body chakra corresponds with a Hindu *bija,* also called a seed syllable. These tones activate the healing qualities of its particular chakra, attune it to your original energetic signature, and release negative physical, psychological, and spiritual energies.

In this technique, you'll focus on attuning a traumatized self and their related chakra to that chakra's bija. After tracking the cocooned self (whether Refugee, Protector, or Distractor) to its corresponding in-body chakra, you'll conduct Spirit-to-Spirit and then spend about a minute humming or chanting the bija internally or externally. If your matching chakra is one of the five out-of-body chakras, select the seventh chakra instead of the ninth and the heart chakra instead of the eighth, tenth, eleventh, or twelfth. If your intuition indicates, request that the Spirit deliver the tone through healing streams with a generative force to bolster it.

The tones are as follows:

First chakra: Lam, pronounced *lum*.

Second chakra: Vam, pronounced *vum*.

Third chakra: Ram, pronounced *rum*.

Fourth chakra: Yam, pronounced *yum*.

Fifth chakra: Ham, pronounced *hum*.

Sixth chakra: Om, pronounced with a long O sound.

Seventh chakra: No specific syllable. However, it is associated with two different breathing sounds: visarga (pronounced with a breathy *ahhh*) and ng (which sounds like the end of the word *sing*).

You can conduct this technique anytime you desire.

Technique 19
Becoming Centered: Assisting Energetic Anxiety and Depression

As explained in chapter 5, energetic anxiety occurs when our soul is frontward in relation to one or more chakras. Energetic depression happens when our soul has shifted toward the back side of one or more chakras.

There is an easy fix to both states: you simply want to center all of your soul in your sushumna. However, a traumatized self might not so easily agree to the change. Perhaps it is scared to forgo predicting the future or processing the past.

You can conduct this technique after you've already dealt with a good many of the traumatized self's issues by using the earlier techniques in this chapter. Follow these steps:

1: Prepare. Bring yourself into your healing haven and breathe deeply.

2: Perform Spirit-to-Spirit. Acknowledge your spirit, the Spirit, and any helping spirits.

3: Ask for Centering. Request that the Spirit send healing streams from beyond your ninth chakra through the top of your head, through your sushumna, and then through your feet and tenth chakra. These beams of light will connect you in the core of the earth and adjust your soul so it fully occupies your body and is centered in the middle of your in-body chakra wheels and the sushumna. These energies of love will radiate from this plumb line throughout all aspects of you, holding you in the present and encompassed by the Spirit.

If any issues arise, simply reprocess them using technique 13 or any other techniques you are drawn to, then return to the flow just established.

4: Close. Breathe deeply and, with gratitude, ask the Spirit to hold you in this center line with love and grace. Go back to your life when ready.

· · · · ·

Synopsis

In this chapter you learned several processes for healing a traumatized self. Along the way, you created a healing haven, became clear about your genuine self and original energetic signature, and walked through a five-step process for recovering from trauma. Additional exercises provided subtle anatomy activities that can be used at any time to assist you in trauma recovery. All in all, you learned that no matter what, you deserve to take the time and attention needed to heal and become all that you can be.

And now, let's look at how you can address chronic illnesses and their related conditions in particular, including how to further assist the Distractor, a particular aspect of a traumatized self, whom we met in this chapter.

CHAPTER 9

Subtle Energy Healing Techniques
for Chronic Illnesses

Treat the fire, not the smoke.
—Mark Hyman, *The UltraMind Solution*

This chapter will address some of the factors that can compound the stress-response cycle triggered by trauma and set someone on a path to developing chronic illnesses. To recap what we know, from a medical point of view, chronic illnesses arise when the body mistakenly responds in a way that causes self-injury. From a subtle energy point of view, chronic illnesses follow in the wake of unhealed trauma. Primary forces cause the initial trauma, but when our body, mind, or soul remains stuck in a continually repeating stress-response cycle, it can create a secondary internal force—or set of forces—that further the stress and cause inside-to-inside damage. This secondary force connects the wounded, self-harming self to someone or something else, such as a person, entity, or power, an addiction pattern, or even a food or other substance. (These secondary forces are one of the factors that can contribute to the development of a chronic illness. For more, refer back to chapter 5.) Hence, if you have a chronic illness, you'll want to make sure you revisit the trauma-healing techniques shared in chapter 8 if needed, but also work with those techniques featured in this and the next chapter.

The first technique in this chapter will show you how to uncover and address self-created secondary forces. You'll then probe another vital factor that often contributes to chronic illnesses, the co-impact of epigenes, miasms, and mast cells, before you adapt the first technique in this chapter to address energetic codependency. In that pursuit, you'll also assist your Distractor self, a type of traumatized self introduced in technique 13 in chapter 8. After this, you'll be provided several additional subtle energy practices. The capstone of this chapter is a list of some of the major chronic illnesses and an energetic work tip for each.

In the end, I hope this chapter will leave you able to excavate and assist the aspects of the self caught in any inside-to-inside loops. You can do it! You can care enough about yourself to douse the fire underneath the smoke.

Technique 20
Uncovering and Healing the Self-Injurious Self

If you're still feeling stuck in a pattern of self-injury, it's time to search for—and unwrap— any secondary forces and free yourself from any self-injurious responses and loops plaguing you. You can follow the next steps and then use the additional processes offered in this and the next chapter to continue improving.

1: Prepare. Ensconce yourself in your healing haven, as you were shown how to do in technique 11 in chapter 8. Make sure you set aside several minutes and have writing tools on hand to keep track of your process and progress.

2: Conduct Spirit-to-Spirit. Affirm your vital spirit and the Spirit. Request that the Spirit assign you imaginal helpers if necessary.

3: Focus On the Symptom. Pinpoint the major symptom causing you hardship. It might be physical, such as occurs with a condition, illness, addiction, or environmental reactivity. It could be psychological, involving negative self-talk, an avoidance of intimacy, a hatred of aging, an inability to accept a learning challenge, or a codependent pattern. It could even be spiritual, involving the effects of a cult or a deep disconnect from the Spirit. No matter the presentation of the challenge, it will appear as a form of sabotage. Either an aspect of you will seem to be sabotaging yourself, or you'll be vulnerable to external sabotage—or both.

If there are several presenting symptoms, select the one that unifies the other issues. For instance, if you overeat because you are in pain, choose pain as your symptom. If your stomach often hurts because you overeat, label food issues as the problem.

4: Request Insights. First, ask the Spirit to reveal the original trauma that created this self-damaging pattern. If you've already worked on it, continue with substep A below.

If you don't know what the original trauma is, you can use technique 13 in chapter 8 to uncover it. (Remember that technique 13 employs several of the techniques presented in chapter 8.) Conduct your healing and then return to this technique to perform the following substeps.

A: Find the self-injurious self and the secondary force. Request that the Spirit assist you with locating the self-injurious self.

From a psychic point of view, this self will appear caught in a spun web or a thick beam of brackish energies. These threads will form a matrix. That matrix is the secondary force. It might be an extension of the same force that caused the initial trauma, but it might also be constituted from a different one.

Make note of the type of force it is, asking the Spirit for insights. As you might recall, your choices are environmental, physical, psychological, modern, spiritual, or missing. In this situation, a missing force will appear like a blank or near-invisible set of threads—like a force field. Figure 18 will give you an idea of how this secondary force looks and operates.

B: See what the secondary force is linked to. This matrix will encompass both the self-injurious self and also something or someone else. For instance, it might incorporate a body part, chakra, internalized entity, ancestor, miasm, microchimeric cell, microbe, or another soul aspect. It might also reach into the environment and connect with a certain type of food, an alcoholic beverage, a person, or an externalized entity.

C: Ask the captured self what it perceives the benefit of this link to be. The self-injurious self will believe it's benefiting from its connection to the object, being, or energy the secondary force links it to. Ask the Spirit to inform you about this gain.

Is this relationship preventing the self-injurious aspect from dealing with their deeper feelings (much as I described a Distractor as doing in chapter 8)? Is the matrix stopping your attempts to gain intimacy? Is it serving the family system? If it's connected to an entity, might this darker entity be considered the self's only friend? If it's connected to a microbe, what job might the microbe believe it's fulfilling?

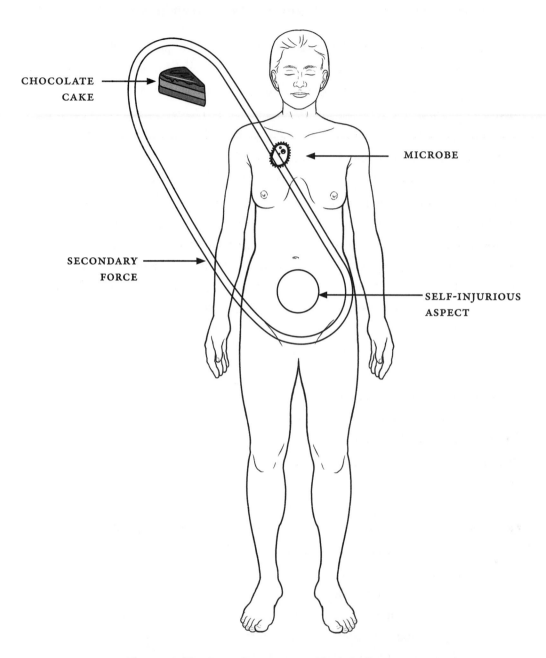

CHOCOLATE
CAKE

MICROBE

SECONDARY
FORCE

SELF-INJURIOUS
ASPECT

Figure 18: The Secondary Force in Chronic Illnesses. *A secondary force encapsulates the self-injurious aspect of a self that can form in the wake of unhealed trauma. This secondary force forms an energetic matrix that encompasses the self-injurious aspect and an additional person, object, entity, microbe, or even food item. There can be several such matrices or even one that is tied to many situations and things.*

You can mix and match techniques already provided in this book to help you work through this step.

D: Figure out the actual effects. Now request that the Spirit point out the actual results of being caught in the self-injurious loop. How is the captured self losing out on life? What pain, illness, dysfunctional beliefs, and challenging emotions are being continually retriggered? What is the real cost of this disruptive secondary force? Write down responses to these and similar questions.

E: Reduce the problem to one of connection. No matter what, the self-injurious self holds the subconscious belief that they don't deserve to be in a healthy connection—connection to self, others, or the Spirit. In fact, the unhealthy link to the object, being, or substance constitutes a replacement for a genuine connection and could therefore be seen as creating an energetic codependent relationship. The self-wounding loop is simultaneously a way to remain in shame.

Shame is actually a belief, not an emotion. It asserts that there is something so wrong with the self that bonding should be disallowed. Ask the Spirit to show the encapsulated self that this belief is a lie—that this self, no matter what, deserves authentic connection. Then ask the Spirit to bring about whatever bonding is required, both immediately and over time.

F: Pinpoint the central feeling. This self-injurious aspect is essentially holding on to a feeling that must be listened to and respected. Let the Spirit unearth this formative feeling, which has never been heard or harkened to. All feelings belong to one of these five constellations, which each present an important message:

Fear: It's time to act differently in order to become safer.

Anger: It's necessary to set a boundary.

Sadness: Love seems to be lost, and it's important to find a renewed
or new source of it.

Disgust: Something or someone is unhealthy and must be unhealthy.

Happiness: I want more of the same.

G: Summarize. Now put together a statement that will describe the self-injurious situation.

233

This declaration will label the negative pattern, the type of connection needed, and the feeling to respond to. For instance, if you're linked to a microbe by a secondary force, you could relay the following: "My self-injurious self is caught in a secondary force with a virus so it can remain bonded with the family; it's vital to make genuine connections outside of the family system so the core feeling of sadness, which is prompting the need for authentic love, can be healed."

5: Turn to the Spirit. Ask the Spirit to help you share compassion and care to the captive self. Then request that it show both you and this self a healthy way to be broken out of the secondary force and return to the flow of life. What is needed? An action or set of actions? A new attitude? A therapist to seek out, a doctor to see, a situation to avoid? A group to join? List as many ideas as possible and know that you can continue to request advice from the Spirit.

6: Ask for Healing Streams to Construct New Boundaries. Ultimately, the wounded self is using the secondary force, as well as the shock bubble encasing it, as a means of protection. Ask that the Spirit substitute a different, healthier energetic boundary for this secondary force and bubble. Healing streams will take the place of the energetic webbing and surround the once-afflicted self, delivering love, care, support, and light. In effect, these streams disconnect the self-injurious aspect from all negative attachments. Watch as the webbing dissipates and know that this change will take as long as needed to ensure safety and effectiveness.

7: Close. A deep and ongoing healing process has now been initiated. There might be more to do, which is why additional techniques are provided in this and the next chapter. For now, enjoy the amazing healing you've just received and ask the Spirit to return you to life in a good way.

Technique 21
Healing Epigenetics, Mast Cells, and Miasms

As already explored, the subtle energy patterns within the epigenetic material, mast cells, and auric field miasms are frequently similar and often match. Let me explain this statement.

Triggered epigenes create a specific matrix of subtle energies, as do the mast cells and the components of a corresponding miasm in the tenth auric field. All three are interconnected by electrical, chemical, and subtle energy charges, which, in turn, create lines of energy to formulate an overall matrix. And all three mirror each other, essentially locking you into a three-way self-injurious loop. It doesn't do much good to clear one of these parts without changing all three, which is the purpose of this technique. If you alter the subtle energetic patterns, physical transformation will follow.

1: Prepare. Enter your healing haven, bringing writing instruments with you to keep track of your process and progress.

2: Perform Spirit-to-Spirit. Affirm your personal spirit and the Spirit. Request that the Spirit select imaginal guides with specialties specific to your needs. Most likely you'll want energetic experts in genetics, the physical aspects of the human body, and the subtle energetics of ancestry.

3: Perceive the Pattern. Ask the Spirit to help you perceive the matrix pattern that has been holding you in energetic and chemical bondage. You might psychically spy a net of lines forming a particular shape, although that form will be distorted. For instance, if the threads create a circular shape, it will be lopsided. You might also kinesthetically feel the pattern, perhaps sensing it as a warped noose around your body or a tight constraint in your energetic field. The Spirit might also verbally inform you about this pattern.

Once you've defined the pattern, ask the Spirit to reveal its impact. Is it holding in microbes? Forcing you to process ancestors' emotions? Locking you in a state of panic? Remain in this fact-gathering state as long as needed.

4: Request the Correct Pattern. You now want the Spirit to substitute a healthy energetic patterning for the unhealthy one. What should the new pattern look, feel, or even sound like? Get a sense of it and then ask the Spirit to employ healing streams to weave a beneficial energetic pattern for your epigenes, mast cells, and tenth auric field. All alterations are made in a smooth and easy way and will continue to be made over time.

Also ask the Spirit to inform you if you ought to take specific and practical action. This guidance might come now or as time goes on, such as in a dream or through advice from a friend.

5: Close. Knowing that your healing is in process, thank the Spirit and all the imaginal helpers for their powerful love, then resume your everyday life.

Technique 22
Addressing Energetic Codependency

The secondary force(s) presenting with a chronic illness frequently establish the conditions for energetic codependency. For example, a traumatized self might hold on to a microbe, and perhaps even be corded to a negative entity linked to that microbe, to ensure itself a place in a family.

For example, as long as a young woman requires assistance, her parents will remain together instead of divorcing. A man might continually attract and marry narcissists, who constantly neglect and belittle him, in order to promote the pattern first established with his mother. He might unconsciously believe that pandering to a narcissist is necessary to survival. Someone with a learning issue might hold on to her family's thought that she's stupid in order to make her father feel smarter. A teenager might join a cult and subsume his free will to the leader in order to please a negative entity that attached to him as a child.

As yet another example, a traumatized self could be emotionally imbalanced because she believes she must always tend to the feelings interjected from her mother during childhood. A corollary activity might include the attacking of maternal microchimeric cells by her immune system, which is seeking to eliminate the interference of the mother. In reaction, the body develops cancer, a thyroid disorder, lupus, diabetes, or some other chronic illness.

What do these and thousands of other types of examples have in common? They all describe an inside-to-inside traumatizing cycle that continues because of the perceived value involved within energetic codependency.

As covered in the last chapter, a traumatized self with a Distractor personality often develops codependent behaviors and related conditions in order to avoid dealing with a primary trauma and finishing the grieving process associated with it. This short technique will enable you to assess for the energetic components of codependency and use techniques you've already learned in this book to assist with healing. It is adapted from technique 20.

1: Prepare. Bring yourself into your healing haven. Writing instruments might be useful for recording your observations and feelings.

2: Conduct Spirit-to-Spirit. Acknowledge your personal spirit and the Spirit. Ask for assistance from the imaginal realms if the Spirit deems this necessary.

3: Isolate Your Distractor. Using the term *Distractor* as a label for your codependent self, focus on the major codependent symptom and ask the Spirit to help you isolate this

Distractor, the self-injurious aspect caught in a secondary force or loop. Start with step 4, "Request Insights," in technique 20 and follow all subsequent steps, but know that you are customizing your activities to the codependent pattern.

Continue onward through the request for healing streams (step 6 of technique 20), which will provide new boundaries and love. Know that degenerative and generative forces will be released and applied where needed; attachments will be disintegrated, with healing sent to all; and, if needed, a spiritual guide will attend you and the Distractor to help you with daily choices.

Also let yourself grieve for the time lost by being stuck in the codependent pattern. We can rejoin or change our current life only when we've grieved the lost time.

4: Close and Continue. You might need to use additional healing techniques from chapter 8 or chapter 10 to continue this healing. For now, however, thank not only the Spirit and any imaginal helpers, but also this internal self for being so vulnerable, and then return to your life.

Technique 23
Mining a Microbe

If you know that a specific type of microbe is involved in a chronic illness, this technique can bring about a subtle healing. It can also be used to analyze for a microbe based on subtle energy factors.

Although this process enables you to clean and clear out a single type of microbe, you can conduct it multiple times. This is helpful, as many chronic illnesses, such as Lyme disease and chronic fatigue syndrome, occur with coinfections.

To help this exploration, I've drawn from the biological understandings of microbes presented in the section called "Major Microbes" in chapter 3, and also the section "The Subtle Energy of Microbes" found in chapter 4. During this process you'll also interact with your epigenes, as these often trigger or are triggered by microbial conditions.

To assist you in these microbial pursuits, let me first remind you of the physical and subtle properties of each microbe.

Viruses: Simple microbe made of a nucleic acid in a protein coat that multiples quickly and is energetically corded to a larger entity or force outside of the host. Within the system, a virus hijacks the DNA of a host's cells and can therefore remain hidden. In an attempt to destroy the virus, the immune system attacks healthy cells.

Bacteria: Single-cell microorganisms that lack a nucleus and can be helpful or harmful. Energetically, the harmful bacteria hold your own repressed and unacknowledged emotions.

Fungi: Microbes with nuclei that create a network, secrete enzymes, and carry others' emotions.

Protozoa: Single-cell organisms with nuclei that steal a host's physical and subtle energy to keep themselves alive.

Worms: Living organisms that steal a host's physical and subtle nutrients or life energy to survive. When clumped together, as in a communal fashion, they cause physical and subtle blockages. Know that these physical blockages often become storage units for subtle energies brought in through negative forces; in fact, they often congregate along a trauma pathway.

Let me introduce you to one more very interesting type of microbe. *Morphing microbes* are microbes that transform from one type to another—or, at least, the immune system perceives that they are able to do so. For example, chlamydia pneumonia is a lung-ingested bacteria that can remain in the lungs, but it can also travel to—and settle within—other organs, causing further damage. This microbe has been linked to pneumonia and bronchitis but also cardiovascular diseases (atherosclerosis and strokes), multiple sclerosis, Alzheimer's disease, chronic neurological disorders, and persistent inflammation and infections, including brain infections. It has been suggested that chlamydia pneumonia is also a co-factor in schizophrenia and autism.

One difficulty in treating the organism is that it morphs, or changes, from one form into another. In fact, it appears in two distinct forms, which makes it hard for the body to find and attack it. In one specific stage, it actively promotes the growth of cytokines, which evade our antibodies and trigger tissue infections that can last for decades. In another form, it can convince monocytes to carry it across the blood-brain barrier. The monocytes then dump the organism into the nervous system, where it induces neuro-inflammation. Hence, though it is a bacterium, it can also present—and operate as—a virus.[91]

---

91   Stratton, "Association of *Chlamydia pneumoniae* with Chronic Human Diseases," and Stratton, "*Chlamydophila pneumoniae*, A Pathogen Causing More Than Pneumonia," 641–650.

I'm accentuating this organism because it exemplifies the activities of the many morphing microbes that can cause chronic illnesses. I believe that many other organisms might actually morph, but science has yet to figure out how many of them exist and, moreover, how they actually operate. (Researchers already know there are at least eight types of the chlamydia bacteria.)

If you suspect you're dealing with an organism that morphs—the clue being that no matter what you do medically, it doesn't help—know that you need to address the subtle issues involved in each morphing form. For instance, chlamydia pneumonia is best analyzed and cleared as both a bacteria and a virus—in other words, as a microbe that contains your repressed emotions and is also corded to an outside influence.

Now let's put all this information to good use.

1: Prepare. Bring yourself into your healing haven. Have writing instruments available.

2: Perform Spirit-to-Spirit. Affirm your personal spirit, the Spirit, and spirits of any others involved, including any spirits of the imaginal realm that the Spirit may call in to assist you.

3: Specify the Microbe(s) You're Addressing. If you already have a biological diagnosis for a microbial condition, write down its name and whether the microbe is a virus, bacteria, fungi, protozoa, worm, or morphing microbe. If you don't know what microbe is affecting you, use either of the following two methods to pinpoint it.

> *Method One: Ask the Microbe.* Microbes can communicate because they are alive. Request that the Spirit or an appointed imaginal guide pinpoint the microbe impacting you. Ask next that the Spirit spin a ball of healing streams around a representative of this microbe. Thus enwrapped, the microbe will be able to communicate truthfully. Use your intuition to see, hear, or sense the microbe's response to your question, "What type of microbe are you?" Then work with that answer.

> *Method Two: Review the List.* Review the previous descriptions of the various microbes. Which set of qualifiers best matches your symptoms? Have your life circumstances made it hard for you to embrace and process your own feelings? Then you might be dealing with bacteria. Are you constantly low on life energy? You could be dealing with protozoa. If you also have a lot of physical

or subtle blocks, such as constipation (physical block) or lack of financial flow (subtle block), a worm could be involved.

Also, understand that a microbe might physically disappear or become dormant, but the symptoms might continue. For instance, I worked with a client who experienced parasitic worms over a two-year period. These caused exhaustion, bloating, under-eye circles, and gas. Prescription medicine wiped them out, yet around certain types of people, her physical symptoms would return. These individuals could be characterized as "vampires" in that they steal first chakra, life energy, much as parasites do. Even though my client was no longer affected by microbial parasites, she was impacted by people parasites. I used this technique to address her symptoms, and her problem cleared up.

4: Request Healing Streams. Ask the Spirit or your imaginal helper to send healing streams to you and your healthy cells, but to also surround a spokesperson for the microbe, thus creating a clear bubble that you can psychically see through. Within this bubble of grace, the microbe will be able to communicate with you.

5: Discuss Matters with the Master Microbe. It's imperative that you intuitively interact with the microbe. Given your knowledge of its type, ask questions aimed at finding out what purpose it believes it serves.

Microbes always believe that they are doing something important; for instance, a virus might believe that unless it links you to your deceased great-grandfather, you'll make the same mistakes as your ancestor did. A bacterium will believe that operating like a suitcase for your feelings will ensure your mother, who hates emotions, won't reject you.

With these ideas in mind, relate to the microbe with questions such as the following:

- How have you been serving me?
- What do you think would happen to me if you weren't active?
- What event convinced you to interact with me?
- What positive effects are you having on my life?
- What negative effects are you delivering to me?
- Are there any attachments, entities, forces, or other energetic constructs involved in your assignment?
- What might convince you to let go and leave, to be relieved from duty?

It might seem odd to befriend and have a conversation with a microbe, but in my years of experience, I've found that that's the easiest and most effective way to prompt it to let go.

6: Meet the Need a New Way. The microbe will quit its job once it knows you've selected a healthier way to address the need it was meeting. Work with the Spirit or your guides to arrive at this activity. You might need to perform an energetic action, such as to create a more protective auric field by returning to technique 10. Then again, a relational, emotional, or physical pursuit might be required.

7: Part Ways. Now ask the Spirit to use healing streams to gather all the microbes, along with the spokesperson, and arrive at a solution. Should the Spirit make these microbes evaporate or go dormant? Be passed out through your excretory system? Maybe they ought to be beamed to a different time and space.

Request that the Spirit also tell you how to cleanse your body and the microbial residue. Follow its directions, incorporate professional medical help if needed, and know you can always ask for more marching orders.

8: Close. Thank the microbe for what it's done and know that it's time to change that relationship. Thank the Spirit, and then move on with your life.

Technique 24
Guided Meditation for a Futuristic Sound and Light Machine

I believe that in the future, chronic illnesses will be healed by a machine able to deliver sound and light frequencies customized to a person's distinct chemical signature. This amazing machine will assess the frequencies of a microbial infection and simply cancel them out, even while reinvigorating the subject's natural frequencies. Because this machine doesn't exist, we'll energetically create it. And we'll go one better: we'll employ your original energetic signature.

In this technique you'll be ushered into this futuristic sound and light machine; although it's invisible, the subtle energies will do all the work.

1: Prepare. Enter your healing haven and lie down. If your healing space doesn't allow you to lie down, establish yourself in a quiet place elsewhere that holds a couch or a soft place upon which to settle.

2: Conduct Spirit-to-Spirit. Affirm your personal spirit, then acknowledge the Spirit and any helping spirits. The Spirit will now assign a spiritual technician to your cause. This technician will program and run this invisible machine for you. Sense the presence of this technician. Relax and know that you are in good hands.

3: Observe the Healing Machine. The technician assists you with perceiving the healing machine, a large, long tube that looks and operates like an MRI machine. When you're ready, the technician says, you'll be brought through the machine headfirst. You await this process while the technician programs the machine to zap away unhealthy microbes and negative energies and enhance your original energetic signature.

4: Be Brought into the Machine. You are already lying down, so it's easy for the technician to energetically transform the structure you're on into a moveable pallet. Next, the Spirit and invisible guides gently move this pallet into the machine. You enter it headfirst and find yourself lying within a colorful, humming structure. Breathe deeply as the technician turns on the machine.

5: Enjoy the Healing Process. Suddenly you are encircled within pixels of beautiful and soft frequencies, sparkles of light and music surrounding you. It's easy to enjoy the ease of this process as you begin to feel lighter and brighter.

6: Conclude the Session and Return. Slowly the sounds and lights fade until all is quiet and still. Your spiritual guides now guide you, feet first, still on your pallet, out of the machine. Within a few moments, you are completely out of the machine, but the technician instructs you to continue to lie still until you feel completely refreshed, renewed, and transformed. The Spirit adds healing streams to the mix; these will continue the frequency-based sequencing and healing as long as needed.

7: Close. Breathe deeply and affirm the power of the process you just underwent. Thank the Spirit, the technician, and the other spiritual guides. Your pallet is transformed back into an everyday structure, and the machine disappears. When ready, you can open your eyes and return to your normal life.

Technique 25
Recoding Your Phonons and Photons

As explored in chapter 3, phonons are subatomic particles that can carry negative or positive sounds or messages throughout the body, traveling out from the heart area. Photons are quantum units of light that move at the speed of light through a vacuum. In particular, biophotons are even smaller than photons and appear in certain ranges of the EMF; they are produced biologically. I believe that when you program the phonons and photons in your body with healing streams emanating from the inner wheel of the heart chakra, which will share these healing codes with all chakras and bodily areas, you can alter the energetic formulas causing your challenges and replace them with life-supporting energies.

During this process, you'll employ technique 7, "Illuminating the Internal Chakric Wheel," and, if needed, technique 9, "Uncovering, Moving, and Adding Generative and Degenerative Forces," both found in chapter 7.

1: Prepare. Settle into your healing haven and get comfortable. You can focus on a particular chronic illness issue or an overall challenge.

2: Conduct Spirit-to-Spirit. Affirm your personal spirit, the Spirit, and the spirits of any imaginal realm helpers that the Spirit may call in to assist you.

3: Activate Your Heart Chakra. Bring your conscious awareness to your heart chakra, specifically into the area right under your sternum. Drop your consciousness into the innermost wheel of this chakra. You'll sense it as a region of great beauty and peace, one filled with white light and the humming of love. Within here, your own spirit dwells in joy with the truth and light of the greater Spirit.

4: Sound Love. Request that the Spirit, or the Spirit-appointed imaginal helpers, compose an orchestration of love. This beautiful piece of music will exactly match and support your original energetic signature.

Even as you bask in the tones or sensations of love perfected for you, streams of grace begin to flow from your inner heart chakra wheel to wash over the outer wheel. The streams then capture the fullness of your specially designed song of love and deliver the composition directly into the phonons being produced with every heartbeat and pressure wave. Thus do the phonons flow through your body, into every nook and cranny, carrying the truth of your being beloved by the Spirit. Simultaneously, the Spirit detaches and attaches the appropriate degenerative and generative forces within and outside of your body.

5: Come Together. Phonons and photons now conjoin and merge. Thus do you become an ever-shifting source of your own healing energies.

6: Close. When you feel finished, thank the Spirit and any spiritual assistants for their help, then return to your normal life.

Technique 26
Spinning the Mobius Loop

As explored in chapter 3, Mobius loops are formed when positive energies meet in specific areas in the body and create scalar waves, vectoring fields of light that can create near-miraculous alterations. When these loops fail to form, our cells lose their natural energy, and chronic illnesses can arise. (Figure 8 will remind you what these twisted figure-eight shapes look like.)

This technique will produce Mobius loops throughout your body. You'll bring about the results through healing streams, which will, in turn, harmonize your subtle and physical energies with your original energetic signature.

1: Prepare. Lie down on a solid structure, such as a bed or couch. If you can, do this within your healing haven.

2: Perform Spirit-to-Spirit. Acknowledge your personal spirit and its ability to activate your original energetic signature within your body, mind, and soul. Affirm the power and authority of the Spirit and sense the presence of any healing spirits.

3: Request Healing Streams. Ask the Spirit to send into you, as well as emanate from your inner chakra wheels, the streams of grace needed to create or activate Mobius loops in all the correct places within your body.

You may sense particular cells aligning before they form loops within your DNA, epigenes, and cardiovascular system. The same shapes are also formulated within your chakras and nadis, as well as anywhere else they need to be.

Feel, see, or sense these coils spinning and weaving, creating scalar waves designed to reflect your original energetic signature, as well as the truth that you are unconditionally loved and loveable. All issues underlying a chronic illness are simply cleared and transmuted, leaving you whole and healthy. Know that the healing streams will continue to spin Mobius loops however and whenever needed.

4: Close. Slowly return to your everyday awareness. When ready, rise and stretch and go forward to meet the world in a new way!

Technique 27
Healing Your Meridians

As explored in chapter 4 and illuminated in figure 2, your meridians flow primarily through your connective tissue, intertwining with your cardiovascular vessels, central nervous system, and chakras. Thus, they serve as vehicles that directly or indirectly nourish and clear all parts of your subtle and physical anatomy.

Meridian-based therapies are extremely potent and often quite effective when performed for various chronic illnesses. They are also complex and often hard to self-deliver. In this technique, you will employ light and sound to clear and transform all meridians at once by focusing on one particular meridian access point. This is the Ming Men doorway, also called the Gate of Power, Destiny, Dreams, or Life.

This doorway is activated during preconception and physically manifests at conception. It is found between the kidneys, at your mid-back. Figure 19 shows this area.

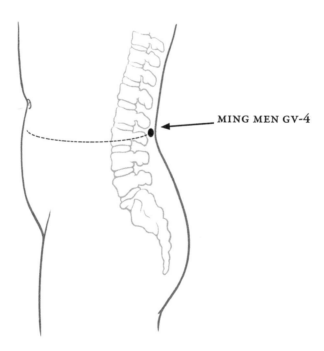

MING MEN GV-4

Figure 19: The Ming Men Doorway. *The Ming Men Doorway is found between the kidneys on your mid-back.*

The most important function of this doorway is to usher in a prenatal energy called *ancestral chi*, or the energies of your ancestors. This particular type of chi is considered the source of good fortune, luck, and the life energy needed to live a long and luscious life. It also blends the often-opposing energies processed within the kidney meridian and enables the cleansing of wastes. However, ancestral chi also stirs the epigenetic material, which, in turn, stimulates mast cell development and establishes harmful miasms. Related disorders, such as microbial, genetic, hormonal, microchimeric, emotional, karmic, and even addiction-related disorders can boil down to the influence of harmful ancestral chi.

No good can come out of ignoring the ancestral chi. But instead of taking in your ancestors' chi, how about relating it to the Spirit's energies? When I use this technique with clients, I invite the Spirit to transform into its Divine Mother Spirit and Father Spirit expressions. Ushered into your Ming Men doorway as these beautiful and empowered female and male forms of itself, the Spirit can replace the negative ancestral chi and enable true transformation.

The process is easy and encapsulated in the following steps:

1: Prepare. Bring yourself into your healing haven, with writing instruments if you want to take notes. I recommend that you sit up so you can best reach the Ming Men area.

2: Conduct Spirit-to-Spirit. Embrace—and be embraced by—your essential self. Affirm your helping spirits, as well as those of your ancestors, and then turn this process over to the Spirit.

3: Touch and Open the Ming Men. Locate the Ming Men area on your back, in between your kidneys. If you're able, physically touch this point, lightly holding your index finger upon it. If you can't reach this point, ask that the Spirit select an imaginal helper to manipulate it for you. Spend a minute or so sensing the opening of this energetic doorway. It might psychically light up, start to vibrate, or simply feel warmer.

4: Request a Substitution. Now ask that the Mother Spirit, the divine feminine, create grace-filled streams of light and sounds that match your original energetic signature. Simultaneously request that the Father Spirit do the same. The Mother Spirit will then sing her streams into your Ming Men point, replete with love and healing. All the maternal energies you've ever needed now pour into you, replacing those that have been harmful or unhelpful.

At the same time, the Father Spirit will send beams of universal light into your Ming Men point. This light is replete with strength and power, also emitting tones full of the same energies. This paternal energy transforms all negative masculine energies into those per-fected for you and your needs. The female and male energies then blend and begin spread-ing throughout your kidney meridian.

Over the next twenty-four hours, the love of the Mother Spirit and the Father Spirit will make their way through the entirety of your meridian system, lighting up your life and pro-viding you the experience of (finally) being lovingly parented.

5: Ask for Further Blessings. Know that the Mother Spirit and Father Spirit will con-tinue to deliver blessings into all areas of your life. Thank your ancestors for what they have given you, even as those ancestors (or their energies) that have been harmful are released. Return to your life when ready.

GUIDE 5

Addressing the Subtle Energy
of Chronic Illnesses
Additional Tips

In order to give you a leg up in addressing a specific chronic illness, here is a list of some of the most common ones, including the ones I've seen most often over the years. After briefly describing the biology of each, I've provided a few energetic tips for working with every illness. My descriptions aren't complete in any way; I simply want to give you a starting place.

▸ *Asthma:* Chronic inflammation of the respiratory airways triggered by allergens and sometimes by stress reactions or self-injurious immune responses by the body. Mast cells and cytokines play a definite role in the disease, causing the related inflammation. Metaphysically, asthma often involves the fear of embracing life, your personal spirit, and the Spirit, as well as an inability to forgive yourself or others for hardships. Forgiveness is key, for it could turn karma into dharma and release the self and others from guilt and shame. Technique 28 in chapter 10 will show you how to perform forgiveness.

▸ *Cancer:* In autoimmune disorders, the immune system is hyperactive. In the case of cancer, the immune system fails to do its job, allowing the cancer cells to grow freely. However, cancer often occurs in inflamed areas that are already suffering from a chronic self-injurious condition. Often cancer is instigated by microbes, imbalanced hormones, and microchimerism. Typically, I also find the presence of disruptive attachments and also an interjection of others' energy. As well, the first chakra is commonly underperforming and needs to be analyzed for traumatized and self-injurious aspects of the self. The related secondary force often involves a fear of one's purpose and an inability to let oneself be creative. A willingness to be unusual and stand out is required.

▶ *Celiac Disease:* Causes gluten to damage the small intestine. Often present with leaky gut syndrome. Related issues include an imbalance in the microbiome and second chakra issues. Regarding the latter, I usually discover that personal emotions are suppressed, which can lead to bacterial issues, and that others' emotions are caught within a fungus such as candida. It's helpful to start uncovering and expressing your own emotions and release others' interjected emotions. Look for forces that set up trauma and self-injurious attitudes or behaviors in the first through third chakras and their related developmental periods. Also address the allergy to gluten using either technique 29, "Programming Your Food and Other Substances for Healing," or technique 30, "Healing a Missing Force for Allergies and Addictive Processes, Including Energetic Codependency"—or both—found in chapter 10.

▶ *Crohn's Disease:* Persistent inflammation of the intestinal lining. See "Celiac Disease" (above) and also search for microbial infections, including fungal (such as candida), bacterial, and viral inflections. Work with first chakra (large intestine) issues regarding an inability to surrender and release waste. Also check the second chakra for emotional issues. To help heal this issue, learn how to let go and flow with life's ups and downs.

▶ *Chronic Fatigue Syndrome:* Possibly caused by a viral condition that, once established, topples the immune system so it overproduces cytokines and debilitates the power of the natural killer cells. Symptoms include severe pain and exhaustion. I typically perceive a low-functioning first chakra and a too-thin first auric layer. Karmic issues carried in from the eighth chakra are typically overriding the ability to perceive life's goodness. Most likely, chronic fatigue patients are also carrying others' pains and emotions. Deal with the karmic reasons you might think you need to codependently assist others with their energies and issues.

GUIDE 5

▶ *Diabetes, Type 1:* Often called juvenile diabetes, type 1 diabetes can actually appear in people of any age. A trigger causes the immune system to destroy the pancreatic cells that make insulin. This third chakra issue is metaphysically caused by an unwillingness to accept the goodness and sweetness of ourselves and the world. I suggest that women also examine the ways that they might be rejecting their feminine powers, such as softness and receptivity.

▶ **Diabetes, Type 2:** With this condition, the body doesn't know how to respond to insulin or is insulin resistant. Look for a resistance to love, connection, and sweetness. Also examine for white blood cell issues; if you find any, deal with trauma or self-injurious patterns that keep you from being safe.

▶ **Endometriosis:** Tissue similar to what normally grows in the uterus grows somewhere else. Work with the second chakra and the displacement of your personal emotions. You might also be corded to people or powers that are trying to get conceived inside of you. Address issues of self-sacrifice, and refuse to do for others what they need to do for themselves.

▶ **Epstein-Barr Virus:** This virus, which causes many fatigue-causing illnesses, including mononucleosis, has also been shown to increase the risk for developing systemic lupus erythematosus, multiple sclerosis, rheumatoid arthritis, juvenile idiopathic arthritis, inflammatory bowel disease, celiac disease, and type 1 diabetes.[92] It has been tentatively associated with fibromyalgia patients, who often inconclusively meet the criteria for chronic fatigue syndrome.[93] As well, it has been associated with Sjogren's syndrome and autoimmune hepatitis, and it is most likely an underlying factor in autoimmune thyroid disorders such as Graves' disease and Hashimoto's. This latter category is quite important, as it impacts about 10 percent of the world's population.[94] Follow the cord attached to the virus to see who or what is stealing your life energy. Then deal with spiritual "shoulds": in what ways are you telling yourself what you should be instead of who you are?

▶ **Fibromyalgia:** Causes widespread pain, fatigue, and tenderness in the body. No one knows exactly what causes this disease, though it's thought that it may

GUIDE 5

---

92   Cincinnati Children's Hospital Medical Center, "Epstein-Barr Virus Linked to Seven Serious Diseases."

93   Reshkova et al., "Evaluation of Antiviral Antibodies Against Epstein-Barr Virus and Neurotransmitters in Patients with Fibromyalgia."

94   Dittfeld et al., "A Possible Link Between the Epstein-Barr Virus Infection and Autoimmune Thyroid Disorders."

be triggered by a virus. I recommend dealing with viral-related issues and also consider the presence of a morphing microbe. As well, assess the microbiome and then search for attachments and others' energies in the eleventh chakra and field. Clear the epigenes, mast cells, and miasm, using technique 21 found earlier in this chapter. Know that mast cells often go awry and become overpopulated when you confuse your needs with those of others.

▶ *Graves' Disease:* The thyroid gland produces extra hormones (hyperthyroidism). Analyze the fifth chakra and look for attachments. Ask the question, "Who or what else am I energetically producing these thyroid hormones for?" Also check for the Epstein-Barr virus and the bacteria Yersinia enterocolitica.

▶ *Guillain-Barre Syndrome:* The immune system attacks the PNS. Because this disease process often starts with a respiratory infection, it's important to examine fourth chakra self-love issues. It's doubly important to probe not only for other fourth chakra issues, but also first and tenth chakra traumas and self-injurious loops, as the disease can paralyze the limbs. (Your arms are an extension of your fourth chakra and your legs of your first and tenth chakras.) Work the polyvagal system to address nervous system challenges and figure out why you don't believe you deserve to own and use your own life energy, but instead give it away.

▶ *Hashimoto's Thyroiditis:* The immune system attacks and seeks to destroy the thyroid. I believe that this disease usually begins as a viral infection. In seeking to kill the virus, the immune system instead attacks the thyroid. In addition to addressing the virus, look for who or what the immune system is really trying to destroy. Usually there is an entity or other type of dark power linked to the thyroid. Specifically check for the Epstein-Barr virus and also the bacteria Yersinia enterocolitica.

▶ *Helicobacter Pylori (H. pylori) Infection:* A bacteria-causing acid eventually eats away the stomach lining. H. pylori can eventually cause stomach cancer, intestinal inflammation, and ulcers. Examine yourself for third chakra issues and repressed feelings, as well as any personal opinions, truths, and thoughts you've been rejecting.

▶ *Hemolytic Anemia:* There is a premature destruction of red blood cells often following problems with the bone marrow. Therefore, address your tenth chakra issues and epigenes, and figure out why you think you should give your life energy away to your ancestors.

▶ *Hepatitis C:* Caused by a virus attacking the liver. Compromised liver function can trigger other chronic illnesses. Examine third chakra issues related to the acceptance or rejection of your masculine power and track the viral cord to an outside source.

▶ *Herpes:* A virus that causes itching and breakouts and can result in a chronic illness. In particular, type 1 and 2, which cause oral and genital herpes respectively, remain latent after the initial infection and stir when the stress response is triggered in the body. Like many viruses, the herpes viruses have evolved to avoid the stress hormones; therefore, they have become almost indestructible. For oral herpes, work with the fifth chakra. Ask yourself what you believe you should or shouldn't be thinking or expressing. For genital herpes, address miasmic-transferred shame and use healing streams to release others' sexual energies.

▶ *Interstitial Cystitis:* Chronic pain in the bladder, typically due to a defect in the lining. Address first chakra rage issues and the reasons you hold back your anger. Also search for bacterial issues and reasons you might be repressing your feelings.

▶ *Irritable Bowel Syndrome:* Address issues related to the microbiome and polyvagal system, and figure out why you want to take care of everyone else, at least in terms of third and second chakra concerns. Ask yourself questions like these: What regrets are eating away at you? What resentments are you holding on to? How can you be more respectful toward yourself?

GUIDE 5

▶ *Lupus:* The four types of lupus cause systemic or area inflammation, swelling, and pain. Work on issues related to safety and letting go. If your lupus is triggered by sunlight, I suggest working on vitamin D–related issues. I would also address leaky gut challenges.

▶ *Lyme Disease, Chronic:* The late stage of a tick-borne bacterial infection that causes body-wide inflammation and organ damage. This complicated malady is best approached through finding the hidden traumatized and self-injurious selves, which have encapsulated themselves in a murky energetic boundary in much the same way the bacteria do. Address the reasons you don't believe you deserve healthy boundaries or protection and ways that you are absorbing others' energies through your tenth chakra.

▸ *Mast Cell Activation Syndromes:* There are a number of chronic illnesses causing serious effects from the over-multiplication of the mast cells. These almost always involve a relationship between the epigenes, mast cells, and miasms. Simply begin by asking yourself, "Why am I allergic to myself?" (meaning, "Why do I respond negatively to myself? Why am I so uncomfortable with/within my own self? Why am convinced that I should feel shame about myself?") I'd also check for a modern force, asking if you are sensitive to EMF and the like.

▸ *Meniere's Disease:* A disorder of the inner ear. Look for fifth chakra issues, particularly those that make you feel guilty for knowing what you aren't supposed to know. Search for what you really need to say or think. Also address second chakra issues, seeking to become more comfortable with your true feelings.

▸ *Multiple Sclerosis:* A nervous system disease causing weakness in the brain and central nervous system. Deal with issues involving the processing of fats, as the disease causes a disintegration of fatty nerve sheaths. Examine the microbiome and polyvagal system and search for morphing microbe issues. Learn how to make spiritual connections through your higher chakras.

▸ *Myasthenia Gravis:* Causes muscle weakness. Begins as a weakness in the acetylcholine at neuromuscular junctions. Consider focusing on issues about your life energy (nerves) and your strength (muscles), as well as how willing you are to take action on your own behalf.

GUIDE 5

▸ *Narcolepsy:* A chronic brain disorder causing disturbances in the sleep-wake cycle. Energetically, this is often a seventh and third chakra issue, as both areas of the body (the gut and the brain stem) are major manufacturing centers of serotonin. Question what you require in order to be able to live according to your own rhythm. Personally, I think that narcolepsy might be a form of ADD and can also be addressed as a third chakra issue.

▶ ***Pernicious Anemia:*** A decrease in red blood cells occurring when the intestines cannot absorb vitamin B$_{12}$. Examine vitamin B issues and the reasons you let others steal your life energy; also search for a self-injurious pattern causing you to refuse life's richness.

▶ ***Psoriasis:*** A skin disease characterized by red, itchy scales on the skin. It can be triggered by infections and stress, but it usually reduces to a first chakra safety issue that allows your system to let others' energies penetrate through your first auric field into your skin.

▶ ***Psoriatic Arthritis:*** An arthritis that is caused by psoriasis (see "Psoriasis"). Also work on repressed anger about having been unconsciously tricked into taking on others' energies.

▶ ***Raynaud's Phenomenon:*** Cold temperatures or strong emotions cause blood vessel spasms. Consider working on your ninth chakra and the reasons that you don't believe you can handle life's vicissitudes.

▶ ***Restless Legs Syndrome:*** The overwhelming urge to move the legs. Address ways you are holding yourself back in everyday life. Ask about the next goal you need to walk toward. I'd work on the tenth and first chakras.

▶ ***Rheumatoid Arthritis:*** A joint-based form of arthritis causing stiffness and pain. Deal with repressed feelings in the second chakra and specifically regrets and resentments. Access eleventh chakra traumatized selves, and forgive yourself for not serving your own higher good. Own your eleventh chakra power!

▶ ***Scleroderma:*** The abnormal growth of connective tissue, resulting in a hardening of the skin. Can impact many other organs as well. Because this disease is caused by an overproduction and storage of collagen, I recommend that you work with eleventh chakra/field issues. Ask yourself why you might be repressing your personal and mystical powers. Because collagen is a protein, I recommend that you examine the related subtle issues. Also probe to see if you've been injured by any environmental forces.

▶ ***Sjogren's Syndrome:*** Dryness of mouth and eyes. In particular, it is caused by immune attacks on the glands making tears and saliva. Examine the second,

GUIDE 5

sixth, and fifth chakra issues. Questions to ask could include the following: What beliefs do I hold about my right to grieve? Do I get to say what I'm thinking?

- **Vasculitis:** Inflammation of the blood vessels, which are being attacked by the immune cells. Deal with reasons you don't believe you can love yourself and related traumas and self-injurious loops. I'd start in the fourth chakra.

- **Vitiligo:** Pigmentation lost in the skin. Seize your spiritual power, which you've probably repressed, and embrace your ability to perform eleventh chakra "magic."

- **Yersinia Enterocolitica:** This bacterium is carried in the intestines of domesticated and wild animals. It can be passed from an infected animal to a person through infected food, water, or fecal material, or through raw meat and unpasteurized milk. Typical symptoms include fever and diarrhea, although this invasive bacterium has also been linked to Graves' disease and Hashimoto's thyroiditis and even a form of reactive arthritis that mainly affects the legs.[95] Basically, it is able to adapt to various environments in the body and form adhesions to the host's cells. I wanted to point this bacterium out to emphasize the ability of many microbes, including Yersinia, to adapt so well to the environment of the human body that their presence can influence or result in the manifestation of chronic illnesses, including some autoimmune disorders. Because this particular infection originates in a person's gut, I would work on the second chakra and the microbiome, even if the resulting disease lies in the thyroid or the legs.

GUIDE 5

---

95 Uliczka et al., "Unique Cell Adhesion and Invasion Properties of Yersinia enterocolitica 0:3."

· · · · ·

Synopsis

On an energetic basis, chronic illnesses occur post-trauma when an internally created secondary force encapsulates the wounded self and begins a self-injurious process. Linked with the self-injurious aspect will be an object, microbe, person, behavior, or some other factor that keeps this self in bondage. In this chapter you learned several techniques, many of which included aspects of other techniques presented in this book, to energetically address these self-injurious issues. As well, you were provided a list of common chronic illnesses and tips on how to start approaching them energetically.

Now it's time to examine additional subtle and physical actions you can take related to addictions, foods, and other situations.

CHAPTER 10

Techniques to Continue and Further Your Recovery

People are like bicycles. They can keep their balance only as long as they keep moving.

—Albert Einstein, in Jürgen Neffe,
Einstein (trans. Shelley Frisch)

In this chapter I'll assist you with addressing both trauma and chronic illnesses from a more physical point of view. We begin energetically, however, by focusing on forgiveness. To release ourselves from the past, we must release the past from us. I'll then focus on physical concerns that can enable transformation, first helping you to examine your relationship with different foods and the missing forces that so often underlie allergies and addictions. Then you'll learn how to energetically balance your sexual hormones. Finally, I'll get you moving and expressing. In the end you'll find yourself exactly where you need to be on the path of your life.

Technique 28
Forgiveness: A Capstone to Grieving

Forgiveness is the capstone for healing from trauma and recovering from chronic illness. It also plays a necessary role in alleviating codependent bonds and moving into the acceptance aspect of grieving.

To forgive is to pardon. When we forgive someone or something else or the factors underlying a situation, we are voluntarily agreeing to alter our attitude and release emotions like resentment and hatred. Forgiveness is far easier if the person we need to forgive is sorry for hurting us, but in many cases they aren't sorry or, if they are, cannot tell us they are (if they've died, for instance). In the case of needing to forgive ourselves, forgiveness becomes easier if we can come to a place of self-compassion, a shift that is sometimes easier said than done.

Fortunately, forgiveness can become easier if we understand that it's a decision, not a feeling—and it's a decision that doesn't imply forgetting. After all, why would we want to forget a lesson learned, such as the need to mistrust a certain type of person? Rather, forgiveness is an act of releasing—releasing oneself and another from the harmful energies binding you together.

Besides being a decision, forgiveness is also a spiritual quality, much like faith, hope, truth, and love. As such, it can be seen to emanate directly from the Spirit. This means that when you call upon forgiveness, you empower the Spirit to deliver this quality to all concerned. If you are unable to fully desire or feel forgiveness, don't worry. The Spirit is in charge of mercy, not us. You have merely to request that the Spirit releases you from the burden of not forgiving and put itself in charge of being merciful. Basically, you make it the Spirit's job, not your own, to figure out what forgiveness needs to look or feel like.

Now it's time to experience the freedom of forgiveness.

1: Prepare. Enter your healing haven or find a quiet place in which you can reflect.

2: Conduct Spirit-to-Spirit. Affirm your spirit. Then recognize and affirm the spirits of others involved in the circumstances leading to the need to forgive. Finally, acknowledge the Spirit.

3: Drop Into Your Feelings. Allow your awareness to deepen into your current feelings about the challenging situation. Don't edit. Feel your pain, despair, hopelessness, rage, and anything else.

Then ask yourself: "Am I ready to be free of all this negativity?" If you are, move to the next step. If you aren't, take more time to focus on that question and move into the next step when ready. Remember, you aren't saying everything was or is "all okay"; rather, you are seeking freedom.

4: Request Forgiveness. Ask that the Spirit deliver to you the spiritual quality of forgiveness. Sense this stream of forgiveness entering all aspects of you—body, mind, and soul.

You are being fully released of the bondage of lack of forgiveness, along with all repetitive negative emotions, patterns, attitudes, and behaviors. If it's hard to release someone else or yourself from fault, give that job to the Spirit.

5: Close with Peace. Sense the ensuing peace and know that this serenity will increase as time goes on. Thank yourself, the other spirits involved, and the Spirit for this gift. When you are ready, continue with your life.

Technique 29
Programming Your Food and Other Substances for Healing

Trauma can throw off our relationship with food and other substances. For instance, a self in a trauma bubble might crave food appropriate to their age, but not your own. You can only eat so many hot dogs for your inner seven-year-old and remain healthy. And chronic illnesses are frequently complicit with reactions to food, causing—or reacting to—cravings, sensitivities, and even allergies and addictions.

Your food and substance choices can progress or regress a healing process. The purpose of this technique, which is actually a conglomerate of techniques, is to help you clear food-related issues and enhance foodstuffs with positive subtle energies.

Getting Started

To begin, review the chakra-based foods and substances chart on the following page, which groups foods and certain other substances by chakra. Every chakra and its corollary hormone gland are situated within a certain band of frequencies. Foods also emanate and impact a particular band of frequencies. Therefore, the frequencies of certain foods and substances will be supportive of a specific chakra and its related functions, while other substances might deliver a neutral or negative effect.

Besides being innately programmed with certain frequencies, foods also take on external frequencies. For instance, beef, which can be beneficial to the first chakra, can become negatively charged if the cows are slaughtered in a violent manner. Thus mistreated, the cows undergo trauma and absorb the violent physical force and subtle charges, all of which can enter your body when you eat that meat. Your first chakra, which relates to the frequencies of beef, might shut down or become hyperactive. Your adrenals could undergo a stress reaction and then become exhausted. You could also act out emotions like fear or rage without even knowing why.

Chakra-Based Foods and Substances

CHAKRA AND ITS IN-BODY CONNECTION	SUPPORTIVE FOODS AND SUBSTANCES	STRESS-INDUCING FOODS AND SUBSTANCES
First chakra Adrenals	Grass-fed and organically raised red meat. Organically produced eggs (if not sensitive or allergic to them), root vegetables, cherries, strawberries (if not sensitive or allergic to them), red grapes, purple grapes, raspberries, and other red and purple fruits. This chakra requires lots of minerals and water.	Beef butchered violently (the adrenal hormones remain in the meat) or raised with antibiotics and growth hormones. Alcohol. Histamine-producing foods, including strawberries, eggs, shellfish, chocolate, certain nuts, cured meats, fermented foods, alcoholic beverages, and vinegar-containing foods. Any life-endangering use of prescription medicine, including opioids, street drugs such as cocaine and heroin, or dangerous performance and diet drugs. Cravings for dangerous amounts of any substance indicate career, sexual, or identity stressors and burnout.
Second chakra Testes and ovaries	Organically raised chicken, turkey, and other fowl. Yams and sweet potatoes, pumpkin, tropical fruits, salmon, tuna, flaxseed, carrots, oranges, quinoa, sprouted grains, orange squash, coconut products, yogurt, nuts.	Cow dairy and soy products, peanuts, gluten (wheat, oats, barley, rye), and other complex and sugary carbohydrates. A craving for rich carbohydrates, white potatoes, and white sugar and flour can indicate emotional stress and the need for comfort.

CHAKRA AND ITS IN-BODY CONNECTION	SUPPORTIVE FOODS AND SUBSTANCES	STRESS-INDUCING FOODS AND SUBSTANCES
Third chakra Pancreas	Non-GMO corn, yellow squash, bananas, plantains, yellow peppers, brown rice, beans, lentils, apples, buckwheat, pineapple, papaya, and many types of nuts and whole grains. To support the pancreas, many people need to eat several small meals a day.	Beer, corn-processed alcohol, processed corn and corn products, including corn syrup, diet soda. Stress can lead to the abusive use of caffeine products, including sodas, coffee, and canned caffeinated stimulants, as well as pain relievers that affect the liver. Might also need to avoid purine-rich foods, including organ meats, anchovies, seafood, red meat, and other foods that stimulate production of uric acid. Cravings for crunchy foods, such as popcorn and chips, might indicate stress. The overuse of caffeine can be a sign of being overscheduled or hatred of a job.
Fourth chakra Heart	Think the Mediterranean diet, including green leafy and cruciferous vegetables, avocadoes, oils (including olive, coconut, and artichoke), teas, herbs, spices, mercury-free fish, whole grains, most fruits.	White sugar, wine, too much salt, canned fruits and vegetables, trans-fatty acids, cured meats, additives, including monosodium glutamate (MSG). Compulsive use of any of the above, or of sugar, chocolate, or sweet alcoholic beverages, can indicate stress related to love and relationship.
Fifth chakra Thyroid	Tart fruits, such as blueberries, blackberries, lemons, kiwi, and grapefruit. Iodine-rich foods, including chlorella and kelp. Magnesium-rich food, such as nuts. Herbal teas, spices, and water. Soups and stews.	Depending on hormonal conditions, might react to soy, cruciferous vegetables, gluten, cow dairy, trans-fatty acids, sugar, alcohol, and processed foods. A compulsive need to constantly chew or drink can indicate fifth chakra stress.

CHAKRA AND ITS IN-BODY CONNECTION	SUPPORTIVE FOODS AND SUBSTANCES	STRESS-INDUCING FOODS AND SUBSTANCES
Sixth chakra Pituitary	Mercury-free fish, leafy greens, nuts, whole grains, dark chocolate, purple berries, and foods high in omega-3.	The pituitary runs our hormonal system; therefore, any craving that throws our endocrine system out of balance can indicate stress in this center or create more stress in other chakras. The underlying challenge, if the stress relates to this chakra, is self-image or confusion about the future.
Seventh chakra Pineal	In general, seventh chakra enhancements involve the use of prayer or blessings when eating or drinking, abstaining from chemically laden foods, and using substances in a worshipful way, such as through rituals, including fasting. Eating foods or taking supplements enabling pineal gland functioning is very important (see a naturopath or nutritionist for advice). Also, select supplements that can cross the blood-brain barrier in the body and be delivered to the brain. This barrier is a protective membrane that separates the digestive system from the brain.	Any unhealthy food or substance can inhibit the functioning of the pineal gland and seventh chakra or indicate a seventh chakra stress. Rigidity in food choices often indicates stress in the seventh chakra and lack of comfort with one's spiritual identity.
Eighth chakra Thymus	Clean and organic foods of any type; if you eat flesh, ask the spirit of that natural being for permission to eat its body. Use healing streams to cleanse the foodstuffs or substances of any or all attachments, dark powers, or entities.	Attachments, dark powers, and entities on substances or foodstuffs can get transferred to the self. Substances can trigger childhood or past-life issues; work on these as traumas, using techniques in chapter 8.

CHAKRA AND ITS IN-BODY CONNECTION	SUPPORTIVE FOODS AND SUBSTANCES	STRESS-INDUCING FOODS AND SUBSTANCES
Ninth chakra Diaphragm	The most enhancing nourishment will fit your values and ideals, whether those be vegan, paleo, or of any other ilk.	Selecting foods and substances that go against your ethics will create negative reactions in any or all organ systems.
Tenth chakra Bone marrow	Favored foods and substances that are grown in or close to the ground, such as all forms of potatoes, nuts, lentils, and peas.	Foods or water affected by genetic modification, fertilizers, and other forms of pollution can cause negative reactions.
Eleventh chakra Connective tissue and muscles	In general, the healthiest foods are more alkaline than acidic or promote a correct balance in the body and empower your strength and agility.	Inflammatory foods indicate a potential issue against owning your personal power and could also keep you from doing so. Usually, these are foods that are white—white flour, sugar, dairy, and the like, and that are also genetically modified or chemically altered.
Twelfth chakra 32 secondary points, such as the liver	Your personal spirit will select the foods and substances best for you.	Your personal spirit will react against the nourishment that fails to support you.

First Steps for All of the Food Techniques

In order to improve your relationship with food, and in particular, more fully recover from trauma and address chronic illnesses, enter your healing haven and conduct Spirit-to-Spirit. Isolate the nourishment issue you'd like to focus on. Then employ the steps of any or all of the following techniques to assist yourself.

Food Technique 1: Healing the Traumatized Self

The following steps will help you heal a traumatized self impacted by food and substance issues. If you are afflicted with a chronic illness, it will help heal the original trauma catching you in a self-injurious loop. You'll then ask for healing streams to release you from second-ary forces.

1: Locate the Causal Chakra. Examining the food chart, track your issue to the chakra it best suits. For instance, if you're struggling with wheat cravings, pinpoint your second chakra. If you believe the foods you eat conflict with your value system, embrace your ninth chakra. If needed, employ your chakra symptoms chart from the personal assessment in chapter 4 or use technique 4, "Locating a Causal Chakra," to figure out the chakra to spotlight.

2: Find and Heal the Traumatized Self. There is a reason that the traumatized self reacts to specific substances. Using skills you've already acquired in previous chapters, relate to this traumatized self, who might be fully or partially enclosed in a shock bubble or already fairly freed up. You can always employ technique 5, "Tracking a Force's Pathway and the Traumatized Self," to find and begin healing this traumatized self, or technique 13, "The Five Stages to Healing a Traumatized Self."

Having located the causal chakra, you can also use technique 6, "Analyzing an External Chakra Wheel," to hone in on the issues related to the nourishment problem, and then ask for healing streams to emanate from the inner wheel, as technique 7, "Illuminating the Internal Chakric Wheel," demonstrates, to perform healing.

If you need further clues for figuring out the reasons a traumatized self began developing food or substance issues, I've provided them below. Read the paragraph pertaining to the age or time period at which the issue developed.

Childhood Issues. Many of our food and substance cravings and reactions stem from childhood wounds and programming. For instance, if your mother gave you muffins instead of hugs, you might have a missing force causing car-bohydrate cravings. If your mother hated making breakfast, you might feel sick when eating breakfast foods. Ask for healing streams to cleanse this program-ming, which will probably involve a psychological force, and eliminate any sub-tle programs you attach to these foods.

Past-Life Issues. Sometimes we react to certain foods in a negative way because of a past-life experience. For instance, our adrenals, which relate to the first chakra, might race because we ate a poisonous and deathly stew in a past life. If your traumatized self or external chakra wheel indicates your issues originated in a past life, ask yourself questions like these: What occurred to cause a harmful reaction? What emotions need to be owned so I don't trigger anymore? How can the Spirit help me heal this issue? Work with the related feelings and concepts as long as needed.

Epigenetic Triggering. Many times our nourishment issue originated in, or has been strengthened by, an ancestral trauma. For instance, if a set of ancestors became sick because all they could eat were moldy nuts during a drought, we might be sensitive to nuts. If your issue emanates from your ancestors, which would involve the tenth chakra, request that the Spirit send healing streams to the souls of all those involved in the challenge and also to you.

Food Technique 2: Assess the Nutrients

As examined in chapters 4 and 5, each of the seven basic nutrients serves us physically and subtly. If you know which type of nutrient is plaguing you, focus on it while using healing streams. If you're not sure, review your responses to the personal assessment in chapter 4. How did you respond to question 6, which asked how your body reacts to each nutrient?

You can also read through the following characterizations of the physical and subtle properties of each food and ask the Spirit to select one to focus on. Then conduct Spirit-to-Spirit and request information and also healing streams.

Carbohydrates: An unhealthy relationship with carbohydrates, which provide sugars for physical energy, can indicate safety and lovability issues. How does your current relationship with carbohydrates provide a false assurance of security and lovability? What might be a better way to meet these needs?

Fats: These calorie-rich acids can establish boundaries but also absorb shame. Is there a shame-related issue that inhibits a healthy relationship with fats? How does it play out? Are you willing to let healing streams release you from this issue and free you from shame (whether it's your own or another's)? If so, allow this clearing and establish more genuine boundaries, such as through technique 10, "Cleaning and Strengthening Your Auric Field."

Proteins: This strengthening nutrient stimulates negative reactions if we believe ourselves to be powerless. How did your traumatized self become convinced into believing yourself a victim? Embrace your rationales. Then take a bold step: support the powerless self in surrendering to the awareness of being powerless. At one level, we are powerless. The human state is one of interdependence with others and dependence upon the Spirit. As soon as we accept this reality, our traumatized self can stop protesting and simply merge with the Spirit. The truth is that the Spirit and its helpers will assist us when we're defenseless, thus enabling us to process protein in a healthy way.

Fiber: Our relationship with indigestible material can be faulty if our traumatized self struggles with letting go. Maybe we hang on to wastes or problems too long, scared of being left without. Maybe we release too soon, unsure about what would happen if we mine all the goodness out of life. Give permission for the traumatized self to release others' energies and clear and clean the related trauma pathway, along with any entrance and exit wounds. Let healing streams remove the energies that don't belong to you, and give permission to be ushered into the cycle of life and fully activate your ability to receive, reap, and let go. Every cell and aspect of self can now engage with this cycle.

Minerals: Are we failing to process a few—or many—inorganic but necessary elements? This issue often lies within the kidney meridian and can be cleared with technique 27, "Healing Your Meridians," which initiates healing through the Ming Men doorway. Once you've opened to the divine feminine and masculine, ask the Spirit to cleanse your physical and subtle bodies of all mineral-based issues, as well as any generative or degenerative forces that get misappropriated to specific minerals. Sense how the healing streams will assist you with metabolizing these crystal energies of the earth and cosmos.

Vitamins: Each of these water- or fat-soluble nutrients reflects a quality we need to accept, process, and use. Request that the Spirit determine how to best deliver a particular spiritual truth to a traumatized self to clear up the following types of issues:

- Vitamin A—willingness to see truth
- Vitamin Bs—support for passions and goals
- Vitamin C—allowance of meaningful connections and intimacy
- Vitamin D—entrance into the flow of life and love
- Vitamin E—willingness to let go of old and others' energies
- Vitamin K—acceptance of personal strength and control of negative thoughts and behaviors

Water: The molecules in this nutrient carrier and cleansing agent are shaped by beliefs. Are we willing to accept ourselves as pure, innocent, and loved? Let healing streams replace all lies with truths.

Food Technique 3: Neutralize Microchimeric Factors

I've discovered that microchimeric factors are frequently complicit in food and substance issues. Others' cells within our body—whether internalized when we were in utero, through blood transfusions, or even through sex—can dictate our reactions to specific substances. In other words, we might crave third chakra diet soda because someone else's cells carry that craving. As well, our cells, if still animate in another person's body, can pick up and transfer their substance issues into us. Perhaps our mom craves sugar, and whenever she's eating it, the subtle charges between our cells makes us do the same.

Look back at your personal assessment results from chapter 4. Did you identify microchimeric cells as perhaps contributing to your trauma or challenge at the cellular level? If so, ask for healing streams to neutralize the microchimeric cells or effects. If you're unsure whether microchimeric cells are involved, use your intuitive skills to let the Spirit show you.

Food Technique 4: Releasing Others' Energetic Constructs and Others' Energy

Are we *sure* that a substance issue is our own? That an aversion or craving started within ourselves? Often an issue clears up because we let go of the energies negatively impacting us. For instance, I had a client who constantly overate second chakra carbohydrates. He had a cord linking him with a dark entity through his fifth chakra. This entity was constantly whispering messages that made him feel unlovable and insecure, hence his craving for soft and loving foods. Once we released this cord, his cravings stopped. You can employ technique 8: "Releasing Others' Energies and Energetic Constructs," found in chapter 7, to address this causal issue.

Food Technique 5: Shift Degenerative and Generative Forces

Sometimes, we unconsciously put a force on a certain type of nourishment to boost or reduce its effects; other times, our family system, an ancestor, an entity, or some other being does this to our food.

How could this happen?

Imagine that your parents were consistently mean and critical. To compensate, you strove to eat more protein to empower yourself, to the point of unconsciously attaching a generative force to the proteins you consumed. But now you have a kidney disorder because you can't fully process proteins, even though now you only eat a nominal amount. In this case, the generative force is constantly super-powering your proteins, causing your kidneys (and immune system) to think that you're devouring more protein than you really are. Use technique 9, "Uncovering, Moving, and Adding Generative and Degenerative Forces," to alleviate this situation.

Technique 30
Healing a Missing Force for Allergies and Addictive Processes, Including Energetic Codependency

As discussed at several points in this book, chronic illnesses, as well as codependency, often result in allergies or addictive challenges. These issues all hold a common theme: the challenge of a missing force.

Missing forces are empty—meaning that an aspect of us knows we are supposed to receive an essential energy, such as love, care, proper nutrition, an education, or some other vital factor, but we don't receive it. Nature abhors a vacuum and can establish secondary forces to help us find something to fill in the missing force, even if that substance is unhealthy. Plus, when we're given a poor substitute, such as food instead of love or a fundamental value system instead of spiritual support, our physical and subtle systems will desire that substance, activity, or object and attack it at the same time. Sooner or later, the body will slip into a chronic self-injurious loop or illness, or an energetic codependency, and a secondary force will hold us in bondage to the negative substitute.

From an energetic perspective, it's imperative that we clear a missing force. We do this by figuring out what we should have been given and providing it in the form of a spiritual quality. We then cleanse ourselves of any inappropriate relationship, whether it involves subtle factors, physical factors, or both, and then, finally, heal ourselves of related secondary forces.

This technique draws from those you've already become acquainted with, such as techniques 4, 13, and 20, which respectively assist you with locating a causal chakra, healing a traumatized self, and recovering from a secondary force. I'll summarize these major processes so you can move through them quickly.

As a cautionary note, this technique will only address subtle issues; in no way is it to become a substitute for receiving professional assistance.

Getting Started

To figure out the purpose of—and the chakra affiliated with—an allergy or addictive process, you can examine the foods and substances listed in the chakra-based foods and substances chart from earlier in this chapter.

You can also use the following chart, which highlights the addictive behaviors or substances that can be chakra-related and also the need that a traumatized self is seeking to satisfy. Regarding the latter, the chart describes the metaphysical purpose for participating in the addictive process and also the fear that could be causing the addiction.

Both charts will help you logically pinpoint what issue you are facing and uncover a causal chakra. Remember, factors listed on both charts can also establish an allergic challenge.

Chakras and Their Related Addictions

CHAKRA	POSSIBLE ADDICTIONS	NEED BEING SOUGHT AND FEAR CAUSING THE ADDICTION
First	Hard drugs or opioids, work, sex, exercise, constant illness, spending and overspending, masochistic and sadistic behaviors, cutting, getting into accidents, hard alcohol such as vodka	To find an identity, fear of facing a primal trauma and subsequent unworthiness
Second	Grain-based alcohol, emotionalism, methamphetamines, opioids, codependency in general	To feel personal feelings, fear of one's own feelings
Third	Corn-based alcohol, work, carbonated beverages, caffeine, marijuana, corn-processed sugars, beer, perfectionism	To raise self-esteem, fear of personal power
Fourth	Sugar, wine, "love" (have to always be in relationship), smoking, Ecstasy, fake sugars (e.g., saccharin, aspartame)	To feel loveable, fear of intimacy
Fifth	Compulsive talking, overeating, reading, tobacco chewing	To express oneself, fear of being bold

CHAKRA	POSSIBLE ADDICTIONS	NEED BEING SOUGHT AND FEAR CAUSING THE ADDICTION
Sixth	Body-image issues (food-related and otherwise), fixation with appearance, obsessive-compulsive behaviors, chocolate, compulsions related to aging such as getting an unhealthy number of anti-aging injections or surgeries	To clarify a confused self-image, shame about genuine self
Seventh	"Uppers" and "downers," fanaticism, use of meditation or religion to avoid reality, self-shaming because of mental illnesses or learning issues	To have spiritual purpose, fear of being rejected by the Divine
Eighth	Any and all addictive substances, including tobacco, alcohol, sugar, and coffee	To discover or recover mystical powers, fear of mystical powers
Ninth	Poverty and scarcity, self-recrimination	To change the world, fear of being inadequate to do so
Tenth	Sacred plant medicines (Ayahuasca, magic mushrooms, marijuana), obsession with nature or natural beings	To achieve oneness with nature, judgment about what's not of nature
Eleventh	Power and leadership, bullying, negativity	To accept one's practical and magical powers, fear of committing evil
Twelfth	An addiction that is unique to you	To find one's uniqueness, fear of being different

Next Steps

1: Prepare. Settle into a quiet space or your healing haven. If you want, bring writing instruments.

2: Conduct Spirit-to-Spirit. Affirm your spirit and the Spirit. Request that the Spirit appoint imaginal helpers if they would be helpful in dismantling any negative attachments or assisting with the healing of any traumas or chronic illnesses or challenges, including food issues, allergies, addictions, and energetic codependent patterns.

3: Focus On the Issue. What issue are you facing? Review it and, if you want, write it down on your paper. Figure out which chakra that challenge relates to, either logically or by using technique 4. Then surrender to the issue—the reasons for it, the effects of it, the nature of the trauma, and any secondary forces that were established. When you feel fully aware of the traumatic and self-injurious aspects of the situation, surrender the entire set of circumstances and all facets of it to the Spirit.

4: Ask for Information. Request that you be intuitively shown any particulars you need to know to assist with your healing. Are there others' energies involved? Holds or attachments? Microchimeric cells? Is there any additional data needed?

5: Hone In. No matter what its appearance and symptoms, the situation most likely involves a missing force. Allow the Spirit to reveal to you the force or type of energy you missed that has resulted in the issues you're addressing. What was supposed to be provided you? What exactly was your actual need? Who or what should have met your need? What, if anything, was substituted for that required force? How have the circumstances around this issue resulted in your focus issue? Remain in this process as long as needed to gain a full awareness.

6: Request Healing Streams and the Missing Qualities. Ask that the Spirit provide you though healing streams of the qualities you've been missing. This spiritual energy will be sent into the "you" of the past, any aspect of you caught in a secondary force, and to all other people or energies involved in the stuck pattern. Know that all related negative parts of this situation are being healed and every aspect of you is being assisted. Be embraced by this love and sense the subsequent changes occurring on every level of your being.

7: Ask for Guidance. Request that the Spirit provide insight and advice as to where to go from here. Do you need therapy or further professional help? Is there a group to seek out or join? A special program to follow? A specific exercise to follow (for this, you can reference technique 32, "Get Moving—and Expressing!"). Know that the Spirit will continue to provide you with further assistance as time goes on.

8: Close with Gratitude. Feel gratitude for any and all traumatized or self-injurious aspects of the self that have been waiting to finally have their needs met. They always knew they deserved better; so do you. And then give forgiveness to yourself or all involved. If you need to, employ technique 28 to enable this forgiveness. When you're ready, breathe deeply and return to your life renewed.

Technique 31
Subtle Sexual Hormone Balancing

Hormones are a major part of our functioning, the sexual hormones especially. After exploring our issues, we must sometimes address and rebalance our sexual hormones. Energetically clearing the subtle energies impacting them can also assist us in becoming healthier and mitigate cravings and other challenges.

I encourage anyone experiencing sexual hormone issues to find a good holistic doctor who will run blood or saliva tests. That information can be brought into this technique. You can also examine for the subtle matters that might be involved in hormone imbalances.

1: Prepare. Settle into your healing haven and relax.

2: Conduct Spirit-to-Spirit. Affirm your own spirit, others' spirits, and the Spirit.

3: Assess and Address Your Testosterone. This male hormone, present in both men and women, encourages strength and empowerment. You might already know your testosterone level, but if you don't, ask the Spirit to assess your current production level. Is it energetically too high or too low? Is your body able to metabolize your testosterone or not?

Then request that the Spirit show you if there is an unconscious reason you are over- or under-empowered. Are you comfortable with being empowered? With being muscular? With keeping yourself safe? Did something occur with a man or male energy to cause you to mistrust your masculine traits, perhaps to the point of affecting your own testosterone production? Is there an outside person, energetic construct, or force underscoring this issue? Ask the Spirit to help you process all underlying issues and assist you with healing them. Streams of grace will initiate this healing.

4: Power Up Your Estrogen. Estrogen enables feminine power and protectiveness. What do you know about your current production levels? You can always ask the Spirit if it's too high or too low, or if you're able to access your estrogen or not.

If your relationship with your own feminine authority is off, request to know the reason. Did something happen to cause an issue or are you being influenced by energies that are not your own?

Remain in a contemplative space until you are clear, and then ask what might happen if you were to be brought into balance. What feminine characteristics might emerge or submerge? How might this shape your life and moods? Request healing streams to bring about change so you can awaken into your feminine powers.

5: Calm with Progesterone. Progesterone is the other face of estrogen. While estrogen encourages and emboldens, progesterone calms and soothes. It is the feminine energy of grace and ease coursing through your life. How would you characterize your relationship with the peaceful feminine aspects of yourself and the world? Do you overdo your need for ease or reject the serenity that is yours to embrace? Ask the Spirit to show you whatever issues might be impacting you and how you can work through them. Let the streams of grace do the rest.

6: Balance the Triad and More. Now request that the Spirit enable a loving and supportive relationship between all three sexual hormones, as well as any others necessary for bodily and spiritual communion. Every single chakra hormone gland will be assisted, as will the secondary endocrine glands in your system.

Then ask that the Spirit reveal what you might need to do physically to further and continually balance your hormones. Are there foods to eat or abstain from? Specific exercises to perform? Would it be helpful to work with an endocrinologist? Get a sense of your path forward.

7: Close. Thank the Spirit and your own body for enabling a balance in your sexual hormones. When you're ready, return to your world.

Technique 32
Get Moving—and Expressing!

Movement and expression are two sides of the same coin—both are ways to release ourselves from long-held trauma and start loving ourselves back from a chronic illness. The key with choosing what physical activity or form of self-expression will best support our healing is to select the activities and expressions that match the chakra most in need of restoration.

In general, movement encourages the reintroduction of our once-traumatized or self-injurious self back into our body. Creative expression releases our inhibitions and reveals ourselves to the external world, as well as the self. If you've already figured out the best chakra to focus on, conduct Spirit-to-Spirit and review the following chakra-based activities chart. If you have any doubt, use technique 4, "Locating a Causal Chakra." You can always select two chakras and mix and match activities or try styling your life to one chakra for a month and a new one the next month.

Chakra-Based Activities

CHAKRA	PHYSICAL ACTIVITIES	CREATIVE ACTIVITIES
First	Running, walking, lifting weights, dancing, sex, any aerobic activity, including skiing and biking	Building and constructing, watching sports, collecting objects, drumming, playing hard
Second	Swimming, yoga, tai chi, qigong, Pilates, water activities	Painting, drawing, cooking, decorating, any activity that involves the use of color, receiving or giving massages, acting and theater activities
Third	Exercise classes, anaerobic activities, tap and ballroom dancing, circuit training	Mental gymnastics, meditation, study-based travel trips, orienteering, inventing an idea or product
Fourth	Exercise programs with a partner, walking, hiking, kayaking, any heart-healthy (cardio) exercise	Participating in relationship support groups, cross-cultural trips, volunteering, writing, singing
Fifth	Walking, rowing, working out with a partner	Singing, listening to music, writing, taking philosophical classes or trips, journaling, acting, using mantras or chanting
Sixth	Walking in beautiful settings, yoga	Painting, drawing, visiting museums, decorating, clothes shopping, taking a clairvoyance class
Seventh	Moving while meditating, yoga, exercise in the sun	Prayer, attending worship classes or services, researching spirituality, teaching spirituality, coaching others about spiritual topics
Eighth	Working out long and short muscles (bulk and stretch), aerobic and anaerobic exercise	Studying or practicing mysticism, communing and intuitively talking with animals (including pets), analyzing dreams
Ninth	Yoga, martial arts, weight lifting, aerobics	Volunteering for a values-based organization, meditating, following a guru

CHAKRA	PHYSICAL ACTIVITIES	CREATIVE ACTIVITIES
Tenth	Exercising or moving outside, walking, hiking, taking adventure trips	Training pets, gardening, researching ancestry, landscape design, organic cooking, learning about herbs, crystals, and natural healing
Eleventh	Doing full-body exercises, martial arts, interacting with the environment	Inventing recipes, taking psychic development classes, volunteering for a leadership position
Twelfth	Select activities meaningful to you	Select expressions unique to you

• • • • •

Synopsis

In this chapter you learned how to support your body and make choices to support your ongoing recovery. First, you learned a method for inviting forgiveness, a key to releasing codependent bonds and bringing yourself into the present. You then acquired practices to effect change in other areas of your everyday life, such as diet and exercise. In short, your historical self has moved into the present, and you are ready to move into your future.

Conclusion

*I will not follow where the path may lead, but I will
go where there is no path, and I will leave a trail.*
—Muriel Strode, "Wind-Wafted Wild Flowers"

When you started this journey, you probably didn't know exactly where you'd end up. You knew, however, that you were ready to feel and live better.

Life is full of challenges, but some are more problematic than others. These are energetic challenges—those that can adversely impact us on both the physical and subtle levels. As you learned, especially hard struggles are delivered through forces, fields of energy that can transfer subtle energies into us and set off a long-term, disruptive stress cycle. Whether our most damaging events involved environmental, physical, psychological, modern, spiritual, or missing forces, the resulting strain went beyond the common in-the-moment stress response and led to at least one traumatic condition.

Trauma isn't a one-time phenomenon. Unless the event and our feelings about it are brought into the light of awareness and healed from the outside to the inside, the traumatized self remains stuck within us, caught within an energetic bubble of shock. If this self isn't freed, and if that trapped self isn't allowed to grieve and heal, chronic illnesses, including autoimmune disorders, can develop.

On the physical level, chronic illnesses develop when the body responds to the subtle energy of trauma in a self-injurious manner. On an energetic level, a secondary force develops around a self locked within a shock bubble, linking that self to an external object, behavior, entity, or even a source of nourishment. Unless that self and its unhealthy link are healed from the inside, we will remain stuck.

In this book you were taught and able to practice dozens of subtle healing techniques aimed at helping you to energetically recover and transform through any number of life's traumas, as well as the self-injurious patterns that can develop when the effects of trauma are left unattended.

And now you are here.

Here, at the junction of yesterday and tomorrow. Here, where you are empowered and loved, where there is one more challenge to receive: the challenge of dreaming.

What are you going to do—or further become—now that your traumatized selves are free from the energies of trauma, stress, and chronic illness or challenges? What are you able to do now that these challenges are no longer keeping your dreams from coming true?

The choices and the challenges are now yours.

APPENDIX

Four-Part Energy Healing of SARS-CoV-2

There are four basic steps to take when seeking to heal from SARS-CoV-2. You can conduct these steps if you are sick, have been stricken, or want to energetically keep yourself from catching the virus. You can also undergo them if you have caught the energy involved in the disease. For instance, you might experience symptoms when thinking of an ill friend or become anxious when grocery shopping. Maybe some of the fear is your own; perhaps some of it belongs to others. You can also employ these steps when working on a loved one or friend.

These four phases are sequenced to walk you through all factors involved in fending off or healing from COVID-19. You can also undertake any of these phases on an as-needed basis. Imagine that you are well and feel great but are going to visit a sick friend. Perhaps you only want to conduct phase 4 and establish protection for yourself. Likewise, maybe you have done a lot of self-healing work and only want to rescue another self who is stuck in a shock bubble; then focus on phase 3. Mix and match these phases as you see fit.

In a nutshell, you'll journey through these stages of healing:

Phase 1: Detaching Cords. All viruses connect to an external source of energy and direction through a cord. To work on the virus, you must first unhook it from its source.

Phase 2: Energetically Collapsing the SARS-CoV-2 Virus and Any Coinfections. This precise energetic technique involves disempowering the virus energetically and doing the same for any coinfections.

Phase 3: Clearing the Forces and Freeing a Stuck Self. Once we collapse the virus and its coinfections energetically, we must recover from all forces involved in a primary and secondary injury. This activity includes finding the forces, cleaning out all negative subtle energies delivered on them, and freeing and healing any aspect of us stuck in a shock bubble.

Phase 4: Energetic Protection for SARS-CoV-2 and Its Effects. Let's make sure our energetic field keeps us safe and secure. Of course, we also want it programmed to flow with our original energetic signature. You'll accomplish these goals in this phase.

Now you're ready to progress through the energy healing.

Phase 1: Detaching Cords

As you know, all viruses link to an external source. They most frequently do this via a cord. It will be far easier to energetically heal from SARS-CoV-2, and keep yourself safe from it and the side effects, if you disconnect from that outside source.

Most frequently I perceive the cord to link with some aspect of the family system. Often the cord attaches to a familial or ancestral miasm in the tenth auric field. If a cord is present in this auric field, it is also operational in our epigenetic material. The programming of that chemical soup is anchored in our tenth chakra, the bone marrow, and the actual epigenome around our genes. If a strong familial cord is present, I believe we can actually catch the virus, or even the symptoms of it, through the epigenome. After all, the originating corona-virus has been around for thousands of years. What if one of our ancestors was stricken with it and also reacted emotionally to it?

Another common source for the cord is to a loved one. We might unconsciously think "I'd rather get sick than them." *Voilà*—we might get sick and they don't. We might even display symptoms for a sick person because we're internally saying "I'll take on some of their challenges so they will survive." I also believe there are many dark forces instigating the presence of this virus. They want to instill terror and fear, racism and judgment, death and destruction. I've worked with many clients whose major attachment is to this type of dark force.

Although you might think you must have the virus to detach a cord, that is not true. You can also erase cords that could attract the SARS-CoV-2 to you! Therefore, this exercise is designed to help you release cords linking you to an "alive" virus or to a potential infection.

1: Activate Spirit-to-Spirit. Feel into your own spirit, the helping spirits, and the Spirit. Acknowledged also are spirits involved in any SARS-CoV-2 associations or relationships. This includes those you are, have been, or could be involved in.

2: Focus on the Viral Cord. Through your intuition, the Spirit or a guide will assist you in honing into a SARS-CoV-2 cord or set of cords. If the virus currently dwells within your body or has already affected you physically, this cord will emanate from some aspect of your body. Psychically it will appear as solid as a garden hose, and it will feel substantial. It will also emit a strong but buzzy sound. If you are only taking on viral issues to help others or you might get the virus in the future, the cord will appear thin and faint, almost ghostly. It will feel vaporous and give off only a slight sound. You can always ask a guide to tell you what type of cord you might be dealing with (present or potential).

3: Ask for Streams to Clean the Cord. Upon your request, streams of grace are now formed by the Spirit. Watch and feel these streams flow through and around the cord, and also any tributaries. Sites reached will include the external force (such as a miasm, entity, or the like) and any internal connections within or outside of you. All involved will be offered grace and healing.

4: Fill In with Grace. The same or different healing streams will make all necessary energetic repairs inside and outside of you, forming protection as needed. If there is a learning you need to acquire about the presence of the cord, ask the Spirit to tell you what it is or provide insight over the next few days.

5: Gratitude. Feel grateful for this opportunity to assist yourself and any loved ones. Close and return to your world.

Phase 2: Energetically Collapsing the
SARS-CoV-2 Virus and Any Coinfections

The goal of this stage is to energetically collapse the RNA strand inside the viral containment. Once you do this to a single virus, we'll then use healing streams to transfer that destruction to the other viruses. We then ask for similar alterations to be carried out on any coinfections. You can conduct this exercise for yourself even if you haven't contracted the virus. It will help you teach your immune system how to perform this activity should you ever come in contact with the virus.

The basis of this activity lies in understanding the mechanics of this particular virus. As covered in chapter 1, the virus is composed of a positive single strand of RNA, which is bunched within a layer of fat and glycoproteins. The latter looks like spikes, and it is through these spikes that the virus can bind to an enzyme on certain bodily cells. The power of the virus lies in the RNA. Destroy or shatter the RNA and the virus is disempowered.

In this exercise you'll be shown how to perform such a maneuver energetically. Basically, you'll be directed to find an energetic "back door" into one of the viruses in order to safely undergo this activity. We'll then ask for equivalent changes for the coinfections.

1: Perform Spirit-to-Spirit. Affirm your spirit, the helping spirits, and the Spirit, then breathe deeply.

2: Ask to Perceive the SARS-CoV-2 Virus. Whether the virus is already inside of you, is potentially going to impact you, or is found in someone else, ask for healing streams to completely protect you and your cells from it. Then ask to perceive it. You'll see, sense, or be informed by your guides about its structure. It will look like a spiked ball that contains a single strand of RNA, which is helical in shape. Now notice that it *seems* big and scary, like the face in *The Wizard of Oz*. You can feel it warning you to back off.

3: Shift to the Back Side. We don't deal with the virus's scary face. Rather, we ask the Spirit or our guides to bring us to its back side. There you'll spot a thin and flimsy covering, rather like the curtain hiding the tinker in *The Wizard of Oz*. This is the weak spot of the virus. It barely hides an energetic tunnel that leads directly to the RNA.

4: Ask for the Spirit to Pierce the RNA. Let the Spirit swish away the curtain and send healing streams through the unprotected tunnel to pierce the viral RNA. The streams will dismantle the RNA and disintegrate the leftovers so they have no power. The other viruses are then collapsed by additional healing streams. In the meantime, the Spirit fills you with your own personal streams, thereby reducing your vulnerability to SARS-CoV-2.

5: Dismantle the Coinfections. The Spirit now carries healing streams to any co-infections. While the streams collapse the remainder of the SARS viruses, it does the same to other microbes.

6: Ask for an Immune Boost. It's also smart to request immune-boosting spiritual qualities and energies. This will make it easier for the body to continue to cleanse and renew your system.

7: Close. When you feel complete, thank the Spirit for the assistance and ask that the work keeps occurring. Return to your life.

You can repeat this exercise if you feel it's necessary.

Phase 3: Clearing the Forces and Freeing a Stuck Self

As covered in chapter 1, SARS-CoV-2 can inflict damage through many different forces. As a coronavirus, it is always delivered through a natural environmental force. If it was developed in a laboratory, it can also be considered subject to a human-made environmental force. Even if you don't agree with this suggestion, the virus at large is mutable because of its interactions with human beings, which infers a secondary human-made environmental force. As this phase of healing will show you, other forces can also become involved. You'll be given the opportunity to address them, if need be. Just follow these steps:

1: Conduct Spirit-to-Spirit. Call upon your spirit, the helping spirits, and the Spirit.

2: Scan for the Entry Sites of Forces. Using your intuitive abilities and contacts available through the imaginal realms, scan for forces. I'll name the possible point of entries for each type of force. I'll also give you a few prompts in the section about natural environmental forces for what you might find or feel. Use these same promptings to scan for other forces. Know that you might or might not find any force beyond the natural environmental force.

Your main choices are as follows:

- *Natural Environmental Forces: Tenth Chakra/Field.* SARS-CoV-2 always enters as a natural environmental force. If you're psychically visual, you'll perceive a dark hole that was an entry point in the tenth chakra or somewhere in the tenth auric field. The place of viral piercing in the tenth field will also show you exactly where the virus (or the energy of the virus) entered your system. For instance, if you have actually contracted the virus, you'll find a black or brown stain near your mouth or nose (fifth chakra/field) or over and in the lungs (where the virus landed in the fourth chakra/field). Be observant. Perhaps you brought the virus in through your hands, such as if you touched something (eleventh chakra/field). If you've only been impacted by the idea of the virus or the aftermath of it in your life, you will still assess

283

the tenth chakra/field and also try to discover how the energy entered, such as through your brain (seventh chakra/field) or a global concern (ninth chakra/field) or the news media and a digital force (third or sixth chakra/field). If you are more kinesthetic, simply let your body help you feel the entry point. If you are verbally intuitive, ask that the Spirit, a guiding spirit, or your spirit alert you as to the entrance site/s.

- *Human-Made Environmental Forces: Tenth Chakra/Field.* Undergo the same scanning process as you did above.

- *Physical Forces: First Chakra/Field.* Perhaps you picked up the virus through touch. In this case, you'll notice a physical force wounding. Damage will also incur in your first chakra/field. In real life, this injury might show up as the viral illness, difficulty in recovering, or survival challenges, such as financial issues. If these issues followed a viral exposure or exist because of the pandemic, the physical force might be a secondary injury.

- *Emotional Forces: Second or Third Chakras/Fields.* Whether you have suffered from the virus or not, the fact of having been affected by it can produce a secondary emotional force. These will damage the feelings of your second chakra/field and your thinking processes as reflected in your third chakra/field. (You might also incur energetic depression or anxiety, for which I recommend you conduct technique 19.)

- *Spiritual Forces: Seventh or Ninth Chakras/Fields.* The pandemic has caused many to question the presence of the Spirit or the role of negative energies in its spread. You can look for secondary forces that have created chaos or confusion for you in the named chakras/fields.

3: Track the Forces and the Incoming or Leftover Harmful Subtle Energies. Intuitively follow the path of each force that has impacted you. As you have been taught to do, start at the entrance site, search for a possible exit site, and flow along the pathway. The force might also have become stuck somewhere in the physical or subtle anatomy. You especially want to focus on the negative subtle energies.

4: Analyze the Negative Subtle Energies. Which of the force pathways contains the most disturbing and potent subtle energies? You can ask this question about all the force pathways, but it's most vital to understand those that have affected you the most. Ask for guidance to determine the nature of these problematic energies, their influence and impact, and how to best understand them.

5: Check for a Shock Bubble. Especially as related to the strongest negative energies, check to determine if there is a part of you stuck in a shock bubble. Is that aspect of you alone in there or did you bring in subtle energies or aspects of another being's reality? Send love to any part of you that is stuck—and to the energies of the "other," too!

6: Ask for Universal Streams of Grace. It's now time to ask for help. Allow the Spirit, your helpers, and your own spirit to beam healing streams through all force pathways, cleansing you of negative subtle energies. These or different streams will softly surround any stuck part of you to create a better energetic protection than the shock bubble. These streams (or the beings connected to them) will help that stuck self process what you've gone through. They'll also return others' energies to them. Give permission for this process to take as long as needed.

7: Request Personal Streams of Grace. Finally, let the Spirit engage personal streams of grace throughout the entirety of your system, bringing it from the heavenly realms downward into your sushumna, or spinal nadi. This stream will continue to disintegrate any energies that don't match your original signature and restore you physically, psychologically, and spiritually.

Phase 4: Energetic Protection for SARS-CoV-2 and Its Effects

Many of the challenges of SARS-CoV-2 demand that we establish a new layer of protection around ourselves. There is a beautiful and easy way to do this. It will involve streaming grace via our chakras' inner wheels and asking that these streams form crystalline points of light within our energy field.

Why should the streams create crystals? Scientists are making fascinating discoveries about crystals. For quite some time, researchers have known that the molecular structures of crystals are spatially symmetric. Because of this, crystals can be used to insulate (think "protect") and act like conductors of energy. But now scientists are starting to believe that they can create "time crystals," or crystals that interact with the fourth dimension through their molecular structure and their quanta. Space crystals show us how a system behaves in a certain space at a given time, but time crystals show how a system can act in the flow of time when it's in a certain spatial area.[96]

Why am I going on about something so hard to understand? Because, as energy workers, we can request that streams of grace formulate tiny subtle crystals in our field that can activate in both space and time. They can go off whenever we are in a certain space—say, for instance, in the presence of SARS-CoV-2, or when around someone with fear about the virus. But these energetic crystals can also be programmed to go off at certain times. How would the latter look? Let's say we want our energy field swept of the energetics of the virus, others' fears, and our own issues every hour on the hour.

It's actually really simple to put this concept to work. Simply follow these steps:

1: Conduct Spirit-to-Spirit. Acknowledge your own vital spirit that dwells most brightly within the inside wheels of your chakras. Affirm the presence of guardian spirits that seek to assist you, then affirm the indwelling presence of the Spirit.

2: Focus on the Inner Wheel of Your Heart Chakra. This is the area in which your spirit and the Spirit dwell most powerfully. Ask that universal and personal healing streams of grace be formulated for your highest protection in regard to the virus and all considerations involved with it. Know too that in here lies the codes of your original energetic signature.

3: Allow Distribution of the Streams. You'll now watch as these streams emanate from the center of the heart chakra, carrying grace but also the energy of your original signature to the outside of that chakra. Simultaneously the same event occurs for all your chakras. Finally, these streams move throughout the remainder of your subtle and physical self before they flow right into your energetic field, the auric fields in particular.

4: Ask for the Formation of Crystals. Request that the streams manufacture tiny subtle energetic crystals within all layers of your energetic fields. Each will be programmed to do what is needed to keep you safe on a spatial level, such as if you are around the virus or the effects of the virus. For instance, they might zap the virus or allow your system to send compassion to a person struggling with pandemic-related problems. If you are sensitive to EMF or other digital issues, these crystals will bounce off any unhealthy human-made

---

96 Hannaford and Sacha, "Time Crystals Enter the Real World of Condensed Matter."

energies and only allow in what supports your true being. These crystals are also automatically programmed to follow a timely schedule of cleansing and renewing your field.

5: Let the Energies Settle. Take a few deep breaths and allow this change to settle into your physical and subtle self. Thank the Spirit for this alteration and continue with your day.

You can conduct this protection exercise any time you think you should renew your field. For instance, imagine that you are feeling an effect from the SARS-CoV-2 virus years later, or it has mutated, or another virus is creating a pandemic or endemic. Simply renew this boundary with the fresh desire in mind.

Bibliography

Aguilera, Greti. "HPA Axis Responsiveness to Stress: Implications for Healthy Aging." *Experimental Gerontology* 46, no. 2–3 (February 1, 2012): 90–95. www.ncbi.nlm.nih.gov/pmc/articles/PMC3026863/.

American Academy of Pediatrics. "Electromagnetic Fields: A Hazard to Your Health?" Accessed September 5, 2019. www.healthychildren.org/English /safety-prevention/all-around/Pages/Electromagnetic-Fields-A-Hazard-to-Your -Health.aspx.

American Cancer Society. "Infectious Agents and Cancer." Accessed July 31, 2019. www.cancer.org/cancer/cancer-causes/infectious-agents.html.

American Psychological Association (APA). "Stress Effects on the Body." Psychology Help Center. Accessed September 5, 2019. www.apa.org/helpcenter /stress-body.aspx.

Anxiety and Depression Association of America (ADAA). "Symptoms of PTSD." Fact sheet. Accessed September 5, 2019. www.adaa.org/understanding-anxiety /posttraumatic-stress-disorder-ptsd/symptoms.

Azab, Marwa. "The Brain on Fire: Depression and Inflammation." *Psychology Today*. October 29, 2018. www.psychologytoday.com/us/blog/neuroscience-in-everyday -life/201810/the-brain-fire-depression-and-inflammation.

Badenoch, Bonnie. *The Heart of Trauma*. New York: W. W. Norton & Norton, 2018.

Baerbel, ed. and trans. "Russian DNA Discoveries." June 17, 2013. www .abundanthope.net/pages/Environment_Science_69/Russian-DNA -Discoveries-Explain-Human-Paranormal-Events_printer.shtml.

Bair, Puran. "Visible Light Radiated from the Heart with Heart Rhythm Mediation." *Subtle Energies & Energy Medicine Journal* 16, no. 3 (2005): 211–217. http://journals.sfu.ca/seemj/index.php/seemj/article/viewFile/56/44.

Barnes, John F. "What Is Fascia?" Myofascial Release Treatment Centers and Seminars. Accessed September 5, 2019. www.myofascialrelease.com/about/fascia -definition.aspx.

Bender, James. "What Are the Differences Between PTS and PTSD?" Updated July 25, 2019. www.brainline.org/article/what-are-differences-between-pts-and-ptsd.

Beyond Blue Support Service. "What Is Grief?" Accessed September 5, 2019. www.beyondblue.org.au/the-facts/suicide-prevention/understanding -suicide-and-grief/suicide-and-grief/what-is-grief-.

Blaser, Martin J. "Understanding Microbe-Induced Cancers." June 2008. www. cancerpreventionresearch.aacrjournals.org/content/1/1/15.

Bonaz, Brono, Thomas Bazin, and Sonia Pellissier. "The Vagus Nerve at the Interface of the Microbiota-Gut-Brain Axis." *Frontiers in Neuroscience.* Accessed August 13, 2019. www.ncbi.nlm.nih.gov/pmc/articles/PMC5808284/.

Bowen, Richard A. "The Enteric Nervous System" in *Pathophysiology of the Digestive System: Digestive System Function.* Colorado State University Hypertexts for Biomedical Sciences. Accessed September 5, 2019. www.vivo.colostate.edu /hbooks/pathphys/digestion/basics/gi_nervous.html.

Breit, Sigrid, et al. "Vagus Nerve as Modulator of the Brain-Cut Axis in Psychiatric and Inflammatory Disorders." *Front Psychiatry* 9, no. 44 (May 13, 2018). www.ncbi.nlm.nih.gov/pmc/articles/PMC5859128/.

California Department of Public Health. "CDPH Issues Guidelines on How to Reduce Exposure to Radio Frequency Energy from Cell Phones." Office of Public Affairs. Updated December 22, 2017. www.cdph.ca.gov/Programs/OPA/Pages /NR17-086.aspx.

Cedars-Sinai. "Connective Tissue Disorders." Conditions and Treatments. Accessed September 5, 2019. www. cedars-sinai.edu/Patients/Health-Conditions /Connective-Tissue-Disorders.aspx.

Centers for Disease Control and Prevention (CDC). "Chronic Disease in America." CDC's National Center for Chronic Disease Prevention and Health Promotion (NCCDPHP). Updated April 15, 2019. www.cdc.gov/chronicdisease/resources /infographic/chronic-diseases.htm.

Cincinnati Children's Hospital Medical Center. "Epstein-Barr Virus Linked to Seven Serious Diseases." April 16, 2018. www.medicalxpress.com /news/2018-04-epstein-barr-virus-linked-diseases.html.

Columbia University Medical Center. "Parkinson's Is Partly an Autoimmune Disease, Study Finds: First Direct Evidence That Abnormal Protein in Parkinson's Disease Triggers Immune Response." June 21, 2017. www.cuimc.columbia .edu/news/parkinsons-partly-autoimmune-disease-study-finds.

Crime Victims Center, Inc. "Statistics: Child Sexual Abuse." Accessed July 28, 2019. www.parentsformeganslaw.org/statistics-child-sexual-abuse/.

Crosbie, Rita, and Phil Crosbie. "The Role of Quantum Physics: The Body and the 'Field.'" Accessed September 5, 2019. www.soundbeings.com/?page_id=910.

Davis, Devra. "The FCC Needs to Update Its Cellphone Tests for Radiofrequency Radiation." Commentary originally posted by the *Chicago Tribune*. Environmental Health Trust. August 26, 2019. www.ehtrust.org/scientific -research-on-5g-and-health/,ehtrust.org/wp-content/uploads/5g-emf-hazards -dr-martin-l.-pall-eu-emf2018-6-11us3.pdf.

Dittfeld, Anna, et al. "A Possible Link Between the Epstein-Barr Virus Infection and Autoimmune Thyroid Disorders." *Central European Journal of Immunology* 41, no. 3 (October 25, 2016). www.ncbi.nlm.nih.gov/pmc/articles/PMC5099387/.

Eustice, Carol. "Cytokines and How They Work." November 30, 2018. www.verywellhealth.com/what-are-cytokines-189894.

Ferguson, Richard. *A Real-Life Christian Spiritual Journey*. Bloomington, IN: iUniverse, 2011.

Fisher, Tim. "5G Spectrum and Frequencies: Everything You Need to Know." Updated July 1, 2019. www.lifewire.com/5g-spectrum-frequencies-4579825.

———. "How are 4G and 5G Different?" Updated September 3, 2019. www. lifewire.com/5g-vs-4g-4156322.

Fortson, Leigh. "Bruce Lipton, PhD—Epigenetics" in *Embrace, Release, Heal: An Empowering Guide to Talking About, Thinking About, and Treating Cancer*. Boulder, CO: Sounds True, 2011. Accessed September 5, 2019. www.brucelipton.com/resource/article/epigenetics.

Fraser, Jack. "How the Human Body Creates Electromagnetic Fields." November 3, 2017. www.forbes.com/sites/quora/2017/11/03/how-the-human-body-creates-electromagnetic-fields/#6783d42a56ea.

Fraser, Peter H., and Harry Massey. *Decoding the Human Body-Field: The New Science of Information as Medicine*. New York: Simon and Schuster, 2008.

Friedland-Kays, Eric, and Deb Dana. "Being Polyvagal: The Polyvagal Theory Explained." Windhorse Integrative Mental Health. December 8, 2017. Accessed September 5, 2019. www.windhorseimh.org/mental-health-education/polyvagal-theory-explained/.

GreenMedInfo Research Group. "Epigenetic Memories Are Passed Down 14 Successive Generations." October 13, 2018. www.greenmedinfo.com/blog/epigenetic-memories-are-passed-down-14-successive-generations-game-changing-resea.

Hadhazy, Adam. "Think Twice: How the Gut's 'Second Brain' Influences Mood and Well-Being." February 12, 2010. Accessed August 13, 2019. www.scientificamerican.com/article/gut-second-brain/.

Hannaford, Peter, and Krzysztof Sacha. "Time Crystals Enter the Real World of Condensed Matter." March 17, 2020. https://physicsworld.com/a/time-crystals-enter-the-real-world-of-condensed-matter/.

HeartMath Institute. "The Making of Emotions." May 30, 2015. Accessed September 5, 2019. www.heartmath.org/articles-of-the-heart/science-of-the-heart/making-emotions/.

Hurley, Dan. "Grandma's Experiences Leave a Mark on Your Genes." *Discover*. June 25, 2015. Accessed August 24, 2019. https://www.discovermagazine.com/health/grandmas-experiences-leave-a-mark-on-your-genes.

Iliades, Chris. "How Stress Affects Digestion." Everyday Health. Last updated October 16, 2018. www.everydayhealth.com/wellness/united-states-of-stress/how-stress-affects-digestion/.

Krans, Brian. "6 Surprising Facts About the Microbes Living in Your Gut." September 7, 2013. www.healthline.com/health-news/strange-six -things-you-didnt-know-about-your-gut-microbes-090713#1.

Kshatri, Jay. "Sound Healing: More Than Just a Good Vibration." July 5, 2015. www .thinksmarterworld.com/sound-healing-more-than-just-a-good-vibration/.

Kübler-Ross MD, Elisabeth, and David Kessler. *On Grief and Grieving: Finding the Meaning of Grief Through the Five Stages of Loss*. Reprint edition. New York: Scribner, 2014.

Kurtzman, Laura. "Scientists Discover Autoimmune Disease Associated with Testicular Cancer: Technology That Uncovered Antibody Has Potential to Identify Other Autoimmune Diseases." University of California San Francisco. July 5, 3019. www.ucsf.edu/news/2019/07/414876/scientists -discover-autoimmune-disease-associated-testicular-cancer.

Kwon, Diana. "Does Parkinson's Begin in the Gut?" May 8, 2018. www .scientificamerican.com/article/does-parkinsons-begin-in-the-gut/.

Lehrer, P. "Anger, Stress, Dysregulation Produces Wear and Tear on the Lung." *Thorax* 61, no. 10 (October 2006): 833–834. www.thorax.bmj.com /content/61/10/833.

Levine, Beth. "Stress-Related Disorders Linked to Autoimmune Diseases, Study Finds." June 19, 2018. www.everydayhealth.com/rheumatoid-arthritis/stress -related-ders-linked-autoimmune-diseases-study-finds/.

Linsteadt, Stephen. "Scalar Waves and the Human Mobius Coil System." Excerpts from *The Heart of Health: The Principles of Physical Health and Vitality*. Accessed September 5, 2019. www.scalarheartconnection.com/articles/scalar-waves-and -the-human-mobius-coil-system-1018/.

MacLean, Paul D. *The Triune Brain in Evolution: Role in Paleocerebral Functions*. New York: Springer, 1990.

Makin, Simon. "New Evidence Points to Personal Brain Signatures." April 13, 2016. www.scientificamerican.com/section/news/new-evidence -points-to-personal-brain-signatures1/.

Matone, Robert. "Scientists Discover Children's Cells Living in Mothers' Brains." December 4, 2012. www.scientificamerican.com/article/scientists-discover -childrens-cells-living-in-mothers-brain/.

McCraty, Rollin. "Energetic Communication." Chapter 6 in *Science of the Heart: Exploring the Role of the Heart in Human Performance*. Vol. 2. Boulder Creek, CA: HeartMath, 2015. www.heartmath.org/research/science-of-the-heart /energetic-communication/.

———. "Resilience, Stress & Emotions." Chapter 2 in *Science of the Heart: Exploring the Role of the Heart in Human Performance*. Vol. 2. Boulder Creek, CA: HeartMath, 2015. www.heartmath.org/research/science-of-the-heart /resilience-stress-and-emotions/.

McLeod, Saul. "Stress, Illness and the Immune System." Simply Psychology. Last updated 2010. www.simplypsychology.org/stress-immune.html.

Mercola, Joseph. "Your Body Literally Glows with Light." August 15, 2009. www. articles.mercola.com/sites/articles/archive/2009/08/15/your-body-literally -glows-with-light.aspx.

Merriam-Webster Dictionary. "Electromagnetic Wave." Accessed August 20, 2019. www.merriam-webster.com/dictionary/electromagnetic%20wave.

Merrick, Melissa T., Derek C. Ford, and Katie A. Ports. "Prevalence of Adverse Childhood Experiences from the 2011–2014 Behavioral Risk Factor Surveillance System in 23 States." *JAMA Pediatrics* 2018; 172 (11): 1038–1044. www .jamanetwork.com/journals/jamapediatrics/article-abstract/2702204.

Moskowitz, Joel M. "5G Wireless Technology: Millimeter Wave Health Effects." Electromagnetic Radiation Safety. Updated February 22, 2019. www.saferemr .com/2017/08/5g-wireless-technology-millimeter-wave.html.

———, et al. "What You Need To Know About 5G Wireless and 'Small' Cells." 2017 PDF. Environmental Health Trust. www.ehtrust.org/wp-content /uploads/5G_What-You-Need-to-Know.pdf.

Muehsam, David. "The Energy That Heals Part II: Biophoton Emissions and the Body of Light." April 22, 2018. www.chi.is/energy-heals-part-ii -biophoton-emissions-body-light/.

Myers, Amy. "9 Signs You Have Leaky Gut." February 9, 2019. www.amymyersmd
.com/2019/02/9-signs-you-have-leaky-gut/.

National Cancer Institute, "Cell Phones and Cancer Risk." Cell Phones Fact sheet.
Updated January 9, 2019. www.cancer.gov/about-cancer/causes-prevention/risk
/radiation/cell-phones-fact-sheet.

National Cancer Institute. "Electromagnetic Fields and Cancer." Updated January 3,
2019. www. cancer.gov/about-cancer/causes-prevention/risk/radiation
/electromagnetic-fields-fact-sheet.

National Institute of Environmental Health Sciences. "Autoimmune Disease."
Updated July 31, 2019. www.niehs.nih.gov/health/topics/conditions
/autoimmune/index.cfm.

National Institute of Mental Health. "Post-Traumatic Stress Disorder." Updated May
2019. www.nimh.nih.gov/health/topics/post-traumatic-stress-disorder-ptsd
/index.shtml.

Neeld, Elizabeth Harper. "The Physical Stress of Grieving." Accessed September 5,
2019. http://connect.legacy.com/inspire/physical-stress-of-grieving.

Oaklander, Mandy. "New Hope for Depression." *Time*. July 27, 2017. Accessed
September 5, 2019. http://time.com/4876098/new-hope-for-depression/.

Office of National Statistics. "People Who Were Abused as Children Are
More Likely to Be Abused As an Adult: Exploring the Impact of What
Can Sometimes Be Hidden Crimes." Updated September 27, 2017. www.
ons.gov.uk/peoplepopulationandcommunity/crimeandjustice/articles/
peoplewhowereabusedaschildrenaremorelikelytobeabusedasanadult/2017-09-27.

Ogloff, James, Margaret Cutajar, Emily Mann, and Paul Mullen. "Child Sexual
Abuse and Subsequent Offending and Victimization: A 45-Year Follow-Up
Study." *Trends & Issues in Crime and Criminal Justice*, no. 440 (June 22, 2012).
Accessed July 28, 2019. Canberra: Australian Institute of Criminology. www.aic
.gov.au/publications/tandi/tandi440.

Paul, Marla. "How Traumatic Memories Hide in the Brain, and How to Retrieve
Them." *Northwestern Medicine*. August 17, 2015. www.news.feinberg
.northwestern.edu/2015/08/how-traumatic-memories-hide-in-the-brain/.

Porges, Stephen W. *The Polyvagal Theory*. New York: W. W. Norton & Company, 2011.

Radiation Safety Institute of Canada. "Cell Phones and Radiation: What You Should Know." Accessed September 5, 2019. www.radiationsafety.ca/wp-content /uploads/2009/05/cellphones_emf_factsheet.pdf.

Rajiv. "Is 5G Technology and Millimeter Waves Safe?" November 24, 2018. www .rfpage.com/is-5g-technology-and-millimeter-waves-safe/.

Reshkova, V., et al. "Evaluation of Antiviral Antibodies Against Epstein-Barr Virus and Neurotransmitters in Patients with Fibromyalgia." *Journal of Neurology and Neuroscience* 6, no. 3 (November 14, 2015). www.jneuro.com/neurology -neuroscience/evaluation-of-antiviral-antibodies-against-epsteinbarr-virus -and-neurotransmitters-in-patients-with-fibromyalgia.php?aid=7360.

Ropp, Thomas. "12 Ways to Unlock the Powers of the Vagus Nerve." Accessed September 5, 2019. www.upliftconnect.com/12-ways-unlock-powers-vagus-nerve/.

Rosenberg, Stanley. *Accessing the Healing Power of the Vagus Nerve*. Berkeley, CA: North Atlantic Books, 2017.

Shute, Nancy. "Beyond Birth." *Scientific American*. April 30, 2010. www .scientificamerican.com/article/fetal-cells-microchimerism/.

Smith, LeCain W. *Our Inner Ocean: A World of Healing Modalities*. Bloomington, IN: Balboa Press, 2014.

Song, Huan, Fang Gang, and Gunnar Tomasson, et al. "Association of Stress-Related Disorders with Subsequent Autoimmune Disease." *JAMA* 319, no. 23 (June 19, 2018): 2388–2400.

Stratton, Charles W. "Association of *Chlamydia pneumoniae* with Chronic Human Diseases." *Antimicrobics and Infectious Diseases Newsletter* 18, no. 7 (July 2000). www.pdfs.semanticscholar.org/e049/1a9cce6bea12d351156e30acd743a0f04f01 .pdf.

———. "*Chlamydophila pneumoniae*, A Pathogen Causing More Than Pneumonia." In *Reference Module in Biomedical Sciences: Encyclopedia of Microbiology* (4th Edition). Elsevier. January 2018.

Sukakov, K. V. "Connective Tissue Under Emotional Stress." *Aviakosm Ekolog Med* 34, no. 3 (2000): 27–33. Accessed September 5, 2019. www.ncbi.nlm.nih.gov /pubmed/10948405.

Tarasuik, Joanne C., Con K. K. Stough, and Joseph Ciorciari. "Understanding the Neurobiology of Emotional Intelligence: A Review." In *Assessing Emotional Intelligence: Theory, Research, and Applications*, 307–320. Springer, April 2009. www.researchgate.net/publication/225310877_Understanding_the_ Neurobiology_of_Emotional_Intelligence_A_Review.

Tiller, William A. "What Are Subtle Energies?" *Journal of Scientific Exploration* 7, no. 3 (1993): 293–304. www.pdfs.semanticscholar.org /c82e/35d051ca75a2327af27975d216f498ff05b9.pdf.

Uliczka, Frank, et al. "Unique Cell Adhesion and Invasion Properties of Yersinia enterocolitica 0:3." *National Institute of Allergy and Infectious Diseases*. July 7, 2011. www.journals.plos.org/plospathogens/article?id=10.1371/journal .ppat.1002117.

van der Kolk, Bessel. *The Body Keeps the Score*. New York: Penguin Books, 2014.

Walia, Arjun. "Precognition: Science Shows How Our Body Reacts to Events Up to 10 Seconds Before They Happen." November 28, 2014. www.collective-evolution .com/2014/11/28/precognition-science-shows-how-our-body-reacts-to-events -up-to-10-seconds-before-they-happen/.

Walker, Peter. "Codependency, Trauma and the Fawn Response." *The East Bay Therapist* (Jan/Feb 2003). www.pete-walker.com/codependencyFawnResponse .htm.

Weinhold, Bob. "Epigenetics: The Science of Change." *Environmental Health Perspectives* 114, no. 3 (March 2006): A160–167. www.ncbi.nlm.nih.gov/pmc /articles/PMC1392256/.

Wonderopolis. "Why Does Everyone Have a Unique Voice?" Accessed September 5, 2019. www.wonderopolis.org/wonder/why-does-everyone-have-a-unique-voice.

World Health Organization. "Depression." Updated March 22, 2018. www.who.int /en/news-room/fact-sheets/detail/depression.

———. "Electromagnetic Fields and Public Health: Mobile Phones." October 8, 2014. Accessed September 5, 2019. www.who.int/en/news-room/fact-sheets /detail/electromagnetic-fields-and-public-health-mobile-phones.

———. "Electromagnetic Fields and Public Health: Electromagnetic Hypersensitivity." December 2005. Accessed September 5, 2019. www.who.int /peh-emf/publications/facts/fs296/en/.

———. "What Are the Health Risks Associated with Mobile Phones and Their Base Stations?" Online Q&A. September 20, 2013. www.who.int/features/qa/30/en/.

Yury, Carrie. "Your Heartbeat May Soon Be Your Only Password." *Wired*. June 2014. Accessed September 5, 2019. www.wired.com/insights/2014/06 /heartbeat-may-soon-password/.

Zhu, Xiqun, et al. "Microbiota-Gut-Brain Axis and the Central Nervous System." *Oncotarget* 8, no. 32 (August 8, 2017). www.ncbi.nlm.nih.gov/pmc/articles /PMC5581153/.

Zimmermann, Kim Ann. "Endocrine System: Facts, Functions and Diseases." February 15, 2018. www.livescience.com/26496-endocrine-system.html.

Index